The Vegetarian Mother's Cookbook

Whole foods to nourish pregnant
and breastfeeding women

– and their families

By Cathe Olson

GOCO Publishing / Nipomo, CA

GOCO PUBLISHING
9975 Danford Canyon Road
Santa Maria, CA 93454
www.simplynaturalbooks.com

Cover and interior design: Jane Kutcher, Sidekick Creative
www.sidekickcreative.com

LCCN: 2001012345
ISBN: 0-9724690-6-0

Printed in the United States of America.

For my mom, Christa Fein,
and for all mothers — past, present, and future

Contents

Acknowledgments

I am deeply grateful to Dina Aronson, MS, RD, for answering numerous questions and poring over multiple drafts of my manuscript to ensure my information was accurate and up to date. I am thankful to Lisa Saslove, MS, RD; Brenda L. Ramler, LM; and Herb Kandell, OMD, LAc, for taking time from their busy schedules to review my manuscript. Your input and suggestions were invaluable.

I would also like to extend my gratitude to Shawna Galassi, Laurie Woodward, Lynnette Kelley, Jessica Devereaux, and Cindy Cleveland from my writers' group for their support and input. I am also grateful to Jean Ann Williams for her editing help. Thanks so much to Brenda Koplin for doing an excellent job copy editing this book.

I am grateful to Jane Kutcher for the amazing book and cover design, and to Daniel Nevins for the beautiful illustrations. You both surpassed my highest expectations. I am thankful to Lissie Fein and Peter King for updating the Cathe's Kitchen Web site and helping in many other ways. A heartfelt thank you to Sarah Brownlee for taking care of my children when I needed uninterrupted time to write.

Most of all, I am enormously grateful to my family. Gary, my husband and best friend, your support and reassurance helped to make my dream come true. Aimie and Emily, my precious daughters, I could not have written this book were it not for you. Thank you all so much for your encouragement, your understanding, your honest evaluation of my recipes, and for your unconditional love.

Preface

I wrote this book because what you eat makes a big difference in how you feel physically and emotionally during pregnancy and lactation. Your diet also directly affects the health of your baby. Vegetarian women must take extra care to ensure they are getting the nutrients they need in order for mother and baby to thrive.

I experienced a major difference between my two pregnancies. During my first pregnancy, I frequently ate out because I did not feel like cooking. Although fresh fruit, vegetables, and whole grains made up a large part of my diet, I did not pay attention to protein and fat. Consequently, my blood sugar levels were unstable, causing me to be forgetful, lightheaded, moody, and tired. I was consistently underweight in my pregnancy and I went into labor six weeks early. Fortunately, my baby and I were fine.

My second pregnancy was much better. I rarely dined out. (I did have a toddler, after all.) I read a lot of books on pregnancy nutrition and came up with a good eating plan. I regularly ate concentrated protein foods like tempeh, tofu, beans, legumes, nuts, seeds, and homemade yogurt. We had our own hens so I consumed two eggs almost every day. I also ate a lot of dark green leafy vegetables, whole grains, cultured foods, and other Super Mommy Foods (see page 24).

I thrived during this pregnancy. My weight gain was always right at the recommended levels. I had energy; I was clearheaded; and I felt good. I kept a food log that my midwife, Edana Hall, reviewed at every prenatal appointment. She was so impressed that she passed the log on to her other vegetarian clients to give them ideas for nourishing meals.

My second daughter was born close to her due date. There was some stress on the baby during the birth because of a minor complication, so when my daughter emerged she was slightly blue, but within seconds she returned to normal color. Edana said my baby was able to recover so quickly because she was well nourished.

Good nutrition is important postpartum too. With my first pregnancy, I did not arrange for postpartum help or meals. Since my baby came early, I hadn't stocked up on food or prepared meals in advance. It was very difficult to eat right under those circumstances and I ended up eating processed and convenience foods. I was usually tired and moody, and often frantic and stressed. Once I began to cook whole foods again, I felt much better physically and emotionally and life with a newborn became enjoyable.

During my second pregnancy, I arranged for postpartum help and meals in advance. I stocked up on food two months before the baby was due (just in case), and prepared and froze meals. It was wonderful to have hot, nourishing meals after the baby was born.

The recipes in this book are dishes my family and I love. Each recipe is packed with nutrients to help you and your baby thrive. I have included tips to make it easier for you to eat well when you don't have much time or energy. I hope this book will help you to have a wonderful pregnancy and postpartum experience.

Introduction

What a miracle to have a baby growing inside you! Isn't it amazing that your body can produce and carry a child, and even give you the means to feed your infant after it is born. As wonderful as our bodies are, they need to be properly fueled to perform this demanding feat. The nutrients needed for baby's organ and brain development come from what you eat, so a balanced diet is essential. Good eating habits also make pregnancy, labor, and postpartum experiences easier and more enjoyable.

You may be wondering if your vegetarian or vegan diet is adequate to sustain this new life. Or maybe you are not vegetarian but want to eat less meat and dairy. Plant foods, optionally supplemented with eggs and/or dairy products, are more than adequate to nourish you and your baby, although care must be taken to ensure you are getting the necessary nutrients. This book contains healthy recipes for mom, as well as the rest of the family. Each dish is packed with protein, vitamins, and minerals so that every bite nourishes. By following the recipes and advice in this book, you can feel secure that you are getting the sustenance you need.

Pregnancy and lactation are wonderful, special times in a woman's life, but can be difficult emotionally. Hormone fluctuations, body changes, and new responsibilities can take their toll. I found myself craving many of my favorite foods from childhood and was constantly on the phone with my mom to get recipes. Since these comfort foods were usually high in sugar, fat, refined products, or contained meat, I have included healthy vegetarian versions of many favorites like Shepherd's Pie, Mushroom Stroganoff, Tapioca Pudding, and Carob Brownies.

During pregnancy, it is often difficult to stand for long periods of time cooking or washing dishes. After the baby comes, there isn't time to prepare complicated menus, especially if you have other children to care for. Most of the recipes in this book can be prepared in stages, so if you are interrupted, you can continue later. I have also included many quick fix ◑ meals that can be prepared in 35 minutes or less. There are also many dishes that can be assembled and frozen ❄ for after the baby comes, so all you or your partner need to do is heat them up.

Enjoy this celebration of your womanhood. The new life that you are nurturing is truly an incredible gift, and the experience of pregnancy and breastfeeding is something you will always remember and cherish. Don't be overwhelmed by advice, much of which may be conflicting. Trust your instincts. If you make mistakes, look at them as learning experiences. A peaceful, loving environment is just as important to your baby as what you eat.

Health Benefits of a Vegetarian Diet

A whole foods vegetarian diet is typically high in fiber, complex carbohydrates, vitamins, minerals, and antioxidants, and low in saturated fat. Studies show that vegetarians who follow a balanced diet are 24% less likely to die of coronary heart disease and have a 90% lower than average risk of developing type 2 diabetes. They typically suffer less from other diseases associated with the typical Western diet, including obesity and diet-related cancers.[1] In addition, nonorganic meat often contains hormones, antibiotics, pesticides, and herbicides. Beef and beef by-products could be infected with Mad Cow Disease and many types of fish contain high levels of heavy metals such as mercury.

Nutrition for Pregnancy and Lactation

Preconception

Take a look at your diet before you become pregnant and make changes if necessary. A healthy diet and lifestyle will prepare your body for the demands of pregnancy. If you smoke, quit. If you are under or overweight, the recipes in this book will help you to get closer to your ideal weight before you become pregnant. Folate (folic acid) is very important in the early stages of pregnancy to prevent birth defects such as spina bifida. Eat plenty of fresh fruits and vegetables, especially dark green leafy vegetables, as well as whole grains and legumes to prevent deficiencies.

Recipe suggestions for preconception:

Zucchini-Corn Omelet
Cantaloupe Surprise
Caesar Salad
Sunny Cole Slaw
Chunky Vegetable Soup
Ginger-Lentil Soup
Veggie Wrap

Mexican Rice
Braised Greens with Sesame
Tofu Vegetable Pot Pie
Spanakopitta
Cranberry-Date Bars
Ambrosia
Everything Smoothie

Pregnancy

What you eat makes a big difference during pregnancy. You will feel better physically as well as emotionally if your body is getting regular meals and adequate nutrients. Protein, carbohydrates, and fat are important to keep your energy levels constant and for the growth of new tissue. Iron is essential for the production of hemoglobin which carries oxygen to your cells, as well as your baby's. Calcium is essential for baby's bones and teeth. Zinc is important for fetal development. Omega-3 fatty acids are important for baby's brain and nervous system development. Properly nourished women are also less likely to have complications like anemia, preeclampsia, or premature labor.

First Trimester

The first trimester can be difficult if you are experiencing morning (and afternoon and evening) sickness. You may not feel like eating, much less like cooking. While extra calories are not mandatory the first couple of months, it is important to eat nutrient-rich foods. Also, keeping food in your stomach can help prevent nausea. Most women prefer bland, starchy foods so keep crackers, breads, soups, and grains on hand but be sure to eat them with a protein like nuts, seeds, tofu, or eggs. Look in the breakfast section for porridges that cook overnight in your slow cooker so you will have something ready to eat as soon as you wake up. Drink plenty of water so you won't become dehydrated, and try to find foods you can eat so that you don't lose weight.

Folate is essential for cell formation. Vitamin B6 may help reduce nausea and vomiting. Potassium-rich foods (e.g., fruit, vegetables, whole grains, nuts, seeds) are important for those who vomit frequently. Cooked whole grain porridges with fruit and nuts or flaxseed oil can usually be tolerated by a queasy stomach and will supply those vitamins and minerals.

Recipe suggestions for the first trimester:

Slow-Cooker Oatmeal
Cream of Millet Cereal
Overnight Rice Porridge
Tabouli
Miso-Noodle Soup
Soothing Mint Soup
Creamy Parsnip Soup
Millet Mashies
Mashed Potatoes
Broccoli-Noodle Casserole
Shepherd's Pie

Baked Ginger-Orange Tofu
Raw Seed Wafers
Brown Rice Crackers
Millet-Coconut Pudding
Ginger-Peach Smoothie
Fresh Fig and Orange Smoothie
Better Than Ginger Ale
Morning Sickness Tea
Anti-Nausea Tea
Ginger Tea
Chia Energy Drink

Second Trimester

Around the end of the fourth month of pregnancy, most women begin feeling better physically and have a bigger appetite. Blood volume, fat stores, and breast tissue increase during the second trimester. Additional calories (about 300 extra per day) are recommended at this time to keep up with your body's expanding needs. Be sure to eat regular meals and snacks to keep your body fueled. Extra protein and iron are important for expanding blood volume and tissues of mother and baby. Continue to eat foods containing omega-3 fatty acids like flaxseeds, chia seeds, walnuts, and/or omega-3 enriched eggs for baby's brain and nervous system development.

Recipe suggestions for the second trimester:

High-Protein Porridge
Scrambled Eggs or Tofu
Breakfast Potatoes and Veggies
Garbanzo Bean Salad
Winter Squash and White Bean Soup
Tortilla Soup
Mild Yellow Curry Stew
Egg or Tofu Salad Sandwich
Bean Quesadilla
Tempeh Rueben
Wheat Berry Pilaf

Millet-Veggie Burgers
High-Protein Pasta
Yogurt-Spinach Quiche
Nori Rice Balls
Carrot-Bran Muffins
Granola Bars
Lemon-Lime Tofu "Cheesecake"
Super C Smoothie
Iron Booster Tonic
Everyday Pregnancy Tea
Chia Energy Drink

Third Trimester

Your diet during this trimester must nourish the developing baby and prepare you for labor, delivery, and breastfeeding. The third trimester is when your baby gains the most weight. Be sure to eat calcium-rich foods like nuts, seeds, and dark green leafy vegetables for baby's bones. Eat plenty of whole grains, fruit, vegetables, and other fiber foods to prevent constipation. Small meals, eaten more frequently, can help to prevent heartburn.

Recipe suggestions for the third trimester:

Almond Pancakes

Tomato-Herb Omelet

Cottage Cheese Sundae

Sweet Potato Salad with Peanut Butter Dressing

"Cream" of Watercress Soup

"Cream" of Broccoli Soup

Seitan "Chicken" and Barley Stew

Watercress Sandwich

Falafel with Tangy Tahini Sauce

Black Bean and Sweet Potato Enchiladas

Parsley-Walnut Pesto Pasta

Potato-Kale Quiche

Brussels Sprouts with White Sauce

Meal Shake

Pumpkin Scones

Coconut Sweet Potato Pie

Everyday Pregnancy Tea

Last Trimester Pregnancy Tea

Chia Energy Drink

Postpartum

The first month after your baby is born, your diet should be one of replenishment for healing and recovery. Lack of sleep and the demands of a new baby can be physically and emotionally exhausting. Get as much rest as you can and eat nutrient-rich foods. In many Asian countries, Sea Vegetable Soup (page 156) is traditionally the first food served after delivery because it contains so many vitamins and minerals. Adequate amounts of omega-3 fatty acids are essential to keep your moods steady and prevent depression, and nourish your baby. Foods rich in zinc and vitamins A, C, and E aid the healing of tissue. Eat plenty of fresh fruits and vegetables to supply your body with antioxidants.

Note: Prepare in advance for your postpartum meals. Cook and freeze soups, beans, grains, and main dishes before the baby comes. Enlist family and friends to bring you meals for at least the first month after your baby's birth. Let them know your dietary preferences and even suggest meals that your family likes.

Recipe suggestions for postpartum:

Müesli

Kale-Egg Scramble

Pear-Walnut Salad

Seaweed Soup

Coconut-Tempeh Stew ❋

Chunky Vegetable Soup ❋

Herbed Split Pea Soup ❋

Egg or Tofu Salad Sandwich

Veggie Dog and Sauerkraut

Rice and Bean Casserole ❋

Kasha-Vegetable Casserole ❋

Bean and Nut Loaf ❋

Butternut Lasagna ❋

Lima Bean Lasagna ❋

Tempeh Squash Bake

Tomato-Watercress Blend

Piña Colada Shake

Gingerbread Bars ❋

Tapioca Pudding

Afterpain Tea

Nursing Tea

❋ = *Main courses that can be frozen and reheated*

Healthy Diet for Lactation

Adequate nutrients and calories are just as important while breastfeeding as during pregnancy. Although you may be anxious to lose weight, this is not the time to diet. Don't worry – the weight will come off naturally if you continue to eat a whole foods diet and get regular exercise.

Fats are essential to nourish your baby's brain as it continues to develop. Foods like nuts, seeds, avocados, omega-3-enriched or organic eggs will supply you with essential fatty acids for your infant. It is crucial that you consume a regular source of vitamin B12 as that nutrient is commonly deficient in pregnant and lactating women.[2] Drink plenty of water to stay hydrated and support your milk production. A good practice is to drink water or herbal tea as you nurse your baby.

Nutrient-dense foods and herbs can help encourage a plentiful breastmilk supply (e.g. carrots, dark green leafy vegetables, nettle, parsley, quinoa, red raspberry leaf, sweet potatoes, and watercress.[3] Certain herbs, like fennel seeds, may help alleviate colic in baby. See Teas and Tonics for breastfeeding tea blends or try Traditional Medicinals® Mother's Milk Tea.

Recipe suggestions for lactation:

Crunchy Buckwheat Cereal
Sesame-Flax French Toast
French Toast Sandwich
Tofu and Udon Noodles with
    Sesame-Peanut Dressing
Curried Rice Salad
Adzuki-Squash Stew
Better Than "Beef" Stew
Ratatouille
Quick Nutritional Yeast Rice
Easy Pasta Lunch
Fried Rice and Veggies

Sesame-Carrot Quinoa Pilaf
Sesame-Tofu Quiche with Broccoli
    and Mushrooms
Seitan "Chicken" and Cashews
Tofu Vegetable Stir-Fry
Creamy Greens Smoothie
Banana-Molasses Muffins
Carob Brownies
Squash Stewed in Coconut Milk
Fennel Tea
Nursing Tea
Chia Energy Drink

Recommended Dietary Intakes for Women

Nutrients per day	Not Pregnant		Pregnant		Lactating	
	<=18	19-50	<=18	19-50	<=18	19-50
Protein, g [a]	46	46	71	71	71	71
Carbohydrates, g	130	130	175	175	210	210
Vitamin A, mcg	700	700	750	770	1,200	1,300
Thiamin, mg	1.0	1.1	1.4	1.4	1.4	1.4
Riboflavin, mg	1.0	1.1	1.4	1.4	1.6	1.6
Niacin, mg	14	14	18	18	17	17
Pantothenic acid, mg	5	5	6	6	7	7
Vitamin B6, mg	1.2	1.3	1.9	1.9	2.0	2.0
Folate, mcg	400	400	600	600	500	500
Vitamin B12, mg	2.4	2.4	2.6	2.6	2.8	2.8
Vitamin C, mg	65	75	80	85	115	120
Vitamin D, mcg [b]	5	5	5	5	5	5
Vitamin E, mg	15	15	15	15	19	19
Calcium, mg	1300	1200	1300	1200	1300	1200
Iron, mg	15	18	27	27	10	9
Magnesium, mg	360	310 [c]	400	350 [c]	360	310 [c]
Zinc, mg	9	8	12	11	13	12

a Protein requirements are an average based on 0.8 g/kg/day for nonpregnant women,
   1.1 g/kg/day for pregnant and lactating women (using pre-pregnancy weight).
b In the absence of adequate exposure to sunlight.
c An extra 10 mg/d are recommended for women over the age of 30.

Sources: Adapted with permission from *Dietary Reference Intakes for Energy, Carbohydrate, Fiber, Fat, Fatty Acids, Cholesterol, Protein, and Amino Acids (Macronutrients) (2002); Dietary Reference Intakes for Calcium, Phosphorous, Magnesium, Vitamin D, and Fluoride (1997); Dietary Reference Intakes for Thiamin, Riboflavin, Niacin, Vitamin B6, Folate, Vitamin B12, Pantothenic Acid, Biotin, and Choline (1998); Dietary Reference Intakes for Vitamin C, Vitamin E, Selenium, and Carotenoids (2000); Dietary Reference Intakes for Vitamin A, Vitamin K, Arsenic, Boron, Chromium, Copper, Iodine, Iron, Manganese, Molybdenum, Nickel, Silicon, Vanadium, and Zinc (2001)* by the National Academy of Science, courtesy of the National Academies Press, Washington, D.C.

Important Nutrients

Protein

Extra protein is necessary for expanded blood volume, formation of amniotic fluid, and for development of the placenta. Your baby needs protein for muscle and tissue formation, as well as brain development. Since no one plant food contains adequate amounts of all essential amino acids, eat a variety of protein sources throughout the day.

The Food and Nutrition Board of the National Academy of Sciences recently updated their Daily Reference Intakes for protein and macronutrients. They now recommend 25 additional grams of protein per day for pregnant and lactating women. The following foods contain between 10 to 15 grams of protein: 4 ounces of tofu, 4 ounces of tempeh, 1 cup of cooked beans, 3 to 4 tablespoons nut or seed butter, 2 eggs, 1 1/4 cups yogurt, or 1/2 cup cottage cheese. You would need to eat two servings of those to get the extra protein required.

Good sources of protein: Beans and legumes, dairy products, eggs, nutritional yeast, nuts, seeds, soy products, whole grains (especially buckwheat, millet, quinoa, amaranth, and oats)

Complex Carbohydrates and Fiber

You must consume adequate amounts of carbohydrates so the protein you consume can be used for your baby's development. Fiber-rich complex carbohydrates allow your body to absorb nutrients and sugars gradually and help the digestive system to function efficiently.

A whole foods, vegetarian diet is naturally high in complex carbohydrates, but those who consume a lot of processed foods and refined grain products may be lacking in fiber and nutrients. Although fiber supplements are available, they are generally unnecessary in a whole foods diet, and can compromise mineral absorption.

Good sources of complex carbohydrates and fiber: Beans and legumes, fruits, nuts, seeds, vegetables, whole grains

Fat

Fat is crucial for cell formation and fetal brain development. It is needed to maintain healthy blood, circulation, and nervous systems. Fatty foods are the main source of the fat-soluble vitamins A, D, E, and K and also provide essential fatty acids. Eating fat does not make you fat. It helps you to feel full so you won't overeat and provides long-lasting energy.

Organic butter is an absorbable source of vitamin A and contains added vitamin D. For those avoiding dairy, coconut oil can be used like butter in baking or for sautéing and has antiviral, antifungal, and antimicrobial qualities. Avoid hydrogenated and partially hydrogenated oils, which are found in many margarines and processed foods. These are trans-fats and have been implicated in a number of health problems. Women who consume large amounts of trans-fatty acids may produce lower amounts of essential fatty acids in their breast milk.[4]

Olive oil is an excellent fat to include in your diet. It is mostly monosaturated and may help control blood pressure and diabetes. Nuts, seeds, and avocados are also excellent fat sources that provide many nutrients.

Omega-3 fatty acids are important for brain and nervous system development. The omega-3 fat docosahexaenoic acid (DHA) is essential for brain function and is drawn from the mother during pregnancy and lactation to nourish the baby. If you do not consume omega-3 fatty acids, your physical and emotional well-being may be compromised. Pregnancy complications and postpartum depression have been linked to low levels of DHA and eicosapentaenoic acid (EPA), another important fatty acid.[5] Even before you conceive, it is important to build up your reserves of omega-3 fatty acids because the typical western diet is often deficient in this nutrient.

Eggs (especially omega-3 enriched), flaxseeds, flaxseed oil, walnuts, pumpkin seeds, and chia seeds supply omega-3 fatty acids; however they contain only the omega-3 fat alpha-linolenic acid (ALA) which must be transformed to DHA and EPA by your body. Too much linoleic acid in your diet can decrease the conversion. The recommended ratio between ALA and linoleic acid is between five and ten to one.[6] In general monosaturated oils (like olive) are lower in linoleic acid than polyunsaturated oils (like corn and safflower). Research is still being done to determine if the body can transform enough ALA to meet the needs of pregnant and lactating woman.[7] You may want to look for high-DHA omega-3 eggs which come from vegetarian hens fed a DHA-rich diet supplemented with algae. If you want to take a supplement for DHA and EPA, there are vegetarian supplements made from algae, such as Neuromins DHA.

Good sources of fat: Avocado, butter, dairy products (full fat), eggs, nuts and nut butters, oils (cold pressed nut, olive, seed, and vegetable oils), seeds and seed butters

Vitamins

Vitamin A: Vitamin A is a fat-soluble vitamin important for formation and growth of baby's cells, tissues, and bones. It is essential for eye development and health of the immune system. Vitamin A is found in dairy products and eggs. In fruits and vegetables, it is found as beta carotene which is converted to vitamin A by the body. Your body's vitamin A needs can be supplied by beta-carotene-rich foods. In fact, too much preformed vitamin A can be toxic so if you are taking supplements and eating vitamin A fortified foods, be sure not to get more than 2,800 to 3,000 micrograms of preformed vitamin A per day.

Good sources of vitamin A: Butter, dairy products, dark green leafy vegetables (kale, spinach, watercress, etc.), orange and yellow fruits and vegetables (apricots, cantaloupe, carrots, papaya, sweet potatoes, winter squash, etc.)

Thiamine (B1), Riboflavin (B2), Niacin (B3): These B vitamins work together as a team and are mostly found in the same foods. They promote healthy nerves, skin, eyes, hair, liver, and muscle tone. These nutrients help the body convert carbohydrates to energy, and protect you from mental disorders such as anxiety and depression. Riboflavin and niacin are important for cell reproduction and growth.

Good sources of thiamine, riboflavin, and niacin: Dairy products, dark green leafy vegetables, eggs, fortified cereals, nutritional yeast, nuts, seeds, whole grains

Pantothenic Acid (B5): Pantothenic acid is needed for the release of energy from carbohydrates. This B vitamin is abundant in most plant foods.

Good sources of pantothenic acid: Beans and legumes, cauliflower, dairy products, dark green leafy vegetables, eggs, fruit, nutritional yeast, tomatoes, whole grains

Vitamin B6 (Pyridoxine): Vitamin B6 is important for the formation of red blood cells and for metabolizing protein and fat. Because of the extra protein being consumed during pregnancy and lactation, vitamin B6 intake must also increase. Vitamin B6 may help reduce nausea and vomiting as well so be sure to get adequate amounts during the first trimester.

Good sources of vitamin B6: Avocado, bananas, brown rice, dark green leafy vegetables, dried fruit, eggs, fortified cereals, nutritional yeast, sweet potatoes, sunflower seeds

Folate: The B vitamin folate (or folic acid) is essential for the formation of cells in your growing baby. Meeting the nutritional recommendations for folate prior to and after conception is imperative to reduce the risk of some types of birth defects. Cooking can destroy some of the folic acid, so include raw fruits and vegetables in your diet.

Good sources of folate: Asparagus, avocado, beans and legumes, broccoli, brussels sprouts, dark green leafy vegetables, fruit, nutritional yeast, nuts, romaine lettuce, root vegetables, seeds, wheat germ, whole rye, whole wheat

Vitamin B12: Vitamin B12 is vital for formation and growth of red blood cells. It is also important for the growth of your baby's nervous system; however, it is one of the most commonly deficient vitamins during pregnancy and lactation, especially among vegans. Vitamin B12 is found only in animal products but vegans can get vitamin B12 from fortified nutritional yeast like Red Star® Vegetarian Support Formula, nondairy milks, and cereals. You can also obtain vitamin B12 from supplements. Eating cultured foods (like yogurt or sauerkraut) helps maximize the reproduction of vitamin B12 in the digestive tract.

Good sources of vitamin B12: Dairy products, eggs, fortified cereals, fortified nutritional yeast, fortified soy milk

Vitamin C: Vitamin C is essential for healthy tissue, teeth, and gums. It's also needed for maintaining resistance to infection and for absorption of iron.

Good sources of vitamin C: Berries, broccoli, cabbage, cantaloupe, cauliflower, citrus fruits, dark green leafy vegetables, kiwi, papaya, parsley, potatoes, red bell peppers, tomatoes, watercress

Vitamin D: Vitamin D is needed for absorption of calcium and phosphorous. The only plant food containing Vitamin D is mushrooms. You can also get this nutrient from sunlight and vitamin D-fortified foods. 10 to 15 minutes of sun daily will satisfy your vitamin D needs. If you are not able to get out in the sun (e.g., during winter months), be sure to eat other sources of vitamin D.

Good sources of vitamin D: Eggs, fortified cereals, fortified dairy products, fortified nondairy milks, mushrooms, sunlight

Note: You may want to wear a hat or sunscreen when outside because sun exposure can aggravate melasma (or the mask of pregnancy) and cause skin discoloration during pregnancy.

Vitamin E: Vitamin E is an antioxidant that protects against tissue damage and inflammation. It is needed for circulation, tissue repair, and healing.

Good sources of vitamin E: Nuts, seeds, soybeans, unrefined vegetable oils, wheat germ

Minerals and Trace Elements

Calcium: Calcium is important for bones and teeth of both mother and baby. Be especially conscientious about getting adequate calcium during the third trimester when the fetus experiences rapid growth so your reserves won't be depleted. You do not need to eat dairy products to get adequate calcium, just make sure you are eating plenty of nondairy sources (see list below). Vitamin D aids in the absorption of calcium.

Good sources of calcium: Beans and legumes, blackstrap molasses, broccoli, carob, dairy products, dark green leafy vegetables, figs, nettle tea, nuts (especially almonds, hazelnuts, brazil nuts), quinoa, red raspberry leaf tea, sea vegetables (especially hiziki and kelp), soy milk (fortified), seeds (especially sesame), soy yogurt (fortified), tofu

Iron: Iron is needed for the formation of blood and to transport oxygen to cells. Maternal blood volume increases about 25 percent during pregnancy so increased iron intake is important. Iron from animal sources (heme iron) is more easily absorbed than iron from plant sources (nonheme iron). To aid your body's absorption of nonheme iron, eat vitamin C-rich foods with iron-rich plant foods. Soaking and/or sprouting grains, legumes, and nuts helps to make the minerals more absorbable. It is also beneficial to cook in cast-iron pans.

The tannins in coffee and black tea decrease iron absorption so it's best to avoid them. Drink herbal teas, especially red raspberry leaf and nettle teas, which supply minerals. Iron needs decrease when you are lactating and not experiencing a menstrual cycle.

Good sources of iron: Amaranth, blackstrap molasses, beans and legumes, dark leafy green vegetables, dried fruit, fortified cereal, nettle tea, nuts, quinoa, sea vegetables (especially hiziki), seeds (especially pumpkin and sunflower), tofu

Magnesium: Magnesium is needed for formation of new tissue. Adequate amounts may also help prevent leg tremors and cramps.

Good sources of magnesium: Beans and legumes, blackstrap molasses, dairy products, dark green leafy vegetables, dried fruit, nuts, sea vegetables, seeds, whole grains

Sodium: Sodium intake does not need to be restricted during pregnancy. In fact, some sodium is essential to maintain fluid and regulate electrolytes. Whole foods salted to taste are fine unless your physician or midwife advises otherwise. Use unrefined Celtic sea salt because it contains essential minerals and trace elements, and has no additives.[8] Avoid refined salt. Commercial salt has anticaking agents added and all minerals and trace elements have been stripped from them. Most processed snack foods, canned foods, boxed mixes, frozen dinners, and fast foods contain high amounts of refined salt so it's best to avoid them. There are many recipes in the book for alternatives to processed foods.

Good sources of sodium: Miso, sea salt (unrefined Celtic), sea vegetables, Shoyu or tamari soy sauce

Zinc: Zinc is important for maintaining immunity, healing wounds, and metabolizing fat. Zinc deficiency can cause poor fetal growth or preterm delivery.

Good sources of zinc: Beans and legumes, dairy products, nuts, sea vegetables, seeds, whole grains

A Note on Phytates:

Some plant foods, such as barley, oats, soy, and whole wheat, are high in phytic acid, which can inhibit the absorption of minerals like calcium, iron, magnesium, and zinc. Soaking, sprouting, or fermenting these foods helps to neutralize the phytic acid. These processes have been included in many recipes. In addition, vitamin C-rich foods overcome the inhibitory effect of phytates on iron absorption.

Super Mommy Foods

Following are foods that are especially beneficial during pregnancy and lactation.

Beans and Legumes

Beans and legumes are good sources of protein, fiber, calcium, iron, thiamine, and niacin. They are a crucial part of a vegetarian diet. Make a big batch of beans when you have time and freeze them in small containers (see the Bean and Legume Cooking Chart on page 386). Canned beans are available also. They are just slightly lower in nutrients than home cooked due to the high heat processing. Canned beans usually contain high amounts of sodium, however. Draining and rinsing away the canning liquid will remove a lot of the sodium.

Soybeans provide more protein than any other bean or legume, making them a staple of many vegetarian diets. Soybeans are rich in many nutrients, including calcium and iron. Fermented soy products like tempeh or miso are especially beneficial because they contain healthy bacteria and enzymes that aid digestion, and the phytic acid is neutralized by the culturing process.

Avoid fabricated soy foods (e.g., fake meats, protein powders) made with soy protein isolates or textured vegetable protein, which are created using a highly chemical process and usually have MSG or artificial flavors added. Also, keep in mind that although soy is a great protein source, it is not the only one. Moderation and variety are important in a vegetarian diet and you shouldn't rely on any one food for nutrients.

Blackstrap Molasses

Blackstrap molasses contains high amounts of calcium and iron, plus magnesium, potassium, copper, and chromium. Buy organic, unsulphured molasses and use it to sweeten porridge, smoothies, and baked goods.

Cultured and Fermented Foods

Naturally cultured and fermented foods contain enzymes and bacteria that help digest food and eliminate wastes. They also help build up friendly bacteria in the intestines, which is especially important after taking antibiotics. (Most hospitals give women antibiotics during labor.) Eat plenty of fermented foods during pregnancy when your digestive system may be sluggish. They can help prevent constipation and other digestive problems, and are useful in preventing and treating yeast infections.

Cultured and fermented foods include natural, unpasteurized miso, naturally fermented vegetable pickles and sauerkraut, yogurt, and Rejuvelac. (See Ingredient Guide for more information on specific foods and look for recipes in this book.) Never boil these foods as high temperatures will destroy the beneficial bacteria.

Dark Green Leafy Vegetables and Cabbage Family Vegetables

Dark green leafy vegetables (kale, collard greens, watercress, etc.) are especially important while pregnant or lactating because they supply so many vitamins and minerals, including vitamins A and C, calcium, and iron. Dark leafy green vegetables also are rich in phytochemicals like beta carotein and lutein which protect against many forms of cancer. Certain greens like spinach and Swiss chard are high in oxalic acid, which inhibit the absorption of much of the calcium and iron. Cooking helps to neutralize some of the oxalic acid.

Vegetables from the cabbage family (broccoli, brussels sprouts, cabbage, etc.) are exceptional sources of vitamin A, vitamin C, and calcium. They are also rich in phytochemicals that have anticancer properties.

Dark green leafy vegetables and cabbage family vegetables provide important nutrients that help to promote a plentiful milk supply for your baby. Buy fresh, organic vegetables whenever possible and eat at least one serving every day.

Eggs

Eggs contain highly useable protein as well as almost every essential vitamin (except vitamin C) and mineral needed by humans. Eggs are very nutrient dense, which means they supply a great deal of nutrition for a small number of calories. Experts used to warn against eating too many eggs because of their high cholesterol content, but research has shown that dietary cholesterol doesn't significantly raise blood cholesterol.[9] Look for organic eggs from hens who are allowed to roam. Omega-3 enriched eggs (which come from hens whose feed is supplemented with flaxseeds) and high-DHA omega-3 eggs (which come from vegetarian hens whole feed is supplemented with algae) are excellent choices.

Nutritional Yeast

Nutritional yeast is an exceptional source of almost all B complex vitamins as well as being high in protein. Look for nutritional yeast flakes enriched with vitamin B12 like Red Star® Vegetarian Support Formula. Nutritional yeast flakes can be added to soups, sauces, eggs, cereals, smoothies, and other foods.

Nuts and Seeds

Nuts and seeds are good sources of fiber, protein, minerals, and essential fatty acids. Be sure to eat flaxseeds, chia seeds, pumpkin seeds, and/or walnuts to get omega-3 fatty acids, which are important for baby's brain and nervous system development as well as your own health. Nuts and seeds can be eaten raw or toasted. Small seeds like sesame and flax must be ground in a coffee grinder, seed grinder, or blender in order for nutrients to be utilized. Nut and seed butters are delicious on crackers or toast or used as a dip or sauce.

Peanut Allergies

Allergies to peanut products affect approximately 1% of the U.S. population. Although there hasn't been extensive research on fetal sensitization, recent studies suggest that when a pregnant woman consumes peanut products, the fetus may be exposed to peanut allergens. If there is a predisposition to allergies, the infant could develop a peanut allergy. Therefore, parents with food allergies and/or family histories of nut allergies may want to avoid peanuts while pregnant or breastfeeding. Almond butter, cashew butter, pumpkin seed butter, or tahini (sesame seed butter) can replace peanut butter in any of the recipes in this book.

Whole Grains

Whole grains supply fiber, minerals, B complex vitamins, and protein. Buy the least processed grain types you can find. Many commercially prepared grains have the germ and bran removed to increase shelf life and shorten preparation time. Even if they are "enriched," this does not replace the nutrition that was lost in the processing.

Putting It into Practice

You may feel overwhelmed with all the nutrients required to nourish the new life within you, but planning a balanced diet is not difficult if you keep a few simple rules in mind.

1) **Eat a varied diet.**

    Eating a variety of whole grains, beans and legumes, nuts, seeds, vegetables, fruit, and optionally eggs and dairy products will ensure that you are getting the nutrients you need, though special care should be taken to ensure you are getting adequate amounts of vitamins B12 and D. Try not to overdo any one food and avoid processed foods which can rob your body of vitamins and minerals.

2) **Eat protein, complex carbohydrates, and fat at every meal.**

    If each meal and snack contains all three factors, you will get the energy you need and your blood sugar levels will remain stable.

3) **Start taking a prenatal supplement when you are trying to conceive and throughout your pregnancy.**

    Although it's best to obtain nutrients from foods, prenatal supplements are nutritional insurance. Continue to take a supplement while lactating but look for a supplement that has a lesser amount of iron. Ask your physician or midwife to recommend a supplement right for you.

Vegetarian Food Guide for Pregnant or Lactating Women

Grains, Cereals, Breads: 6 to 10 servings (a serving is 1 slice of bread, 1/2 bagel or English muffin, 1 tortilla, or 1/2 cup cooked cereal or grain)

Protein Foods (Beans and Legumes, Soy Products, Nuts, Seeds, Eggs, Dairy Products): 7 to 9 servings (a serving is 1/2 cup cooked beans or legumes, 4 ounces tofu or tempeh, 2 tablespoons nuts or seed butter, 1/4 cup nuts, 1 egg, 1/2 cup dairy or soy milk, 1/2 cup dairy, soy, or cashew yogurt, 1/2 cup dairy or tofu cottage cheese)

Vegetables: 4 or more servings (a serving is 1 cup raw or 1/2 cup cooked). Emphasize high calcium vegetables such as dark green leafy vegetables and broccoli, and vitamin A-rich vegetables like carrots, sweet potatoes, and winter squash.

Fruit: 2 or more servings (a serving is 1 fruit or 1/2 cup fruit smoothie)

Fats: 2 to 4 servings (a serving is 1 teaspoon oil, butter, or mayonnaise, 1 tablespoon cream cheese, 2 tablespoons nuts or seeds, 1/8 avocado)

Vitamin B12 Food: 3 servings (a serving is 1 tablespoon fortified nutritional yeast flakes, 1 cup fortified soy milk, 1/2 cup dairy milk, 3/4 cup yogurt, 1 large egg, 1 ounce fortified breakfast cereal)

Note: Some foods are listed in more than one group (e.g., nuts and seeds are both protein and fat foods). When planning your meals, these foods should be counted in only one group.

Sample Menu for Pregnant or Lactating Women

	Day One	Day Two	Day Three
Breakfast	Oatmeal with dried fruit and nuts/seeds Everyday Pregnancy Tea or Nursing Tea	Scrambled Tofu Whole grain toast Everyday Pregnancy Tea or Nursing Tea	Papaya Delight Everyday Pregnancy Tea or Nursing Tea
Morning Snack	Dairy or nondairy yogurt or cottage cheese Fresh fruit	Fresh Fig and Orange Smoothie	Savory Bagel Sandwich
Lunch	Tempeh Rueben Carrot sticks	Quick Cheesy Rice or Quick Nutritional Yeast Rice Steamed broccoli	Ginger-Lentil Soup (leftover from Day 1 dinner) Pear-Walnut Salad
Afternoon Snack	Carob Cocoa Rye crispbread crackers with tahini	Apple with nut/seed butter for dipping	Raw Vegetables with Hummus Dip
Dinner	Ginger-Lentil Soup Spanakopitta	Tamale Pie Green Salad	Quiche (dairy or tofu version) Braised Greens
Evening Snack	Orange and almonds	Crunchy Buckwheat Cereal with dairy or nondairy milk	Sunflower-Sesame Molasses Cookies Rose Hip Tea

Note: Don't forget to drink plenty of water and take a supplement daily.

Whole Foods Shopping List

A well-stocked pantry is essential when following a whole foods diet. Keep a variety of ingredients on hand so you won't have to make unplanned trips to the market. It is also helpful to have some prepared food for when you need to make a meal quickly. Following is a list of foods to use as a guide when shopping. You don't need all the items on this list, but you should try to have several from each category. Descriptions of unfamiliar items along with nutritional, storage, and purchasing information can be found in the Ingredient Guide.

Beans and Legumes
Adzuki beans
Black beans
Garbanzo beans
Kidney beans
Lentils
Lima beans
Navy beans
Split peas

Whole Grains
Amaranth
Barley
Buckwheat groats
Bulgur
Millet
Oat groats
Oats, rolled
Polenta
Quinoa
Rice, brown
Wheat berries

Whole Grain Flours
Arrowroot powder
Barley flour
Brown rice flour
Carob powder
Cornmeal

Whole wheat flour
Whole wheat pastry flour

Pastas
Brown rice pasta
Quinoa pasta
Whole wheat pasta

Whole Grain Breads and Crackers
Bagels
Bread, whole grain
Crackers, whole grain*
English muffins
Flatbread
Pita bread
Rye crispbread crackers
Tortillas

Concentrated Plant Protein
Seitan
Tofu
Tempeh

Nuts and seeds
Almonds
Cashews
Chia seeds
Coconut, unsweetened shredded
Flaxseeds

Pecans
Pine nuts
Pumpkin seeds
Sesame seeds
Sunflower seeds
Walnuts

Nut and seed butters
Almond butter
Cashew butter
Peanut butter
Pumpkin seed butter
Tahini

Fruit (best to buy local, in season)
Apples
Apricots, fresh/dried
Avocados
Bananas, fresh/frozen
Berries
Cantaloupe
Cranberries, fresh/dried
Figs, fresh/dried
Mangos, fresh/frozen
Oranges
Papaya
Peaches, fresh/frozen
Pears
Plums
Prunes
Raisins
Strawberries, fresh/frozen

Vegetables (best to buy local, in season)
Beets
Broccoli
Brussels sprouts
Cabbage
Carrots
Cauliflower

Corn, fresh/frozen
Cucumbers
Garlic
Kale
Lettuce (not iceberg)
Onions
Parsnips
Peas, fresh/frozen
Potatoes
Pumpkin, fresh/canned
Spinach
Sweet potatoes
Tomatoes, fresh/canned
Watercress
Winter squash
Zucchini

Prepared Juices (unsweetened)
Apple juice
Pineapple juice
Pineapple-coconut juice
Prune juice

Cultured Foods
Amasake
Apple cider vinegar
Brown rice vinegar
Cottage cheese
Kefir
Miso
Pickles, naturally fermented*
Sauerkraut*
Soy sauce (Shoyu or tamari)
Yogurt (dairy or nondairy)*

Dairy Products
Cottage cheese
Cream or Neufchâtel cheese
Feta cheese
Hard cheese

Milk
Parmesan cheese
Ricotta cheese
Yogurt*
Yogurt cheese*

Nondairy Products
Amazake
Coconut milk
Soy, rice, or almond cheese
Soy, rice, or almond milk*
Soy or cashew yogurt*
Tofu cottage cheese*

Eggs
Ener-G® Egg Replacer

Sea Vegetables
Agar agar
Arame
Hiziki
Kelp, granulated
Kombu
Kuzo
Nori
Wakame

Sweeteners
Agave nectar
Blackstrap molasses
Brown rice syrup
Evaporated cane juice
Honey
Liquid stevia extract
Maple syrup

Butter and Oils
Butter (salted and unsalted)
Coconut oil
Ghee

Grapeseed oil
Olive oil
Safflower oil, high-oleic
Sunflower oil, high-oleic
Toasted sesame oil

Condiments and Flavorings
Balsamic vinegar
Brown rice vinegar
Nutritional yeast flakes
Red wine vinegar
Salad dressing*
Sea salt, unrefined Celtic
Tabasco sauce
Vegetable bouillon
Vegetable stock*

Spices
Black pepper
Cardamom, ground
Chili powder
Cinnamon, ground
Cloves, ground
Cumin powder
Curry powder
Ginger, fresh/powdered
Nutmeg, ground
Pumpkin pie spice
Turmeric, ground

Herbs (fresh or dried)
Basil
Cilantro, fresh or frozen
Oregano
Parsley, fresh or frozen
Rosemary
Sage
Tarragon
Thyme

Herbal teas (loose or in bags)
Chamomile
Fennel
Ginger root
Nettle
Nursing-blend tea*
Peppermint

Pregnancy-blend tea*
Red raspberry leaf

Other
Pancake and waffle mix*
Marinara sauce*

* = Items can also be made from recipes in this book

Tips and Timesavers

- Cook brown rice, barley, and/or other long-cooking grains and store in meal-size portions in freezer. They can be added to soups or salads or used for burritos, etc.
- Cook and freeze a variety of beans and store in two-cup portions in your freezer. You may also want to keep some canned beans on hand.
- Mince hardy greens like kale, collards, etc. (I use my food processor.) Store in containers or bags in your freezer. Frozen greens can be added to scrambled eggs, rice, soups, and smoothies.
- Freeze minced parsley and cilantro in freezer containers or ice cube trays.
- Make and freeze marinara sauce or stock up on prepared sauce. Pasta and sauce with some beans, tofu, or cheese for protein is always an easy meal.
- Buy a bunch of lemons and juice them all at once. Pour juice into ice cube trays and freeze. When frozen, transfer to freezer bag or container. Each cube equals about two tablespoons of lemon juice.
- Whenever you cook grains or beans for a meal, make double what you need. Refrigerate the leftover for morning porridge or next day's meals. You can also freeze them.
- Eat dinner leftovers for lunch or freeze them in individual-size portions for another day. (Many of the soup recipes make a big enough portion that you will have leftovers.)
- Hard-boil a bunch of eggs and keep them in the refrigerator. Add them to salads, sandwiches, or eat as a snack.
- Make a batch (or two) of cookies or muffins and store in the freezer. You will appreciate having a wholesome treat on hand when you want one.
- Plan plenty of time to make a meal, especially after the baby comes when you may not always have a big chunk of time to spend in the kitchen. Chop vegetables for soup in the morning or the night before so when it's time to make dinner you just have to throw everything in the pot.
- If you want to bake muffins or cookies, you can do it in several sessions. First, get out the ingredients. Later, mix all the dry ingredients; later, prepare the liquid ingredients. When you are ready to bake, preheat the oven, combine liquid and dry ingredients and bake.

Cravings

You may find yourself experiencing strong cravings and aversions during pregnancy. Here are some healthy ways to satisfy cravings for certain tastes and textures.

When you crave:	Eat:
Sweet foods	Adzuki-Squash Stew, bars or cookies, Butternut Lasagna, cakes, English Muffin Cheesecake, fruit, Molasses Toast, Müesli, muffins, porridge, puddings, smoothies, Squash and White Bean Soup, Trail Mix
Salty foods	Cheese and crackers, Miso-Noodle Soup, pickles, popcorn, Quick Nutritional Yeast Rice, Sauerkraut, Sea Vegetable Soup, Tempeh Rueben, tortilla chips with Easy Bean Dip
Sour foods	Creamsicle Smoothie, pickles, Rejuvelac, Sauerkraut, Sugar-Free Lemonade, tart oranges or other fruit, tea with lemon, yogurt (plain)
Creamy foods	Better than Ice Cream, cottage cheese, "Cream" of Broccoli Soup, "Cream" of Watercress Soup, "Cream" of Spinach and Millet Soup, Creamy Parsnip Soup, Creamy Watercress Dip, Hummus, Lentil Puree (Dahl), Mashed Potatoes, Millet Mashies, Müesli, Saucy Noodles and Vegetables, smoothies, sorbet, Tapioca Pudding, yogurt
Crunchy foods	Crackers, Crunchy Buckwheat Cereal, Garbanzo Crunchies, Millet Crunch Granola, nuts or seeds, popcorn, toast, toasted English muffin, tortilla chips with Easy Bean Dip, trail mix
Bland foods	Bagels, Broccoli-Noodle Casserole, cooked grains, crackers, Creamy Parsnip Soup, English muffins, Kasha-Potato-Carrot Casserole, Mashed Potatoes, Millet Mashies, Müesli, oatmeal or porridge, Pasta with Vegetables and Pine Nuts, Saucy Noodles and Vegetables, Scrambled Eggs Plus, Scrambled Tofu, Tapioca Pudding, toast
Spicy foods	Black Bean and Sweet Potato Enchiladas, Fajitas, Kung Pao Tofu, Mild Yellow Curry Stew, Seitan "Chicken" and Cashews, Tamale Pie, tortilla chips and salsa, Tofu Enchiladas, Tortilla Soup, Veggie Breakfast Burrito

Common Pregnancy Discomforts

Morning Sickness

Prevention:
- Eat small, frequent meals to prevent low blood sugar.
- Get adequate amounts of vitamin B6 (see page 20 for sources).
- Eat a protein-rich snack before bed.
- Have something to eat as soon as you get up (crackers, bread, or one of the overnight porridges in this book).

Treatment:
- Drink teas made from red raspberry leaf, peppermint, ginger, or fennel (pages 374–381).
- Drink Better Than Ginger Ale (page 360).
- Drink water or tea with lemon.
- Drink Lemonade or Mint Lemonade (page 358).
- Eat a bowl of cooked millet or Cream of Millet Cereal (page 49).

Constipation

Prevention:
- Eat fiber-rich foods like whole grains, legumes, fruits, and vegetables.
- Drink plenty of water.
- Exercise regularly (walking, swimming, and yoga are good choices).

Treatment:
- Eat a bowl of oatmeal with or without 1 teaspoon ground flaxseeds before bed or first thing in the morning.
- Eat pears, prunes, or figs.
- Drink prune or pear juice.
- Drink Unblocker Tea (page 379).
- Drink Apple Cider Vinegar Tonic (page 382).
- Drink Chia Energy Drink (page 382).
- Drink plenty of water.
- Move around (walk, swim, do yoga, etc.).

Heartburn

Prevention:
- Eat small, frequent meals.
- Chew food slowly and thoroughly.
- Drink beverages between meals rather than with meals.
- Keep track of and eliminate foods that cause you heartburn.
- Don't lie down after eating.
- Drink fennel tea after meals.
- Eat papaya or pineapple with meals (they contain digestive enzymes).

Treatment:
- Eat yogurt or drink kefir.
- Eat soaked, raw almonds. Chew them slowly.

Fatigue

Prevention:
- Eat regular, nutrient-rich meals.
- Include protein foods at all meals and snacks.
- Avoid sugar and refined foods.
- Get adequate rest.
- Take time to relax or meditate.
- Get regular exercise.

Treatment:
- Take a nap.
- Drink Chia Energy Drink (page 382).
- Drink tea made from red raspberry leaves, peppermint, or spearmint.
- Eat a protein-rich snack.
- Take a walk.
- Talk to your physician or midwife about testing for anemia or thyroid disorders.

Common Postpartum Discomforts

Colicky Baby

Prevention:
- Nurse in a relaxed manner and environment to promote good digestion.
- Drink Nursing Tea (page 376) daily.
- Avoid gas-promoting foods like garlic, onions, beans and legumes, and cabbage family foods if they seem to cause baby distress (usually only necessary for the first month or two).
- Avoid any foods that seem to cause baby distress.

Treatment:
- Drink fennel or catnip tea before breastfeeding. Diluted, room-temperature tea can also be fed directly to baby.
- Eliminate sugar, chocolate, and white flour from your diet.
- Systematically eliminate possible allergens like dairy, wheat, soy, corn, citrus, and peanuts from your diet. (It takes 3 to 5 days for the food to be out of your system. After that time, reintroduce food to see if reaction occurs in baby.)

Lack of Breastmilk

Prevention:
- Eat nutrient-rich meals and snacks.
- Eat plenty of dark green leafy vegetables.
- Drink tea made from fennel, fenugreek, blessed thistle, or red raspberry leaf tea daily (or try Nursing Tea on page 376).
- Get adequate rest.

Treatment:
- Drink Nursing Tea (page 376) before you breastfeed.
- Drink Creamy Green Smoothie (page 372).
- Eat dark green leafy vegetables.
- Eat nutrient-rich meals and snacks.
- Drink fenugreek tea or ask your physician or midwife about a fenugreek supplement.

Moodiness or Depression

Prevention:
- Eat foods containing essential fatty acids like nuts and seeds (e.g., walnuts, flaxseeds, chia seeds, pumpkin seeds).
- Eat foods containing B-vitamins like nutritional yeast, whole grains, dark green leafy vegetables, and eggs.
- Eat lots of fresh fruits and vegetables to supply your body with antioxidants.
- Eat regular nutrient-rich meals and snacks to avoid low blood sugar which can cause mood swings.
- Drink red raspberry leaf tea daily.
- Avoid refined sugars and processed foods.
- Get regular fresh air and exercise.
- Get enough rest and sleep (e.g., nap when baby naps or ask someone to watch your baby so you can take an uninterrupted nap).
- Take time to care for yourself. (Ask your partner, family member or friend to watch your baby for an hour or two so you can take a bath, get a massage, read a book, etc.)

Treatment:
- Increase your consumption of omega-3 fatty acid-rich foods (e.g., walnuts, flaxseeds, chia seeds, and pumpkin seeds).
- Drink 2 cups lemon balm tea daily.
- Drink blessed thistle tea or Nursing Tea (page 376) several times daily.
- Eat regular nutrient-rich meals and snacks.
- Eliminate sugar and processed foods from your diet.
- Get fresh air and exercise.
- Get a massage.
- Do yoga or Tai Chi.
- Talk to your physician or midwife about testing for anemia or thyroid disorders.

What to do if you are not thriving on a vegetarian diet:

Occasionally, pregnant or lactating women do not thrive on a vegetarian or vegan diet. Women who are allergic to grains, soy, nuts, eggs, and/or dairy may have difficulty getting the nutrients they need. If you are having trouble maintaining your proper weight, are feeling overly lethargic or moody, are feeling generally unhealthy, or your physician or midwife has concerns about your diet, you may want to consider supplementing your diet with some animal foods.

Fish is a good choice, particularly wild salmon, cod, sardines, anchovies, herring, and mackerel, which are excellent sources of DHA. Avoid shark, king mackerel, tilefish, swordfish, and tuna, which tend to retain high levels of toxins in their flesh. Organic poultry is another option. If you are vegan, you might consider eating eggs. Look for eggs from hens that you know are not being mistreated and are allowed to roam free. Most hens are raised without a rooster and are not fertilized. You may even consider raising your own hens. Chickens are easy to take care of and make wonderful pets.

The decision to eat animal foods can be a difficult one, especially for those who are vegetarian for ethical reasons. If you decide to eat some animal foods, pay attention to how you feel. If you feel more energetic and grounded, acknowledge the fact you are doing what's best for the health of your child. If you don't feel better after a few weeks (or feel worse), talk to your doctor or midwife about other possible causes.

About the Recipes

The recipes in this book call for whole foods wherever possible. I offer alternatives to dairy products in every recipe and alternatives to eggs where I can. All ingredients can be found at natural foods stores. Most supermarkets carry some organic and natural foods. If you can't find certain ingredients (e.g., sea vegetables or nutritional yeast flakes), refer to the Ingredient Guide for substitution ideas or simply omit them from the recipe. You can also go to the Web site www.simplynaturalbooks.com. The Resources page lists online sources for natural foods.

The recipes in this book were analyzed using Nutribase EZ Edition, version 5, software from CyberSoft, Inc. Each recipe analyzed contains breakdowns for calories (cals.), protein (grams), carbohydrates (grams), fiber (grams), fat (grams), and sodium (milligrams) rounded to the nearest whole number. If a recipe supplies 10 percent or more of the daily recommended dietary intake (RDI) for nonpregnant women for any of the vitamins or minerals listed on the chart on page 17, they are listed under KEY NUTRIENTS.

All ingredients, including (optional) ingredients, are included in the analysis. Optional additions or optional toppings listed at the end of the recipe or in the instructions are not included in the nutrient analysis. When a recipe calls for variable amounts (e.g. 1 to 2 tablespoons), analysis is calculated using the first or lower quantity. If a recipe suggests alternative ingredients (e.g., whole wheat or spelt flour), the analysis is based on the first listed ingredient (in the case of this example, whole wheat flour). Many recipes call for "milk (dairy or nondairy)." Full-fat dairy milk was used for the nutrient analysis. Using reduced-fat dairy milk, soy milk, rice milk, or almond milk will alter calories, protein, fat, and other nutrients.

If a recipe suggests variable serving amounts, the first listing is the one used for the nutrient analysis. Nutrient information was not available for some ingredients (such as sunflower sprouts and Rejuvelac) so they are not included in the analysis. In other cases, nutrient analysis was not available for ingredients in the exact form specified in a recipe. In that case, nutrient information was calculated using the closest form. For example, nutrient information for carrots was only available for raw or boiled carrots. In recipes calling for steamed carrots, nutrient analysis was based on boiled carrots.

Unless the recipes specify otherwise, the following ingredients were used in nutrient analysis. If you choose alternate or reduced fat ingredients, the nutrient and fat contents will differ.

Bread, bagels, English muffins, tortillas: whole wheat
Brown rice: long grain
Butter: salted butter
Dairy products (milk, yogurt, cheese): full fat versions
Eggs: large eggs
Fruit (apples, oranges, bananas, etc.): medium size
Garlic cloves: medium size
Lettuce: romaine
Mayonnaise: full-fat version
Nutritional yeast flakes: Red Star® Vegetarian Support Formula
Oil: grapeseed oil
Olive oil: extra virgin
Pasta: whole wheat
Tofu: firm tofu prepared with calcium sulfate
Vegetable stock: because prepared and homemade stock are so variable, water was used for nutrient analysis
Vegetables (onions, carrots, cucumbers, etc.): medium size

BREAKFASTS

Breakfast is an important meal at any time of your life, but essential while you are nurturing a baby. Unfortunately, it's the meal we often skimp on. While you may have been able to get by on a cup of juice or a slice of toast before, a more substantial breakfast will help you to feel your best while pregnant and breastfeeding.

Mornings can be rushed and hectic, especially when you have children. The recipes in this section require minimal preparation. Organization and planning help to make breakfast stress-free. Think about breakfast at night. Soak rolled oats overnight so oatmeal just takes a few minutes to cook, or start some porridge in your slow cooker. Keep one of the pancake and waffle mixes (pages 66 – 67) on hand. When you make pancakes, French toast, or waffles, freeze the leftovers so you'll have a quick, homemade breakfast on rushed mornings.

Be sure to include protein and fat in your morning meal. A completely carbohydrate breakfast, even of whole grains, will leave you tired, hungry, and maybe even light-headed an hour or two later. Limit or avoid sweetened foods in the morning. They cause your blood sugar to shoot up causing you to feel drained and weak soon after. Protein and fat give you energy and help sustain you throughout the morning.

First trimester mornings can be especially challenging so it is helpful to have something already prepared. Keep hard-boiled eggs, yogurt, cottage cheese, or Müesli in the refrigerator so you won't have to worry about cooking. Overnight Rice Porridge (page 55) or Slow Cooker Oatmeal (page 47) are good choices because they cook overnight. When you are really pressed for time, toast or a bagel with nut or seed butter can get you started quickly.

These breakfast recipes are designed to nourish you at this important time of your life but they are also excellent for the whole family. Your partner and children will benefit from the protein and nutrients in these dishes. Remember, these recipes are just ideas. You can adjust them according to what you have on hand and to suit your family's tastes.

Don't be limited to the choices in this section for breakfast. Smoothies (see Beverages) are also a good choice and easy to make. I find soup very comforting in the morning. Keep leftover soup in the refrigerator or freezer and warm it up for breakfast.

Hot Cereals

Basic Oatmeal
Soaked Oatmeal
Slow Cooker Oatmeal
Instant Oatmeal
Cream of Millet Cereal
High-Protein Porridge
Cranberry-Pear Crunch Cereal
Brown Rice and Miso
Polenta Porridge
Multigrain Grits
Overnight Rice Porridge
Savory Rice and Bean Porridge
Savory Bean Mash

Cold Cereals

Winter Müesli
Summer Müesli
Cold Grain Cereal
Crunchy Buckwheat Cereal
Millet Crunch Granola
Papaya Delight
Cantaloupe Surprise
Cottage Cheese Sundae

Pancakes, Waffles, and French Toast

Whole Wheat Pancake and
    Waffle Mix
Multigrain Pancake and Waffle Mix
Whole Grain Pancakes
Whole Grain Waffles
Mush Cakes
Sesame French Toast
Vegan French Toast
French Toast Sandwich

Eggs, Tofu and Potatoes

Scrambled Eggs Plus
Broccoli-Mushroom Scramble
Curried Spinach Scramble
Basic Omelet
California Omelet
Herbed Cottage Cheese Omelet
Veggie Omelet
Tomato-Herb Omelet
Veggie Breakfast Burrito
Scrambled Tofu
Golden Tofu on Toast
Breakfast Potatoes and Veggies

Toast, Bagels, and English Muffins

Molasses Toast
Savory Bagel Sandwich
English Muffin Cheesecake
English Muffin Melt

Hot Cereals

There is nothing more soothing than a bowl of hot porridge on a cold morning. The cereals in this section require hardly more than mixing grain and liquid in a pot. They cook without much intervention. Since some have cooking times of 20 minutes or longer, start the cereal when you first get up and by the time you are showered and dressed, you'll have a hot breakfast waiting. During the first trimester, you may want something to eat as soon as you awaken. Try Overnight Rice Porridge or Slow Cooker Oatmeal – they cook in your slow cooker while you sleep.

Add protein and fat to your cereal to keep your blood sugar levels stable and to sustain you through the morning. Nuts and seeds are an excellent addition to cereals, as well as a little oil or butter to help your body absorb fat-soluble vitamins. You can sweeten your cereal with a little honey, molasses, or maple syrup if desired, but I don't recommend much sugar in the morning. Try using fresh or dried fruit or fruit-sweetened jam instead. For something different, try seasoning your porridge with naturally fermented soy sauce or miso for a savory taste.

Basic Oatmeal

Mixing oats with cold water results in a creamy porridge. Oatmeal supplies some protein but if you top it with a couple tablespoons of nuts, seeds, yogurt or milk, you can boost the protein further.

1 cup rolled oats
3 cups water
1/4 teaspoon sea salt
Pinch ground cinnamon, cardamom, or pumpkin pie spice (optional)

Mix all ingredients together in pan. Bring to a boil over high heat. Reduce heat to low and simmer uncovered 15 minutes, or until desired consistency.

Makes 3 to 4 servings

Variation: Use steel cut oats instead of rolled oats. Increase cooking time to 30 minutes.

APPROXIMATE NUTRITIONAL INFORMATION FOR 1 SERVING: Calories: 104 cal; Protein: 4 g; Carbohydrates: 18 g; Fat: 2 g; Fiber: 3 g; Sodium: 185 mg.

KEY NUTRIENTS: Thiamine: .2 mg; Iron: 1.13 mg; Magnesium: 39.96 mg; Zinc: .83 mg.

What to do with leftover porridge:

I always seem to have some oatmeal left after breakfast and can't bear to throw it away. Here are a few ideas to use up that extra porridge.

- Add it to bread, cookies, muffins, etc.
- Reheat it with milk (dairy or nondairy) for breakfast or snack.
- Use it to thicken soup.
- Make Mush Cakes (page 71) or Leftover Oatmeal-Raisin Muffins (page 301).

Soaked Oatmeal

Oats contain a lot of phytates that can inhibit mineral absorption. Soaking the oats overnight helps to neutralize the phytic acid. It also reduces the cooking time.

1 cup rolled oats
2 1/2 cups water
1/4 teaspoon sea salt

In medium-size pan, mix oats, water, and sea salt and let sit overnight or up to 24 hours. When ready to cook, bring to a boil and simmer 3 to 5 minutes, or until desired consistency. Top with almonds, walnuts, or ground flaxseeds for protein, minerals, and essential fatty acids.

Makes 3 to 4 servings

Note: Add 2 tablespoons yogurt, whey, or lemon juice to water when soaking oats if desired.

Variation: Use steel cut oats instead of rolled oats and use 3 cups water. Increase cooking time to 10 minutes.

APPROXIMATE NUTRITIONAL INFORMATION FOR 1 SERVING: Calories: 104 cal; Protein: 4 g; Carbohydrates: 18 g; Fat: 2 g; Fiber: 3 g; Sodium: 185 mg.

KEY NUTRIENTS: Thiamine: .2 mg; Iron: 1.13 mg; Magnesium: 39.96 mg; Zinc: .83 mg.

Slow Cooker Oatmeal

You'll love waking up to this creamy cereal. You may need to alter the amount of water slightly to work with your slow cooker.

1 cup rolled oats
4 cups water
1/4 teaspoon sea salt

Place all ingredients in slow cooker. Cover and set to low. Cook overnight (10 to 12 hours).

Makes 3 to 4 servings

Variation: Substitute steel cut oats for rolled oats and use 4 1/2 to 5 cups water.

APPROXIMATE NUTRITIONAL INFORMATION FOR 1 SERVING: Calories: 104 cal; Protein: 4 g; Carbohydrates: 18 g; Fat: 2 g; Fiber: 3 g; Sodium: 185 mg.

KEY NUTRIENTS: Thiamine: .2 mg; Iron: 1.13 mg; Magnesium: 39.96 mg; Zinc: .83 mg.

Following are some of our favorite flavor combinations for oatmeal:

Apple-Walnut Oatmeal: Core and shred 1 apple. Mix apple and 1/3 cup chopped walnuts into oatmeal.

Coconut-Banana Oatmeal: Place oatmeal in serving dishes. Top with sliced bananas and cover with coconut milk. Sprinkle shredded coconut over top.

Dried Fruit and Seed Oatmeal: Mix any combination of dried fruit (raisins, cranberries, apricots, prunes) and seeds (sunflower, pumpkin, ground sesame or flax) into oatmeal. Top with milk (dairy or nondairy).

Cashew Yogurt and Molasses Oatmeal: Place oatmeal in bowl. Top with scoop of Cashew Yogurt (page 272) and drizzle on a little blackstrap molasses.

Instant Oatmeal

Store-bought instant oatmeal is usually loaded with sugar. This version is just as convenient but much healthier.

Mix together 4 cups quick-cooking oats, 1 cup dried fruit (e.g., raisins), 3/4 cup chopped nuts or seeds (e.g., almonds). Store in covered container.

To serve: Pour about 1/2 cup of mixture into bowl. Cover with boiling water. Let sit one minute. Top with milk or yogurt if desired.

Makes 5 1/2 cups

Note: For extra chewy cereal, use regular rolled oats.

Try the following combinations:
- Chopped dried apple, cinnamon, and walnuts
- Raisins, coconut, and sunflower seeds
- Dried bananas and almonds
- Dried cranberries and pumpkin seeds

APPROXIMATE NUTRITIONAL INFORMATION FOR 1/2 CUP: Calories: 204 cal; Protein: 7 g; Carbohydrates: 32 g; Fat: 6 g; Fiber: 5 g; Sodium: 3 mg.

KEY NUTRIENTS: Thiamine: .27 mg; Riboflavin: .12 mg; Pantothenic Acid: .44 mg; Vitamin E: 2.42 mg; Iron: 1.94 mg; Magnesium: 73.82 mg; Zinc: 1.3 mg.

Cream of Millet Cereal

Millet porridge has been said to help alleviate morning sickness. The taste and texture is similar to Cream of Wheat®. To save time in the morning, toast the grains the night before.

1 cup millet
Pinch sea salt
5 cups water

Toast millet in dry skillet, stirring occasionally, until mixture begins to pop (about 5 minutes). Cool and grind to powder in blender or coffee grinder. Place water in pan. Whisk in ground millet and salt. Bring to a boil and simmer uncovered for 20 minutes, or until mixture is thickened and millet is soft. Stir occasionally to keep mixture from scorching. Serve with milk, cream, butter, flaxseed oil, and/or dried fruit if desired.

Makes 4 servings

Note: For a richer cereal, substitute milk for half of the water in the cereal.

Variations

Cream of Rice Cereal: Substitute brown rice for millet.
Cream of Barley Cereal: Substitute barley for millet.
Cream of Wheat Cereal: Substitute wheat or spelt berries for millet.

APPROXIMATE NUTRITIONAL INFORMATION FOR 1 SERVING: Calories: 189 cal; Protein: 6 g; Carbohydrates: 36 g; Fat: 2 g; Fiber: 4 g; Sodium: 37 mg.

KEY NUTRIENTS: Thiamine: .21 mg; Riboflavin: .14 mg; Niacin: 2.36 mg; Pantothenic Acid: .42 mg; Vitamin B6: .19 mg; Folate: 42.5 mcg; Iron: 1.5 mg; Magnesium: 57 mg; Zinc: .84 mg.

High-Protein Porridge

This cereal is a good source of minerals and B vitamins, as well as protein.

1/3 cup quinoa
1/3 cup millet
1/3 cup amaranth
5 cups water
Pinch sea salt
1/4 cup flax or sesame seeds, ground
1 teaspoon ground cinnamon or cardamom (optional)

Rinse quinoa. Place grains, water, and sea salt in heavy-bottomed pot. Bring to a boil over high heat. Reduce heat and simmer uncovered 25 to 30 minutes, stirring occasionally to prevent cereal from sticking to bottom of pan. Stir in ground seeds and spices.

Makes 4 servings

APPROXIMATE NUTRITIONAL INFORMATION FOR 1 SERVING: Calories: 224 cal; Protein: 8 g; Carbohydrates: 36 g; Fat: 6 g; Fiber: 7 g; Sodium: 45 mg.

KEY NUTRIENTS: Thiamine: .13 mg; Riboflavin: .15 mg; Niacin: 1.55 mg; Pantothenic Acid: .61 mg; Vitamin B6: .22 mg; Folate: 56 mcg; Iron: 3.65 mg; Magnesium: 127.04 mg; Zinc: 1.67 mg.

Cranberry-Pear Crunch Cereal

This cereal is a great way to use leftover grains. It is a good source of B vitamins, vitamin E, and minerals.

2 cups cooked brown rice, millet, quinoa, or barley
1 cup milk (dairy or nondairy)
1 pear, diced
1/4 cup sunflower seeds or chopped almonds
2 tablespoons dried cranberries
Pinch ground ginger or nutmeg

Mix all ingredients in pan and warm over low heat about 10 minutes, stirring occasionally.

Makes 4 servings

Note: See the Grain Cooking Chart in the Appendix for instructions on cooking grains.

APPROXIMATE NUTRITIONAL INFORMATION FOR 1 SERVING: Calories: 235 cal; Protein: 7 g; Carbohydrates: 36 g; Fat: 8 g; Fiber: 4 g; Sodium: 35 mg.

KEY NUTRIENTS: Thiamine: .33 mg; Riboflavin: .16 mg; Niacin: 2.03 mg; Pantothenic Acid: 1.11 mg; Vitamin B6: .24 mg; Vitamin B12: .22 mcg; Vitamin E: 5 mg; Calcium: 97.72 mg; Iron: 1.17 mg; Magnesium: 84.39 mg; Zinc: 1.35 mg.

Brown Rice and Miso

This is an excellent grounding breakfast that is high in B vitamins.

1 cup hot, cooked brown rice
1 teaspoons miso mixed with 2 tablespoons warm water
1 tablespoons toasted sesame seeds

Mix all ingredients together.

Makes 1 to 2 servings

Note: See the Grain Cooking Chart in the Appendix for instructions on cooking rice.

APPROXIMATE NUTRITIONAL INFORMATION FOR 1 SERVING: Calories: 274 cal; Protein: 7 g; Carbohydrates: 48 g; Fat: 6 g; Fiber: 5 g; Sodium: 222 mg.

KEY NUTRIENTS: THIAMINE: .29 MG; RIBOFLAVIN: .1 mg; Niacin: 3.46 mg; Pantothenic Acid: .63 mg; Vitamin B6: .31 mg; Iron: 1.6 mg; Magnesium: 113.94 mg; Zinc: 2.24 mg.

Polenta Porridge

This creamy, golden porridge is a delicious treat. Eat it with fresh, frozen, or dried berries or sliced bananas and milk. You can also top it with butter or Parmesan cheese and serve it with eggs.

5 cups water
1/8 teaspoon sea salt
1 cup polenta (coarsely-ground cornmeal)

Bring water and salt to a boil. Pour polenta into boiling water in a thin stream while stirring with a wooden spoon. When mixture comes to a boil, reduce heat to low and simmer 15 minutes. Stir occasionally to prevent sticking.

Makes 4 servings

Note: If you have leftover Polenta Porridge, spread it in a shallow pan or dish. Refrigerate until firm. Cut into squares and brown in hot, oiled skillet and eat like pancakes.

APPROXIMATE NUTRITIONAL INFORMATION FOR 1 SERVING: Calories: 126 cal; Protein: 3 g; Carbohydrates: 27 g; Fat: 1 g; Fiber: 0 g; Sodium: 70 mg.

Multigrain Grits

This combination of grains has a gritlike taste and texture but is more nutritious than packaged grit mixes. It is delicious eaten with butter alongside eggs or as a porridge.

1/2 cup millet
1/4 cup polenta
1/4 cup amaranth
5 cups water
1/8 teaspoon sea salt
1 tablespoon flaxseeds
1 tablespoon sesame seeds
2 tablespoons sunflower or pumpkin seeds

Place grains, water, and salt in heavy-bottomed pot. Bring to a boil over high heat. Reduce heat and simmer uncovered 30 minutes, stirring occasionally to prevent cereal from sticking to bottom of pan. Grind seeds in coffee grinder or blender. Stir into cooked grains.

Makes 6 servings

APPROXIMATE NUTRITIONAL INFORMATION FOR 1 SERVING: Calories: 150 cal; Protein: 5 g; Carbohydrates: 24 g; Fat: 4 g; Fiber: 4 g; Sodium: 50 mg.

KEY NUTRIENTS: Thiamine: .16 mg; Niacin: 1.12 mg; Pantothenic Acid: .46 mg; Vitamin B6: .14 mg; Vitamin E: 1.76 mg; Iron: 1.66 mg; Magnesium: 63.74 mg; Zinc: .89 mg.

Overnight Rice Porridge

It's convenient to have breakfast ready in the morning especially during the first trimester when you want something to eat as soon as you wake up. Top this cereal with nuts or seeds for protein and fat.

1 cup brown rice
4 1/2 cups water
1/4 teaspoon sea salt

Place rice, water, and sea salt in slow cooker. Cover and set to low. Let cook overnight (about 10 hours). Mix in dried fruit, nuts, and/or seeds if desired and top with milk and blackstrap molasses.

Makes 6 servings

APPROXIMATE NUTRITIONAL INFORMATION FOR 1 SERVING: Calories: 114 cal; Protein: 2 g; Carbohydrates: 24 g; Fat: 1 g; Fiber: 1 g; Sodium: 97 mg.

KEY NUTRIENTS: THIAMINE: .12 mg; Niacin: 1.57 mg; Pantothenic Acid: .46 mg; Vitamin B6: .16 mg; Magnesium: 44.09 mg.

Savory Rice and Bean Porridge

Here's another recipe that you can cook overnight so it's ready when you wake up.

1/2 cup brown rice
1/2 cup adzuki beans
4 1/2 cups water
1/2 strip kombu (optional)

Place rice, beans, water, and kombu in slow cooker. Cover and set to low. Let cook overnight (about 10 hours). Season with miso or soy sauce to taste. Add a dollop of plain yogurt or sour cream if you like.

Makes 6 servings

APPROXIMATE NUTRITIONAL INFORMATION FOR 1 SERVING: Calories: 113 cal; Protein: 4 g; Carbohydrates: 23 g; Fat: 1 g; Fiber: 3 g; Sodium: 17 mg.

KEY NUTRIENTS: Thiamine: .14 mg; Niacin: 1.22 mg; Pantothenic Acid: .47 mg; Vitamin B6: .14 mg; Folate: 105.19 mcg; Iron: 1.04 mg; Magnesium: 46.9 mg; Zinc: 1.14 mg.

Savory Bean Mash

Beans are an excellent morning choice because they are high in protein. Since we tend to move around more during the day, they are less likely to cause digestive difficulties.

2 cups or 1 (15-ounce) can cooked beans (pinto, adzuki, white beans, etc.)
1 teaspoon olive oil
1/4 teaspoon dried sage or thyme
Soy sauce, miso, or sea salt to taste
Black pepper to taste
1 tablespoon minced fresh parsley (optional)

Heat beans with a little water if necessary until warm. Stir in remaining ingredients and mash together.

Makes 4 servings

APPROXIMATE NUTRITIONAL INFORMATION FOR 1 SERVING: Calories: 128 cal; Protein: 7 g; Carbohydrates: 22 g; Fat: 2 g; Fiber: 7 g; Sodium: 20 mg.

KEY NUTRIENTS: Thiamine: .16 mg; Vitamin B6: .13 mg; Folate: 148.5 mcg; Iron: 2.29 mg; Magnesium: 47.5 mg; Zinc: .93 mg.

Cold Cereals

Ready-to-eat cereals are certainly convenient but grains that have been flaked and puffed at high temperatures are nutritionally inferior to unprocessed, whole grains. In addition, most commercial cereals contain sugar, preservatives, artificial colors and flavors. Even if the cereal is labeled "no preservatives added," the package itself may have been treated with the preservatives BHA and BHT.

Although I don't recommend packaged, ready-to-eat cereals on a daily basis, they are nice to have around when you just don't have the time or energy to cook. Buy quality, organic cereals made with whole grains and natural sweeteners. Check the label and look for cereal that contains no more than 4 grams of sugar per serving. Add raw or toasted nuts or seeds (whole or ground) to add nutrients, protein, and essential fatty acids to your breakfast.

Müesli

My Mom used to make big batches of Müesli in the summer when fresh berries and fruit were abundant. We would eat it all day long. Müesli can be made any time of year with whatever fruit is available. It keeps for several days in the refrigerator and makes a great snack. You can make Müesli the night before so breakfast will be ready in the morning.

This is a completely versatile dish. Start with oats and milk and then add whatever fruit is in season and your favorite nuts or seeds. If gluten in oats is a problem, substitute rolled barley or other rolled grain. Following are a couple of versions that we enjoy. Both are good sources of protein and rich in most vitamins and minerals, including calcium and iron.

Winter Müesli

2 cups rolled oats
1 1/2 cups milk (dairy or nondairy)
1 apple, diced
1 pear, diced
1 orange, peeled and sections sliced in half
1 banana, peeled and sliced
1/4 cup coarsely chopped walnuts
1/2 cup raisins or dried cranberries (optional)
1/4 cup pumpkin seeds
1/2 teaspoon ground cinnamon
2 tablespoons chia gel (page 394) (optional)

Mix oats and milk together in large bowl. Let sit while you prepare fruit or place in refrigerator overnight. Mix in remaining ingredients. Eat immediately or refrigerate for later.

Makes 6 servings

Variation:

Replace 1/2 to 1 cup milk with yogurt or kefir.

APPROXIMATE NUTRITIONAL INFORMATION FOR 1 SERVING: Calories: 303 cal; Protein: 10 g; Carbohydrates: 47 g; Fat: 10 g; Fiber: 6 g; Sodium: 34 mg.

KEY NUTRIENTS: Thiamine: .31 mg; Riboflavin: .22 mg; Pantothenic Acid: .72 mg; Vitamin B6: .27 mg; Vitamin B12: .22 mcg; Vitamin C: 17.38 mg; Calcium 116.84 mg; Iron: 2.66 mg; Magnesium 101.58 mg; Zinc: 1.79 mg.

Summer Müesli

2 cups rolled oats
1 1/2 cups milk (dairy or nondairy)
1 peach or nectarine, diced
2 apricots or plums, diced
1 cup berries (raspberries, blackberries, blueberries, strawberries, etc.)
1/2 cup sunflower seeds or chopped almonds
2 tablespoons ground flaxseeds or chia gel (page 394)

Mix oats and milk together in large bowl. Let sit while you prepare fruit or place in refrigerator overnight. Mix in remaining ingredients. Eat immediately or refrigerate for later.

Makes 6 servings

Variation: Replace 1/2 to 1 cup milk with yogurt or kefir.

APPROXIMATE NUTRITIONAL INFORMATION FOR 1 SERVING: Calories: 253 cal; Protein: 10 g; Carbohydrates: 30 g; Fat: 11 g; Fiber: 7 g; Sodium: 33 mg.

KEY NUTRIENTS: Vitamin A: 65.98 mcg; Thiamine: .51 mg; Riboflavin: .2 mg; Niacin: 1.27 mg; Pantothenic Acid: 1.5 mg; Vitamin B6: .21 mg; Folate: 56.92 mcg; Vitamin B12: .22 mcg; Vitamin C: 8.5 mg; Vitamin E: 6.79 mg; Calcium 115.47 mg; Iron: 2.42 mg; Magnesium 110.62 mg; Zinc: 1.98 mg.

Cold Grain Cereal

Mix cold cooked brown rice, barley, millet, or quinoa with fruit and milk, just as you would eat packaged cereal. You'll be surprised how delicious it is.

Crunchy Buckwheat Cereal

Here's a cold breakfast cereal you can feel good about. It is easy to make in advance and will keep in your refrigerator for days. It's delicious sprinkled over fruit, too.

2 cups raw whole buckwheat groats
2 tablespoons maple syrup, brown rice syrup, agave nectar, or honey (optional)
1/4 cup nut or seed butter (almond butter, tahini, etc.)

Preheat oven to 300°F. Spread buckwheat on large baking sheet. Bake for 20 minutes. Stir buckwheat around a bit. Roast for 15 to 20 minutes more until golden. Immediately mix hot buckwheat with sweetener and nut or seed butter until buckwheat is coated. Cool. Store in covered jar in refrigerator. To serve, place 1/2 cup of cereal in bowl, cover with milk. Add fresh or dried fruit if desired.

Makes 4 servings

APPROXIMATE NUTRITIONAL INFORMATION FOR 1 SERVING: Calories: 405 cal; Protein: 13 g; Carbohydrates: 72 g; Fat: 10 g; Fiber: 8 g; Sodium: 12 mg.

KEY NUTRIENTS: Thiamine: .18 mg; Riboflavin: .22 mg; Niacin: 4.21 mg; Pantothenic Acid: 1.01 mg; Vitamin B6: .29 mg; Folate: 34.44 mcg; Iron: 2.15 mg; Magnesium 182.62 mg; Zinc: 2.4 mg.

Millet Crunch Granola

This healthy granola makes a great topping for fruit or yogurt. You can even eat it alone for a crunchy snack.

2 1/4 cups rolled oats
1/2 cup uncooked millet
1/3 cup honey, brown rice syrup, agave nectar, or maple syrup
1/4 cup tahini
2 tablespoons water
1/3 cup pumpkin seeds
1/3 cup sunflower seeds
1 tablespoon flaxseeds
1 tablespoon sesame seeds

Preheat oven to 250°F. Place rolled oats and millet on baking sheet. Roast for 1 hour. In small pan, melt sweetener, tahini, and water together over low heat. In large bowl, toss oats, millet, and seeds with tahini mixture until completely coated. Spread on unoiled baking sheet, and bake for 30 minutes. Stir once or twice during baking. Cool completely. Store in airtight container.

Makes 8 servings

Variation: Add 1/2 to 1 cup dried fruit to cooked granola and store as directed. Do not bake fruit.

APPROXIMATE NUTRITIONAL INFORMATION FOR 1 SERVING: Calories: 297 cal; Protein: 10 g; Carbohydrates: 41 g; Fat: 12 g; Fiber: 6 g; Sodium: 9 mg.

KEY NUTRIENTS: Thiamine: .48 mg; Riboflavin: .15 mg; Niacin: 1.65 mg; Pantothenic Acid: .89 mg; Vitamin B6: .17 mg; Folate: 47.48 mcg; Vitamin E: 3.36 mg; Iron: 3.05 mg; Magnesium 116.55 mg; Zinc: 2.14 mg.

Papaya Delight

I first tried this delicious breakfast at a natural foods café when I was pregnant with my second daughter. Both papaya and yogurt contain enzymes to aid digestion.

1/2 papaya, seeds removed
1/2 cup plain yogurt (dairy or nondairy)
1/4 cup granola

Place papaya on plate, cut side up. Fill with yogurt. Sprinkle with granola.

Makes 1 serving

Note: Use Millet Crunch Granola (page 62) or your favorite lightly sweetened granola.

APPROXIMATE NUTRITIONAL INFORMATION FOR 1 SERVING: Calories: 282 cal; Protein: 10 g; Carbohydrates: 41 g; Fat: 10 g; Fiber: 6 g; Sodium: 65 mg.

KEY NUTRIENTS: Vitamin A: 81.96 mcg; Thiamine: .31 mg; Riboflavin: .3 mg; Niacin: 1.43 mg; Pantothenic Acid: 1.25 mg; Vitamin B6: .15 mg; Folate: 90.08 mcg; Vitamin B12: .45 mcg; Vitamin C: 94.65 mg; Vitamin E: 3.49 mg; Calcium: 218.57 mg; Iron: 1.74 mg; Magnesium 88.17 mg; Zinc: 1.9 mg.

Cantaloupe Surprise

1/2 cantaloupe, seeds removed
1/2 cup cottage cheese or plain yogurt (dairy or nondairy)
1/2 cup blueberries, raspberries, or blackberries

Place cantaloupe on plate, cut side up. Fill cavity with cottage cheese or yogurt. Top with berries.

Makes 1 serving

Note: If avoiding dairy products, use Tofu Cottage Cheese (page 273) or Cashew Yogurt (page 272).

APPROXIMATE NUTRITIONAL INFORMATION FOR 1 SERVING: Calories: 273 cal; Protein: 16 g; Carbohydrates: 42 g; Fat: 6 g; Fiber: 5 g; Sodium: 431 mg.

KEY NUTRIENTS: Vitamin A: 898.77 mcg; Thiamine: .15 mg; Riboflavin: .37 mg; Niacin: 1.94 mg; Pantothenic Acid: .55 mg; Vitamin B6: .35 mg; Folate: 52.95 mcg; Vitamin B12: .48 mcg; Vitamin C: 129.54 mg; Vitamin E: 1.42 mg; Calcium: 116.39 mg; Magnesium 35.39 mg.

Cottage Cheese Sundae

This is a super high-protein breakfast.

1/2 cup sliced fresh fruit (e.g., strawberries, bananas, peaches, figs, pineapples, grapes, etc.)
1/2 cup cottage cheese (dairy or nondairy)
2 tablespoons wheat germ
2 tablespoons Toasted Seed Mix (page 283) (optional)

Place fresh fruit in bowl. Top with cottage cheese. Sprinkle with wheat germ and Toasted Seed Mix.

Makes 1 serving

Note: Substitute 2 tablespoons sunflower or pumpkin seeds if you don't have Toasted Seed Mix.

APPROXIMATE NUTRITIONAL INFORMATION FOR 1 SERVING: Calories: 299 cal; Protein: 21 g; Carbohydrates: 21 g; Fat: 15 g; Fiber: 8 g; Sodium: 403 mg.

KEY NUTRIENTS: Thiamine: .37 mg; Riboflavin: .46 mg; Niacin: 1.69 mg; Pantothenic Acid: .79 mg; Vitamin B6: .15 mg; Folate: 82.05 mcg; Vitamin B12: .48 mcg; Vitamin C: 43.35 mg; Vitamin E: 6.34 mg; Calcium: 119.75 mg; Iron: 3.19 mg; Magnesium 108.16 mg; Zinc: 1.21 mg.

Pancakes, Waffles, and French Toast

You may think pancakes, waffles, and French toast are only for special occasions or weekends, but these recipes are easy enough to make any day of the week. Prepare one of the pancake and waffle mixes in advance so making them will be a snap. Freeze extra waffles or French toast, so during the week you can pop them into the toaster for a quick meal or snack.

Be creative with toppings. Try yogurt, nut or seed butters, fresh fruit, fruit-sweetened jam, or applesauce instead of traditional maple syrup. The whole grains, nuts, seeds, and spices give these lots of flavor that doesn't need to be covered up with sugary toppings.

Be sure to include a concentrated protein like eggs, cottage cheese, yogurt, beans, or nut/seed butters to slow the carbohydrate load that can cause a mid-morning energy crash.

Whole Wheat Pancake and Waffle Mix

4 cups whole wheat pastry flour
4 cups whole wheat flour
1/4 cup baking powder
1 teaspoon baking soda
1 teaspoon sea salt
1/4 cup evaporated cane juice (optional)
1 tablespoons ground cinnamon or pumpkin pie spice (optional)

Sift or whisk all ingredients together in large bowl until completely combined. Store in a covered 2-quart container.

Makes about 8 cups

Multigrain Pancake and Waffle Mix

2 cups whole wheat pastry flour
2 cups barley flour
2 cups buckwheat flour
1 cup brown rice flour
1 cup corn flour
1/4 cup baking powder
1 teaspoon baking soda
1 teaspoon sea salt
1/4 cup evaporated cane juice (optional)
1 tablespoon ground cinnamon or pumpkin pie spice (optional)

Sift or whisk all ingredients together in large bowl until completely combined. Store in a covered 2-quart container.

Makes about 8 cups

Whole Grain Pancakes

1 egg
1 1/4+ cups milk (dairy or nondairy)
2 tablespoons oil or melted unsalted butter
1 1/2 cups Whole Wheat or Multigrain Pancake and Waffle Mix

Preheat griddle or skillet to medium heat. Beat egg and milk together in mixing bowl until smooth. Beat in oil or melted butter. Stir in mix. If mixture is too thick, add additional milk. Batter should spread on griddle but not run. Cook on preheated, lightly oiled griddle or skillet until golden brown on both sides.

Makes 6 servings (2 pancakes per serving)

Note: If not using mix, whisk together 3/4 cup whole wheat or barley flour, 3/4 cup whole wheat pastry flour, 1/8 teaspoon baking soda, 1 1/2 teaspoons baking powder, 1/8 teaspoon sea salt, 1/2 teaspoon cinnamon (optional), and 2 teaspoons dehydrated cane juice (optional).

Variations

Almond Pancakes: Add 1 teaspoon almond extract and 1/2 cup chopped almonds to batter.
Apple, Peach, Apricot, Strawberry, or Banana Pancakes: After ladling batter onto griddle, press thin slices of fruit into batter.
Blueberry or Raspberry Pancakes: After ladling batter onto griddle, drop berries onto batter. (Small berries work best.)

APPROXIMATE NUTRITIONAL INFORMATION FOR 1 SERVING: Calories: 316 cal; Protein: 8 g; Carbohydrates: 34 g; Fat: 10 g; Fiber: 4 g; Sodium: 362 mg.

KEY NUTRIENTS: Thiamine: .13 mg; Riboflavin: .17 mg; Niacin: 1.48 mg; Pantothenic Acid: .49 mg; Vitamin B6: .11 mg; Vitamin B12: .27 mcg; Iron: 2.74 mg; Magnesium 38.51 mg; Zinc: .94 mg.

Tips for pancakes

- Heat the pan or griddle before you place the batter on it. To test if pan is ready, flick a drop or two of water on the surface. If the drop jumps, the pan is hot enough.
- Don't turn the pancakes too soon. Wait till the edges are dry and small bubbles appear on pancake surface.
- Don't undercook pancakes. They will be damp and unpleasant. If they are cooking too fast on the outside, turn down the heat.
- Place a plate inside your oven with the temperature set to warm. As pancakes come off the griddle, place them on the plate. That way, everyone can eat hot pancakes together.
- Extra pancakes can be frozen. Heat frozen pancakes in toaster, toaster oven, or on a warm griddle.

Whole Grain Waffles

2 eggs
1 1/4 cups milk
4 tablespoons oil or melted unsalted butter
1 1/2 cups Whole Wheat or Multigrain Pancake and Waffle Mix

Beat eggs and milk together in mixing bowl until smooth. Beat in oil or melted butter. Stir in mix. If mixture is too thick, add additional milk. Batter should pour smoothly from ladle and not drop in clumps. Bake in lightly oiled, preheated waffle iron until golden brown and crisp. Waffles are best served immediately but you can place on rack in warm oven until ready to serve if desired.

Makes 8 servings (2 4.5-inch square waffles per serving)

Note: If not using mix, whisk together 3/4 cup whole wheat or barley flour, 3/4 cup whole wheat pastry flour, 1/8 teaspoon baking soda, 1 1/2 teaspoons baking powder, 1/8 teaspoon sea salt, 1/2 teaspoon cinnamon (optional), and 2 teaspoons dehydrated cane juice (optional).

Variations

Raisin-Walnut Waffles: Gently fold 1/2 cup chopped walnuts and 1/2 cup raisins into batter.

Sunflower-Cranberry Waffles: Gently fold 1/2 cup chopped sunflower seeds, 1/2 cup dried cranberries, and 1 teaspoon grated orange peel into batter.

APPROXIMATE NUTRITIONAL INFORMATION FOR 1 SERVING: Calories: 276 cal; Protein: 7 g; Carbohydrates: 18 g; Fat: 26 g; Fiber: 3 g; Sodium: 280 mg.

KEY NUTRIENTS: Riboflavin: .16 mg; Vitamin B12: .26 mcg; Iron: 2.15 mg; Zinc: .78 mg.

Tips for Waffles

- Make sure waffle iron is preheated completely before cooking waffles.
- Even if your iron is nonstick, lightly spray or brush oil over it immediately before pouring in batter.
- Use the correct amount of batter. The manufacturer's instructions should tell you the right amount, usually about 1/2 cup for regular waffles and 1 cup for Belgian waffles.
- When steam stops streaming out of waffle iron, gently lift the cover to peek. The waffle is ready when golden and crisp. If not ready, replace the cover and cook a little longer.
- Waffles are best eaten immediately. If you want to keep them warm and crisp, place them in a warm oven on a rack that is on a baking sheet. If you place them directly on the baking sheet they will get soggy.
- Waffles can be frozen. To reheat, just toast frozen waffles in a toaster.

Mush Cakes

These are a delicious way to use up leftover porridge. My kids absolutely love them.

3 cups cooked porridge (Oatmeal, Cream of Millet, etc.)
2 eggs, beaten (or equivalent egg replacer)
1/2 teaspoon ground cinnamon

Mix porridge, eggs, and cinnamon together until combined. Oil or butter a hot griddle or skillet. Place 2-inch patties on griddle over medium-low heat. Bake about 5 minutes per side, or until brown and crispy. Serve like pancakes with jam, applesauce, or pure maple syrup.

Makes 4 to 6 servings

Variation: Add grated apple, raisins, chopped nuts, sunflower seeds, etc., to batter.

APPROXIMATE NUTRITIONAL INFORMATION FOR 1 SERVING: Calories: 146 cal; Protein: 8 g; Carbohydrates: 19 g; Fat: 4 g; Fiber: 3 g; Sodium: 33 mg.

KEY NUTRIENTS: Thiamine: .21 mg; Riboflavin: .16 mg; Pantothenic Acid: .66 mg; Vitamin B12: .25 mcg; Vitamin D: 1.3 mcg; Iron: 1.55 mg; Magnesium: 44.62 mg; Zinc: 1.14 mg.

Sesame French Toast

This is especially good made with whole grain raisin bread. Freeze the leftovers and warm in your toaster when ready to eat.

2 eggs
1/2 cup milk (dairy or nondairy)
Pinch ground cardamom
1/2 teaspoon vanilla or almond extract
1/2 cup sesame seeds
6 slices whole grain bread

In shallow bowl, beat together eggs, milk, cardamom, and vanilla or almond extract. Preheat griddle or skillet to medium heat. Spread sesame seeds on a plate. Dip bread into egg mixture, coating both sides. Lay bread on sesame seeds and turn to coat both sides. Place bread on lightly oiled, hot griddle or skillet. Cook each side of bread until golden brown. Repeat with remaining slices. Serve with applesauce, unsweetened jam, chopped fresh fruit, and/or yogurt or cottage cheese.

Makes 3 servings

APPROXIMATE NUTRITIONAL INFORMATION FOR 1 SERVING: Calories: 351 cal; Protein: 15 g; Carbohydrates: 34 g; Fat: 19 g; Fiber: 7 g; Sodium: 360 mg.

KEY NUTRIENTS: Vitamin A: 77.73 mcg; Thiamine: .42 mg; Riboflavin: .41 mg; Niacin: 3.29 mg; Pantothenic Acid: .87 mg; Vitamin B6: .35 mg; Folate: 68.98 mcg; Vitamin B12: .49 mcg; Vitamin D: 1.73 mcg; Vitamin E: 1.41 mg; Calcium: 339.05 mg; Iron: 5.84 mg; Magnesium: 141.02 mg; Zinc: 3.47 mg.

Vegan French Toast

You can have French toast without eggs or dairy. The flaxseeds give an eggy feeling to the toast and supply omega-3 fatty acids.

3 tablespoons flaxseeds
1/3 cup water
1 cup soy, rice, or almond milk
1 teaspoon vanilla extract
1/2 teaspoon ground cinnamon
Pinch ground nutmeg
8 slices whole grain bread

Grind flaxseeds to powder in coffee grinder or blender. Whisk or blend ground seeds, water, milk, vanilla, cinnamon, and nutmeg. Make sure they are well blended. Pour into shallow dish. Dip bread into flax mixture, coating both sides. Place bread on oiled, hot griddle or skillet. Cook each side of bread until golden brown. These are stickier than regular French toast so you may need to add more oil to the pan when you turn. Repeat with remaining slices.

Makes 4 servings

APPROXIMATE NUTRITIONAL INFORMATION FOR 1 SERVING: Calories: 257 cal; Protein: 11 g; Carbohydrates: 36 g; Fat: 9 g; Fiber: 6 g; Sodium: 363 mg.

KEY NUTRIENTS: Thiamine: .27 mg; Riboflavin: .25 mg; Niacin: 2.53 mg; Pantothenic Acid: .74 mg; Vitamin B6: .24 mg; Folate: 71.07 mcg; Vitamin B12: .23 mcg; Calcium: 140.94 mg; Iron: 2.89 mg; Magnesium: 98.80 mg; Zinc: 1.84 mg.

French Toast Sandwich

This is a great idea for a take-out breakfast when you don't have time to eat at home. It's also a yummy snack.

Spread a slice of French toast (regular or vegan) with peanut butter, almond butter, tahini, or cream cheese. Spread a second piece with apple butter, applesauce, mashed bananas, or jam. Press together into a sandwich.

Makes 1 serving

APPROXIMATE NUTRITIONAL INFORMATION FOR 1 SERVING: Calories: 463 cal; Protein: 20 g; Carbohydrates: 40 g; Fat: 27 g; Fiber: 8 g; Sodium: 365 mg.

KEY NUTRIENTS: Vitamin A: 77.73 mcg; Thiamine: .42 mg; Riboflavin: .41 mg; Niacin: 3.29 mg; Pantothenic Acid: .87 mg; Vitamin B6: .35 mg; Folate: 68.98 mcg; Vitamin B12: .49 mcg; Vitamin D: 17.33 mcg; Vitamin E: 1.41 mg; Calcium: 339.05 mg; Iron: 6.2 mg; Magnesium: 141.02 mg; Zinc: 3.47 mg.

Eggs and Tofu

Eggs are an extremely beneficial food during pregnancy and lactation. One egg supplies more than six grams of highly absorbable protein. They are excellent sources of vitamins, especially the fat-soluble vitamins A and D. Eggs are rich in just about all minerals, including iron and zinc. They are good sources of the essential fatty acids which are vital for the development of your baby's nervous system.

Although health experts used to warn against eggs because of their high cholesterol content, studies have proven that dietary cholesterol is not the cause of high blood cholesterol levels so feel free to eat 2 eggs per day if you like. Both of my midwives encouraged me to eat eggs during my pregnancies.

Buy organic eggs from free-range chickens. Not only are the hens treated more humanely, but they are given feed free of pesticide and antibiotic residues. Organic eggs also contain more than three times the vitamin A of commercial eggs.10 Omega-3 enriched eggs (which come from hens whose feed is supplemented with flaxseeds) and high-DHA omega-3 eggs (which come from vegetarian hens whose feed is supplemented with algae) are excellent choices because they supply omega-3 fatty acids.

During pregnancy, it is important to make sure eggs are thoroughly cooked because of the danger of listeria and salmonella. Let soft-boiled, poached, or sunny-side-up eggs wait until after you have the baby. Always check eggs before using them. Discard any cracked eggs to avoid possibility of food poisoning.

Scrambled Eggs Plus

Plain scrambled eggs are fine but I like to give them a nutritional boost.

2 eggs
1 teaspoon cold water or milk (optional)
1 teaspoon nutritional yeast flakes
2 tablespoons minced parsley

In bowl, beat eggs, water, nutritional yeast, and parsley. Warm skillet over medium heat. Add just enough oil to coat pan. Add egg mixture. Push eggs gently around pan until firm.

Makes 1 serving

APPROXIMATE NUTRITIONAL INFORMATION FOR 1 SERVING: Calories: 218 cal; Protein: 16 g; Carbohydrates: 5 g; Fat: 15 g; Fiber: 1 g; Sodium: 347 mg.

KEY NUTRIENTS: Vitamin A: 277.42 mcg; Thiamine: 2.18 mg; Riboflavin: 2.66 mg; Niacin: 12.52 mg; Pantothenic Acid: 1.26 mg; Vitamin B6: 2.26 mg; Folate: 100.95 mcg; Vitamin B12: 2.7 mcg; Vitamin C: 10.35 mg; Vitamin E: 1.73 mg; Calcium: 97.11 mg; Iron: 2.09 mg; Zinc: 2 mg.

Tips for scrambled eggs

- Beat eggs with a fork or a whisk until they are a uniform yellow color. Don't use an egg-beater, mixer, or blender; overmixed eggs will be tough.
- Salt toughens eggs so don't add it until after eggs are cooked.
- Make sure the pan is hot before you add the eggs.
- Lightly oil or butter the pan even if it is nonstick.
- Cook scrambled eggs over medium-low heat to keep them tender.
- Let the eggs sit for one minute after you pour them into the pan. This will help to prevent them from adhering to the bottom.
- Gently push the eggs from side to side using a spatula. Give them time to rest between pushes.
- Remove eggs as soon as they are set, or just a little before. The eggs will continue cooking after you remove them from the pan.

Broccoli-Mushroom Scramble

3 white mushrooms, thinly sliced
1/2 cup chopped broccoli
1 teaspoon olive oil
2 eggs
2 teaspoons water or milk (optional)

Place mushrooms and broccoli in skillet with olive oil over medium-low heat. Cover and let steam 5 to 10 minutes until broccoli is tender. Beat eggs with water or milk. Pour over vegetables. Let mixture sit for one minute, then push eggs around pan until firm. Serve immediately.

Makes 1 serving

APPROXIMATE NUTRITIONAL INFORMATION FOR 1 SERVING: Calories: 268 cal; Protein: 16 g; Carbohydrates: 7 g; Fat: 20 g; Fiber: 2 g; Sodium: 356 mg.

KEY NUTRIENTS: Vitamin A: 305.66 mcg; Thiamine: .14 mg; Riboflavin: .81 mg; Niacin: 2.56 mg; Pantothenic Acid: 2.25 mg; Vitamin B6: .27 mg; Folate: 74.32 mcg; Vitamin B12: .96 mcg; Vitamin C: 42.49 mg; Vitamin D: 41.04 mcg; Vitamin E: 2.39 mg; Calcium: 110.44 mg; Iron: 2.41 mg; Magnesium: 31.04 mg; Zinc: 1.79 mg.

Curried Spinach Scramble

4 eggs
1/4 teaspoon curry powder
2 teaspoons nutritional yeast flakes
1/2 teaspoon soy sauce
2 teaspoons oil
1 clove garlic, minced
1 cup coarsely chopped fresh spinach

Beat eggs, curry powder, nutritional yeast flakes, and soy sauce together until mixture is uniformly smooth and yellow. Heat oil in skillet over medium heat. Add garlic and sauté for a couple of minutes until golden. Place spinach in an even layer in pan. Cover with beaten egg mixture. Cook, pushing eggs around gently until they are firm.

Makes 2 servings

APPROXIMATE NUTRITIONAL INFORMATION FOR 1 SERVING: Calories: 262 cal; Protein: 16 g; Carbohydrates: 5 g; Fat: 20 g; Fiber: 1 g; Sodium: 431 mg.

KEY NUTRIENTS: Vitamin A: 338.70 mcg; Thiamine: 2.19 mg; Riboflavin: 2.68 mg; Niacin: 12.54 mg; Pantothenic Acid: 1.25 mg; Vitamin B6: 2.3 mg; Folate: 118.55 mcg; Vitamin B12: 2.7 mcg; Vitamin E: 1.88 mg; Calcium: 104.18 mg; Iron: 2.05 mg; Zinc: 2.01 mg.

Need to take your breakfast on the road?

Warm a pita pocket or tortilla and stuff it with scrambled eggs or tofu.

Basic Omelet

Eat this omelet plain or with any of the fillings below. Omelets should be cooked over higher heat than scrambled eggs.

4 eggs
1 tablespoon water or milk
1 teaspoon nutritional yeast flakes (optional)

Beat all ingredients together until fluffy. Pour into hot, oiled or buttered skillet over medium heat. When bottom is set, lift sides of omelet to let uncooked portion flow underneath. As soon as omelet is set, fold omelet in half. For omelet with filling, arrange filling ingredients on half of omelet and fold the other half over. Serve immediately.

Makes 2 servings

Filling Suggestions

California Omelet: Arrange 1/2 avocado (sliced) and 1/2 cup sunflower sprouts over half of omelet before folding.
Herbed Cottage Cheese Omelet: Spread 1/2 cup Herbed Cottage Cheese (page 274) or Herbed Tofu Cottage Cheese (page 274) over half of omelet before folding.
Veggie Omelet: Arrange 1/2 cup sautéed vegetables (onion, mushrooms, broccoli, cauliflower, asparagus, peas, spinach, etc.) over half of omelet before folding.

APPROXIMATE NUTRITIONAL INFORMATION FOR 1 SERVING (without filling): Calories: 209 cal; Protein: 14 g; Carbohydrates: 3 g; Fat: 15 g; Fiber: 0 g; Sodium: 342 mg.

KEY NUTRIENTS: Vitamin A: 237.9 mcg; Thiamine: 1.12 mg; Riboflavin: 1.59 mg; Niacin: 6.26 mg; Pantothenic Acid: 1.23 mg; Vitamin B6: 1.2 mg; Folate: 63 mcg; Vitamin B12: 1.82 mcg; Vitamin E: 1.6 mg; Iron: 1.54 mg; Zinc: 1.57 mg.

Tomato-Herb Omelet

We love this for breakfast, lunch, or even dinner in the summer with tomatoes and herbs from the garden.

4 eggs
1 tablespoon water or milk
10 cherry tomatoes, sliced in half (or 1 to 2 regular tomatoes, sliced)
2 tablespoons minced fresh parsley
2 tablespoons minced fresh chives or green onions
1 tablespoon fresh thyme
2 tablespoons grated Parmesan cheese (dairy or nondairy) (optional)

Preheat a skillet over medium heat. Beat eggs with water or milk until completely combined. Coat pan lightly with oil or butter. Pour in egg mixture. Lay tomato slices evenly in egg mixture. Sprinkle herbs and Parmesan cheese over top. Cook until set. Fold omelet in half as you remove it from the pan.

Makes 2 servings

APPROXIMATE NUTRITIONAL INFORMATION FOR 1 SERVING: Calories: 254 cal; Protein: 18 g; Carbohydrates: 7 g; Fat: 17 g; Fiber: 1 g; Sodium: 479 mg.

KEY NUTRIENTS: Vitamin A: 329.11 mcg; Thiamine: .12 mg; Riboflavin: .59 mg; Pantothenic Acid: 1.47 mg; Vitamin B6: .23 mg; Folate: 58.82 mcg; Vitamin B12: .94 mcg; Vitamin E: 2 mg; Calcium: 193.73 mg; Iron: 2.34 mg; Zinc: 1.82 mg.

Veggie Breakfast Burrito

We love this for dinner too. If you don't eat eggs, makes this with Scrambled Tofu (page 82).

2 teaspoons olive oil
1/2 onion, finely diced
1 small zucchini, finely diced
1/2 cup fresh or frozen corn kernels
2 tablespoons minced kale, spinach, or other leafy green
1 tablespoon minced fresh cilantro
6 eggs
1 teaspoon water or milk
1 tablespoon nutritional yeast (optional)
4 large (burrito-size) or 6 medium whole grain tortillas
1/2 avocado, sliced
1/2 cup salsa

Heat oil in skillet over medium-low heat. Stir in onion and sauté 5 to 10 minutes or until soft. Stir in zucchini and corn. Cover and steam 5 to 10 minutes until zucchini is tender. Stir in greens and cilantro. Beat eggs with water or milk and nutritional yeast. Pour over vegetables. Let mixture sit for one minute. Gently push egg mixture around skillet until firm.

Warm tortillas in dry skillet or oven for a minute or two until soft. Place egg mixture in center of tortilla. Top with avocado slices and salsa. You can also add sea salt and black pepper if desired. Fold tortilla around filling as follows: Fold bottom up, fold in one side, fold in other side, fold top down. Place fold side down on plate to keep it from unrolling.

Makes 4 to 6 servings

APPROXIMATE NUTRITIONAL INFORMATION FOR 1 SERVING: Calories: 428 cal; Protein: 18 g; Carbohydrates: 39 g; Fat: 21 g; Fiber: 6 g; Sodium: 595 mg.

KEY NUTRIENTS: Vitamin A: 224.1 mcg; Thiamine: 1.74 mg; Riboflavin: 2.06 mg; Niacin: 10.38 mg; Pantothenic Acid: 1.35 mg; Vitamin B6: 1.84 mg; Folate: 101.75 mcg; Vitamin B12: 2.04 mcg; Vitamin E: 2.43 mg; Iron: 3.45 mg; Magnesium: 36.54 mg; Zinc: 1.73 mg.

Scrambled Tofu

This is a delicious alternative to scrambled eggs.

1 tablespoon olive oil
1 pound tofu
1/4 teaspoon ground turmeric
1/2 teaspoon curry powder
1 tablespoon nutritional yeast
2 tablespoons water
Sea salt and black pepper to taste
1/4 cup minced parsley

Heat oil in skillet over medium-low heat. Crumble tofu into skillet. Cook and stir, breaking up any large chunks. Add remaining ingredients. Cook and stir 5 minutes, or until mixture is light yellow and completely heated.

Makes 4 servings

Note: This also makes a great filling for tortillas or pita pockets.

Variation: Sauté chopped onions, mushrooms, bell peppers, broccoli, tomatoes, spinach, or other vegetables until tender before adding tofu. Continue as directed.

APPROXIMATE NUTRITIONAL INFORMATION FOR 1 SERVING: Calories: 206 cal; Protein: 19 g; Carbohydrates: 6 g; Fat: 14 g; Fiber: 3 g; Sodium: 19 mg.

KEY NUTRIENTS: THIAMINE: 1.78 mg; Riboflavin: 1.72 mg; Niacin: 9.82 mg; Vitamin B6: 1.71 mg; Folate: 78.66 mcg; Vitamin B12: 1.33 mcg; Calcium: 779.77 mg; Iron: 12.23 mg; Magnesium: 67.67 mg; Zinc: 2.35 mg.

Golden Tofu on Toast

Brush 2 (1/2-inch) slices tofu with Dijon mustard. Brown in oiled skillet over medium heat until crisp and golden on each side. Spread 2 slices of whole grain toast with butter or oil. Place tofu on one slice. Top with tomato slices and second piece of toast.

Makes 1 serving

APPROXIMATE NUTRITIONAL INFORMATION FOR 1 SERVING: Calories: 378 cal; Protein: 16 g; Carbohydrates: 31 g; Fat: 23 g; Fiber: 5 g; Sodium: 616 mg.

KEY NUTRIENTS: Vitamin A: 140.84 mcg; Thiamine: .27 mg; Riboflavin: .2 mg; Niacin: 2.42 mg; Vitamin B6: .17 mg; Folate: 42.46 mcg; Vitamin C: 10.51 mg; Calcium: 434.12 mg; Iron: 8 mg; Magnesium: 85.79 mg; Zinc: 2.02 mg.

Breakfast Potatoes and Veggies

I love this combination with scrambled eggs or tofu instead of toast. It's a great way to get an extra serving of vegetables at breakfast. If you want to make this a meal in itself, add some tempeh, tofu, or beans.

1 tablespoon oil
1 small onion, diced
3 medium potatoes, diced into 1/2-inch pieces
1 bell pepper, seeded and diced
5 to 6 mushrooms, chopped
1 cup chopped broccoli or cauliflower
1 tablespoon minced fresh herbs (thyme, tarragon, etc.)
1/4 cup chopped fresh watercress or parsley
Sea salt and black pepper to taste

Heat oil in large skillet over medium heat. Add onion and potatoes. Sauté about 10 minutes, or until potatoes are golden. Stir in bell pepper, mushrooms, and broccoli or cauliflower. Cover and reduce heat to medium-low. Cook about 15 minutes, or until potatoes are soft. Stir in minced herbs and watercress or parsley. Season with sea salt and pepper to taste.

Makes 4 to 6 servings

Note: When I make this to go with eggs. I cook this dish first and transfer to a covered heatproof dish and keep in warm oven while I use the same skillet to cook the eggs.

APPROXIMATE NUTRITIONAL INFORMATION FOR 1 SERVING: Calories: 99 cal; Protein: 5 g; Carbohydrates: 14 g; Fat: 4 g; Fiber: 6 g; Sodium: 158 mg.

KEY NUTRIENTS: Vitamin A: 65.46 mcg; Thiamine: .17 mg; Riboflavin: .17 mg; Niacin: 3.54 mg; Pantothenic Acid: 1.08 mg; Vitamin B6: .44 mg; Folate: 73.38 mcg; Vitamin C: 76.68 mg; Vitamin D: 1.71 mcg; Iron: 2.29 mg; Magnesium: 50.62 mg.

Toast, Bagels, and English Muffins

Keep whole grain toast, bagels, and English muffins around for quick breakfasts and snacks. I prefer sprouted breads and bagels. (Ezekiel 4:9® or Alvarado St. Bakery® products are excellent.) Be sure to eat them with a topping or food containing protein and fat.

Topping ideas for toast, bagels, and English muffins:

- Almond butter, peanut butter, cashew butter, pumpkin seed butter, or tahini
- Ricotta, cottage, cream, Neufchâtel, or yogurt cheese (page 273)
- Olive oil, flaxseed oil, or butter and ground cinnamon
- Mashed avocado and nutritional yeast flakes
- Any of the dips or spreads beginning on page 263

Molasses Toast

My sister Lissie introduced me to this delicious combination. It's rich in iron and B vitamins.

Toast a slice of whole grain bread. Spread with tahini or butter. Drizzle on a couple teaspoons of blackstrap molasses. Sprinkle with 1 teaspoon nutritional yeast flakes.

Makes 1 serving

APPROXIMATE NUTRITIONAL INFORMATION FOR 1 SERVING: Calories: 212 cal; Protein: 9 g; Carbohydrates: 28 g; Fat: 9 g; Fiber: 5 g; Sodium: 168 mg.

KEY NUTRIENTS: Thiamine: 4.52 mg; Riboflavin: 4.37 mg; Niacin: 26.75 mg; Vitamin B6: 4.39 mg; Folate: 134.43 mcg; Vitamin B12: 3.51 mcg; Calcium: 197.83 mg; Iron: 3.95 mg; Magnesium: 67.15 mg; Zinc: 2.76 mg.

Savory Bagel Sandwich

This is delicious for breakfast, lunch, or a snack.

Spread one side of a whole grain bagel with cream cheese or tahini. Spread the other side with mashed avocado. On the cream cheese or tahini side, place 2 cucumber slices, 1 large tomato slice and top with sunflower sprouts. Sprinkle on a little sea salt or soy sauce if desired. Top with avocado side of bagel.

Makes 1 serving

APPROXIMATE NUTRITIONAL INFORMATION FOR 1 SERVING: Calories: 294 cal; Protein: 10 g; Carbohydrates: 40 g; Fat: 12 g; Fiber: 10 g; Sodium: 259 mg.

KEY NUTRIENTS: Vitamin A: 90.65 mcg; Thiamine: .5 mg; Riboflavin: .59 mg; Niacin: 8.75 mg; Pantothenic Acid: .43 mg; Vitamin B6: .12 mg; Folate: 205.72 mcg; Calcium: 218.07 mg; Iron: 1.69 mg.

English Muffin Cheesecake

Split and toast 1 whole grain English muffin. Spread each half with 1 to 2 tablespoons cottage cheese, tofu cottage cheese (page 273), ricotta cheese, yogurt cheese (page 273), cream cheese, or Neufchâtel cheese. Top each side with 2 tablespoons diced fresh fruit (peaches, apricots, berries, bananas).

Makes 1 serving

APPROXIMATE NUTRITIONAL INFORMATION FOR 1 SERVING: Calories: 182 cal; Protein: 9 g; Carbohydrates: 33 g; Fat: 3 g; Fiber: 5 g; Sodium: 520 mg.

KEY NUTRIENTS: Thiamine: .21 mg; Riboflavin: .17 mg; Niacin: 2.67 mg; Pantothenic Acid: .53 mg; Vitamin B6: .12 mg; Folate: 33.62 mcg; Calcium: 197.02 mg; Iron: 1.66 mg; Magnesium: 49.83 mg; Zinc: 1.12 mg.

English Muffin Melt

Split a whole grain English muffin. Place 2 to 3 apple or pear slices on each half. Cover with cheddar, Monterey Jack, Muenster, or Swiss cheese slices. (You can also use soy or rice cheese.) Bake in toaster oven or conventional oven at 400°F until cheese is melted.

Makes 1 serving

APPROXIMATE NUTRITIONAL INFORMATION FOR 1 SERVING: Calories: 289 cal; Protein: 13 g; Carbohydrates: 38 g; Fat: 11 g; Fiber: 6 g; Sodium: 596 mg.

KEY NUTRIENTS: Vitamin A: 82.26 mcg; Thiamine: .22 mg; Riboflavin: .21 mg; Niacin: 2.33 mg; Pantothenic Acid: .62 mg; Vitamin B6: .16 mg; Folate: 39.51 mcg; Vitamin B12: .23 mcg; Vitamin D: .34 mcg; Calcium: 384.12 mg; Iron: 1.93 mg; Magnesium: 58.25 mg; Zinc: 1.97 mg.

Sandwiches and Quick Lunch Ideas

 Lunch was challenging for me during pregnancy. I tended to ignore hunger pangs when they started because I was busy and didn't want to stop what I was doing. Before I knew it, I would go from a little hungry to spaced-out and shaky. Then I'd end up grabbing anything I could find because I was too disoriented to think about cooking something nutritious.

What worked well for me was to think about lunch at breakfast time. While my porridge was cooking or while I washed the breakfast dishes, I'd make a batch of egg salad or hummus so at lunchtime all I had to do was spread a filling on bread. If your mornings are rushed, make your lunch the night before. Find out what works best for you.

Leftovers make an easy lunch too. Warm up soup or quiche from dinner and eat with salad or fruit. Another good idea is to cook extra rice, pasta, beans, or vegetables when you cook supper. They can be added to a salad, or tossed with cheese or toasted nuts. Check out the Salads section too. Almost any salad can be stuffed in a pita or wrapped in a tortilla for a quick nutritious lunch.

This section contains many sandwich recipes because they are easy to make and can be eaten at home or taken along when you go out. Stock your freezer with whole grain bread, tortillas, flatbreads, pita pockets, and bagels. Prepare fillings in advance whenever possible. Add fresh vegetables like lettuce, cucumbers, tomatoes, grated carrots, sprouts, avocado to your sandwiches for extra nutrients and fiber. To satisfy that pickle craving, try some Sauerkraut (page 195) or Carrot Pickles (page 196) on your sandwich. They provide enzymes and bacteria that aid digestion.

There is also a selection of quick nonsandwich lunches – many of which can be made with dinner leftovers.

Cold Sandwiches
and Wraps

Herbed Cottage Cheese and
    Avocado Sandwich
Bean Salad Sandwich
Egg or Tofu Salad Sandwich
Tahini-Vegetable Sandwich
Avocado-Cheese Sandwich
Almond Butter-Orange Sandwich
Quick Tofu Sandwich
Cucumber-Watercress Sandwich
Veggie Wrap
Spinach-Hummus Wrap
Garbanzo Bean Salad Pocket
Egg and Avocado Sandwich

Hot Sandwiches
and Wraps

Beanball Submarine Sandwich
Bean Quesadilla
Bean and Avocado Tortilla
Open-Face Bagel Melt
Veggie-Apple Melt
Creamy Watercress and Tomato Toast
Tempeh Rueben
Veggie Dog and Sauerkraut

Breadless Lunches

Stuffed Bell Peppers
Baked Potato Lunch
Quick Cheesy Rice
Quick Nutritional Yeast Rice
Easy Pasta Lunch
Quick Asian Noodles

Cold Sandwiches and Wraps

Herbed Cottage Cheese and Avocado Sandwich

Place 1/3 cup Herbed Cottage Cheese (regular or tofu) (page 274) in bread or wrap of choice. Add slices of tomato, slices of avocado, and sunflower sprouts.

Makes 1 serving

APPROXIMATE NUTRITIONAL INFORMATION FOR 1 SERVING: Calories: 267 cal; Protein: 15 g; Carbohydrates: 33 g; Fat: 10 g; Fiber: 6 g; Sodium: 568 mg.

KEY NUTRIENTS: Thiamine: .25 mg; Riboflavin: .34 mg; Niacin: 2.88 mg; Pantothenic Acid: .65 mg; Vitamin B6: .2 mg; Folate: 49.58 mcg; Vitamin B12: .33 mcg; Vitamin C: 12.38 mg; Vitamin E: .97 mg; Calcium: 98.42 mg; Iron: 2.28 mg; Magnesium: 62.36 mg; Zinc: 1.23 mg.

Bean Salad Sandwich

This high-protein bean salad filling will keep for several days in your refrigerator. Try it over greens as a salad, too.

Salad:
2 cups cooked kidney or cannelli beans
1/4 cup minced red onion
1 small bell pepper, seeded and diced
1/2 cup walnuts, chopped
1 tomato, diced
1/4 cup minced fresh parsley

Dressing:
3 tablespoons olive oil
2 teaspoons Dijon mustard
2 tablespoons lemon juice
1 clove garlic, crushed

6 whole grain pita pockets
Lettuce

Place salad ingredients in bowl. Whisk dressing ingredients together. Pour dressing over bean mixture and toss gently to combine. If you have time, let salad marinate at least 30 minutes or overnight. (It will still taste good if you don't marinate it.) Stuff into warmed pita pockets with lettuce.

Makes 6 sandwiches

Variation: Stir in 1 cup frozen corn.

APPROXIMATE NUTRITIONAL INFORMATION FOR 1 SANDWICH: Calories: 375 cal; Protein: 13 g; Carbohydrates: 53 g; Fat: 15 g; Fiber: 10 g; Sodium: 368 mg.

KEY NUTRIENTS: Vitamin A: 59.92 mcg; Thiamine: .38 mg; Riboflavin: .13 mg; Niacin: 2.61 mg; Pantothenic Acid: .8 mg; Vitamin B6: .35 mg; Folate: 131.13 mcg; Vitamin B12: .91 mcg; Vitamin C: 25.69 mg; Vitamin E: 1.21 mg; Iron: 4.37 mg; Magnesium: 90.12 mg; Zinc: 1.96 mg.

Egg or Tofu Salad Sandwich

1 stalk celery
1 carrot
1/2 cup kale or green cabbage
8 hard-boiled eggs (peeled) or 12 ounces firm tofu
1/2 teaspoon sea salt
1/4 teaspoon black pepper
1/4 cup mayonnaise (regular or vegan)
Whole grain bread or pita pockets

Mince celery, carrot, and kale or cabbage in food processor with metal blade. Slice eggs or tofu, and add to vegetables in food processor. Add salt, black pepper, and mayonnaise. Pulse to mix. If not using food processor, mince vegetables with knife or shred with grater. Blend all ingredients in a bowl. Spread salad between slices of bread or stuff in pita pockets.

Makes 4 to 6 sandwiches

APPROXIMATE NUTRITIONAL INFORMATION FOR 1 SANDWICH (using eggs): Calories: 403 cal; Protein: 18 g; Carbohydrates: 29 g; Fat: 24 g; Fiber: 5 g; Sodium: 786 mg.

KEY NUTRIENTS: Vitamin A: 635.55 mcg; Thiamine: .29 mg; Riboflavin: .65 mg; Niacin: 2.43 mg; Pantothenic Acid: 1.76 mg; Vitamin B6: .26 mg; Folate: 78.15 mcg; Vitamin B12: 1.12 mcg; Vitamin C: 7.14 mg; Vitamin E: 1.67; Calcium: 104.09 mg; Iron: 3.23 mg; Magnesium: 62.97 mg; Zinc: 2.2 mg.

APPROXIMATE NUTRITIONAL INFORMATION FOR 1 SANDWICH (using tofu): Calories: 371 cal; Protein: 19 g; Carbohydrates: 32 g; Fat: 21 g; Fiber: 7 g; Sodium: 674 mg.

KEY NUTRIENTS: Vitamin A: 482.01 mcg; Thiamine: .35 mg; Riboflavin: .22 mg; Niacin: 2.69 mg; Pantothenic Acid: .48 mg; Vitamin B6: .22 mg; Folate: 58.81 mcg; Vitamin C: 7.31 mg; Calcium: 634.98 mg; Iron: 10.94 mg; Magnesium: 102.30 mg; Zinc: 2.48 mg.

Tahini-Vegetable Sandwich

2 slices whole grain bread, lightly toasted
Tahini (or other nut or seed butter)
Optional additions: cucumber slices, sprouts, lettuce, tomato slices, grated carrots
    apple slices, pear slices

Spread both slices of bread with tahini. Layer any or all of the vegetables on one slice of bread. Cover with remaining slice.

Makes 1 serving

APPROXIMATE NUTRITIONAL INFORMATION FOR 1 SANDWICH (without additions): Calories: 309 cal; Protein: 11 g; Carbohydrates: 34 g; Fat: 17 g; Fiber: 7 g; Sodium: 317 mg.

KEY NUTRIENTS: Thiamine: .58 mg; Riboflavin: .27 mg; Niacin: 3.93 mg; Pantothenic Acid: .52 mg; Vitamin B6: .14 mg; Folate: 57.4 mcg; Calcium: 166.32 mg; Iron: 2.6 mg; Magnesium: 76.96 mg; Zinc: 2.48 mg.

Avocado-Cheese Sandwich

Avocados are a good source of protein and vitamin E. If you are avoiding dairy products, use soy, rice, or almond cheese – or just leave the cheese off altogether.

1/8 avocado, sliced
2 slices whole grain bread
1 to 2 slices Swiss cheese (or other dairy or nondairy cheese)
Dijon mustard or mayonnaise (regular or vegan)
Optional additions: lettuce, tomato slices, cucumber slices, shredded carrots,
    sprouts, pickles

Mash avocado slices on one slice of bread. Place cheese on avocado. Add any optional additions. Spread remaining slice with mustard or mayonnaise and place on top of sandwich.

Makes 1 serving

APPROXIMATE NUTRITIONAL INFORMATION FOR 1 SANDWICH: Calories: 279 cal; Protein: 13 g; Carbohydrates: 28 g; Fat: 14 g; Fiber: 5 g; Sodium: 468 mg.

KEY NUTRIENTS: Thiamine: .22 mg; Riboflavin: .21 mg; Niacin: 2.63 mg; Pantothenic Acid: .55 mg; Vitamin B6: .17 mg; Folate: 43.58; Calcium: 243.08 mg; Iron: 2.1 mg; Magnesium: 57.96 mg; Zinc: 2.39 mg.

Almond Butter-Orange Sandwich

This may sound like an odd combination but it was my favorite sandwich during the first trimester of my pregnancies when I constantly craved oranges. It is a light sandwich that supplies protein and vitamin C.

2 slices whole grain bread
2 tablespoons almond butter
1/2 orange, peeled and sectioned
Sunflower sprouts
Lettuce (optional)

Lightly toast 2 slices of whole grain bread and spread almond butter on each. Cover one slice with orange sections. Next, place a thin layer of sunflower sprouts over oranges and cover with lettuce. Top with remaining slice of bread.

Makes 1 serving

APPROXIMATE NUTRITIONAL INFORMATION FOR 1 SERVING: Calories: 360 cal; Protein: 13 g; Carbohydrates: 42 g; Fat: 17 g; Fiber: 6 g; Sodium: 301 mg.

KEY NUTRIENTS: Thiamine: .26 mg; Riboflavin: .15 mg; Niacin: 2.38 mg; Pantothenic Acid: .49 mg; Vitamin B6: .14 mg; Folate: 61.25 mcg; Vitamin C: 37.25 mg; Iron: 2.02 mg; Magnesium: 55.31 mg; Zinc: 1.16 mg.

Quick Tofu Sandwich

Try this sandwich with flavored tofu too.

2 slices whole grain bread
Mayonnaise (regular or vegan)
Mustard
2 ounces tofu, sliced
Sea salt and black pepper to taste if desired
Shredded carrots
Sunflower sprouts
Lettuce

Toast bread if desired. Spread mayonnaise on one slice and mustard on the other. Lay tofu on bread. Sprinkle with salt and pepper. Cover with carrots, sprouts, and lettuce. Top with remaining bread slice.

Makes 1 serving

Note: You can also add avocado, cheese, tomatoes, cucumbers, pickles, etc., if desired.

APPROXIMATE NUTRITIONAL INFORMATION FOR 1 SERVING: Calories: 305 cal; Protein: 15 g; Carbohydrates: 31 g; Fat: 15 g; Fiber: 6 g; Sodium: 489 mg.

KEY NUTRIENTS: Vitamin A: 422.43 mcg; Thiamine: .31 mg; Riboflavin: .19 mg; Niacin: 2.54 mg; Pantothenic Acid: .43 mg; Vitamin B6: .18 mg; Folate: 59.97 mcg; Calcium: 434.89 mg; Iron: 7.96 mg; Magnesium: 83.71 mg; Zinc: 2.03 mg.

Cucumber-Watercress Sandwich

Watercress is a good source of vitamin A and minerals.

2 slices of whole grain bread, lightly toasted
2 tablespoons cream cheese, Neufchâtel cheese, yogurt cheese (page 273),
   or mayonnaise (regular or vegan)
4 cucumber slices
1/3 cup watercress leaves

Spread each slice of toast with cream cheese or mayonnaise. Place cucumber slices on one side. Cover with watercress and remaining slice of bread.

Makes 1 serving

APPROXIMATE NUTRITIONAL INFORMATION FOR 1 SERVING: Calories: 244 cal; Protein: 8 g; Carbohydrates: 27 g; Fat: 13 g; Fiber: 4 g; Sodium: 386 mg.

KEY NUTRIENTS: Vitamin A: 166.01 mcg; Thiamine: .18 mg; Riboflavin: .18 mg; Niacin: 2.02 mg; Vitamin B6: .14 mg; Vitamin E: .99 mg; Iron: 2.27 mg; Magnesium: 55.98 mg; Zinc: 1.3 mg.

Veggie Wrap

These wraps are great for lunch, snacks, or picnics. They are convenient to eat on the road also. Get out your food processor or hand grater, and shred a bunch of each vegetable so you can throw a wrap together anytime you want one. Shredded vegetables will keep for 3 to 5 days in a tightly sealed container in the refrigerator.

1 large whole grain tortilla or slice flatbread (lavash)
1 tablespoon of your favorite creamy dressing
2 to 4 tablespoons of any or all of the following:
   Chopped lettuce
   Chopped spinach
   Crumbled tofu
   Shredded carrots
   Shredded beets
   Shredded zucchini
   Shredded cabbage
   Shredded cheese
   Sliced avocado
   Sprouts
   Nuts or seeds
   Raisins, dried cranberries, or currants

Place desired fillings on tortilla or flatbread. Drizzle with dressing and roll up. Wrap tightly with wax paper, foil, or plastic wrap until ready to eat. It will keep for a couple of days wrapped and refrigerated.

Makes 1 serving

APPROXIMATE NUTRITIONAL INFORMATION FOR 1 SERVING: Too many variables for accurate nutrient analysis.

Spinach-Hummus Wrap

1 large whole grain tortilla or slice flatbread (lavash)
1/4 to 1/3 cup Hummus (page 264)
1/2 cup chopped fresh spinach
2 to 3 tablespoons diced cucumbers (optional)
2 to 3 tablespoons diced tomatoes (optional)
2 to 3 tablespoons shredded carrots (optional)

Liberally spread tortilla or flatbread with hummus. Layer vegetables over hummus and roll up. Wrap tightly with wax paper, foil, or plastic wrap until ready to eat. It will keep for a couple of days wrapped and refrigerated.

Makes 1 serving

APPROXIMATE NUTRITIONAL INFORMATION FOR 1 SERVING: Calories: 307 cal; Protein: 11 g; Carbohydrates: 42 g; Fat: 10 g; Fiber: 7 g; Sodium: 504 mg.

KEY NUTRIENTS: Vitamin A: 517.05 mcg; Thiamine: .12 mg; Vitamin B6: .15 mg; Folate: 111.82 mcg; Vitamin C: 18.49 mg; Iron: 3.73 mg; Magnesium: 39.76 mg; Zinc: .81 mg.

Garbanzo Bean Salad Pocket

Cut a warmed pita pocket in half to create two pockets. Spread pockets with cream cheese or mashed avocado. Insert lettuce or spinach greens and stuff with Garbanzo Bean Salad (page 132).

Makes 1 serving

APPROXIMATE NUTRITIONAL INFORMATION FOR 1 SERVING: Calories: 414 cal; Protein: 15 g; Carbohydrates: 70 g; Fat: 10 g; Fiber: 11 g; Sodium: 504 mg.

KEY NUTRIENTS: Vitamin A: 440.22 mcg; Thiamine: .41 mg; Riboflavin: .18 mg; Niacin: 3.52 mg; Pantothenic Acid: 1 mg; Vitamin B6: .39 mg; Folate: 146.01 mcg; Vitamin C: 11.67 mg; Vitamin E: 1.21 mg; Iron: 4.53 mg; Magnesium: 108.19 mg; Zinc: 2.61 mg.

Egg and Avocado Sandwich

1/8 avocado
2 slices whole grain bread, lightly toasted if desired
Mayonnaise (regular or vegan) or mustard
1 hard-boiled egg, sliced
Tomato slices
Lettuce

Mash avocado on one slice of bread. Spread the other with mayonnaise or mustard. Place egg slices on avocado. Place tomatoes and lettuce over egg. Cover with remaining slice of bread.

Makes 1 serving

Note: Fried egg or tofu can be used instead of hard-boiled egg if desired.

APPROXIMATE NUTRITIONAL INFORMATION FOR 1 SERVING: Calories: 332 cal; Protein: 13 g; Carbohydrates: 30 g; Fat: 19 g; Fiber: 6 g; Sodium: 414 mg.

KEY NUTRIENTS: Vitamin A: 150.13 mcg; Thiamine: .29 mg; Riboflavin: .43 mg; Niacin: 2.96 mg; Pantothenic Acid: 1.37 mg; Vitamin B6: .27 mg; Folate: 85.18 mcg; Vitamin B12: .56 mcg; Vitamin C: 12.02 mg; Vitamin E: 1.54 mg; Iron: 2.99 mg; Magnesium: 67.96 mg; Zinc: 1.78 mg.

Hot Sandwiches and Wraps

Beanball Submarine Sandwich

This is a great way to use up leftover Beanballs. You can use a traditional sub roll, pita pocket, tortilla, hot dog bun, or a slice of bread folded in half.

Warm about 4 Italian-style Beanballs (page 228) with sauce. Place beanballs in sub roll or your choice of bread. Top with grated Parmesan or shredded mozzarella if desired. Optionally, place under broiler for a minute or two to melt cheese.

Makes 1 serving

APPROXIMATE NUTRITIONAL INFORMATION FOR 1 SERVING: Calories: 354 cal; Protein: 14 g; Carbohydrates: 67 g; Fat: 6 g; Fiber: 12 g; Sodium: 639 mg.

KEY NUTRIENTS: Vitamin A: 373.78 mcg; Thiamine: .35 mg; Riboflavin: .19 mg; Niacin: 4.1 mg; Pantothenic Acid: .64 mg; Vitamin B6: .26 mg; Folate: 104.64 mcg; Vitamin C: 7.65 mg; Vitamin E: 1.54 mg; Calcium: 126.36 mg; Iron: 4.69 mg; Magnesium: 111.07 mg; Zinc: 2.6 mg.

If you are avoiding dairy products, these vegan cheese alternatives taste great and melt evenly when heated:

- Lisanatti® Almond Cheese
- Vegan Gourmet™ Cheese Alternative

Bean Quesadilla

This delicious melt supplies calcium and protein. Kids love it too.

Whole grain tortilla
2 tablespoons Easy Bean Dip (page 265)
1/4 cup diced tomatoes
1/4 cup shredded Monterey Jack cheese

Preheat toaster oven or conventional oven to 375°F. Spread bean dip over half of tortilla. Spread tomatoes over bean dip. Cover with cheese. Fold the half of tortilla without toppings over cheese side. Place on baking sheet and bake 2 to 3 minutes, or until cheese is melted but tortilla is still soft. Serve with salsa if desired.

Makes 1 serving

APPROXIMATE NUTRITIONAL INFORMATION FOR 1 SERVING: Calories: 318 cal; Protein: 13 g; Carbohydrates: 34 g; Fat: 14 g; Fiber: 5 g; Sodium: 418 mg.

KEY NUTRIENTS: Vitamin A: 123 mcg; Thiamine: .47 mg; Riboflavin: .44 mg; Niacin: 2.71 mg; Vitamin B6: .47 mg; Folate: 43.71 mcg; Vitamin B12: .33 mcg; Vitamin C: 12.26 mg; Calcium: 212.93 mg; Iron: 2.14 mg.

Bean and Avocado Tortilla

This is my vegan version of a quesadilla.

Preheat toaster oven or conventional oven to 375°F. Spread thick layer of bean dip over a large whole grain tortilla. Place on baking sheet and bake 2 to 3 minutes, just until tortilla is hot but not crispy. Place sliced avocado over half of tortilla. Optionally, add diced tomatoes, shredded carrots, lettuce, sprouts, etc. Fold tortilla in half. Serve with salsa if desired.

Makes 1 serving

APPROXIMATE NUTRITIONAL INFORMATION FOR 1 SERVING: Calories: 329 cal; Protein: 10 g; Carbohydrates: 42 g; Fat: 13 g; Fiber: 9 g; Sodium: 248 mg.

KEY NUTRIENTS: Thiamine: .93 mg; Riboflavin: .9 mg; Niacin: 5.82 mg; Pantothenic Acid: .61 mg; Vitamin B6: 1.01 mg; Folate: 125.08 mcg; Vitamin B12: .67 mcg; Vitamin E: 1.08 mg; Iron: 3.05 mg; Magnesium: 43.59 mg; Zinc: .94 mg.

Open-Face Bagel Melt

1 whole grain bagel
2 large tomato slices
1/4 cup alfalfa sprouts
1 large slice (1 ounce) Swiss cheese or nondairy alternative, cut in half

Preheat toaster oven or conventional oven to 375°F. Slice bagel in half. Place tomato slice on each half of bagel. Top with sprouts and cover with cheese slices. Place on baking sheet and bake 5 minutes, or until cheese is melted.

Makes 1 serving

APPROXIMATE NUTRITIONAL INFORMATION FOR 1 SERVING: Calories: 316 cal; Protein: 16 g; Carbohydrates: 39 g; Fat: 11 g; Fiber: 9 g; Sodium: 264 mg.

KEY NUTRIENTS: Thiamine: .49 mg; Riboflavin: .65 mg; Niacin: 8.38 mg; Vitamin C: 10.99 mg; Calcium: 466.46; Iron: 1.4 mg; Zinc: 1.24 mg.

Veggie-Apple Melt

2 slices whole grain bread
2 teaspoons Dijon mustard
2 teaspoons mayonnaise (regular or vegan)
4 apple slices
2 tablespoons shredded carrots
2 to 4 cucumber slices
2 tablespoons alfalfa sprouts
2 thin slices cheddar cheese (dairy or nondairy)

Preheat toaster oven or conventional oven to 375°F. Spread one slice of bread with mustard, the other with mayonnaise. On mustard side, place apple slices and carrots. On mayonnaise slice, place cucumber slices and sprouts. Cover each with a slice of cheese. Place on baking sheet and bake 5 minutes, or until cheese is melted.

Makes 1 serving

APPROXIMATE NUTRITIONAL INFORMATION FOR 1 SERVING: Calories: 366 cal; Protein: 14 g; Carbohydrates: 38 g; Fat: 20 g; Fiber: 6 g; Sodium: 681 mg.

KEY NUTRIENTS: Vitamin A: 391.38 mcg; Thiamine: .19 mg; Riboflavin: .13 mg; Niacin: 2.15 mg; Vitamin B6: .15 mg; Iron: 2.1 mg; Magnesium: 56.51 mg; Zinc: 1.21 mg.

Creamy Watercress and Tomato Toast

Spread 2 slices of whole grain peasant bread with Creamy Watercress Dip (page 266). Top each slice with tomato slices and sprinkle with Parmesan cheese (dairy or nondairy). Broil for 2 to 3 minutes or until cheese is golden.

Makes 1 serving

Variation: Replace Creamy Watercress Dip with Parsley-Walnut Pesto (page 269).

APPROXIMATE NUTRITIONAL INFORMATION FOR 1 SERVING: Calories: 239 cal; Protein: 12 g; Carbohydrates: 31 g; Fat: 9 g; Fiber: 5 g; Sodium: 424 mg.

KEY NUTRIENTS: Vitamin A: 72.75 mcg; Folate: 43.04 m Thiamine: .26 mg; Riboflavin: .19 mg; Niacin: 2.59 mg; Pantothenic Acid: .46 mg; Vitamin B6: .19 mg; Folate: 43.04 mcg; Vitamin C: 23.47 mg; Calcium: 289.67 mg; Iron: 5.28 mg; Magnesium: 76.83 mg; Zinc: 1.73 mg.

Tempeh Rueben

This is a very hearty and delicious sandwich. Tempeh and sauerkraut contain beneficial bacteria and enzymes that aid digestion. Rinse the sauerkraut to eliminate most of the sodium.

2.6 ounces (1/3 of an 8-ounce package) tempeh
2 teaspoons Dijon mustard
2 to 3 teaspoons Thousand Island Dressing (page 136) or mayonnaise
   (regular or vegan)
1/4 cup sauerkraut (page 195)
2 thin slices Swiss cheese

Slice tempeh into 1/2-inch slices. Warm skillet over medium-high heat. Pour in enough oil to coat. Brown tempeh on both sides. While tempeh is cooking, preheat toaster oven or conventional oven. Spread dressing or mayonnaise on one slice of bread and mustard on the other. Place bread on baking sheet. Place cooked tempeh on the mustard slice of bread and sauerkraut on the dressing or mayonnaise side. Place a slice of cheese on each side. Place under broiler for 2 to 3 minutes, or until cheese is melted. Place bread together, filling sides in.

Makes 1 serving

Note: One (8-ounce) package of tempeh makes about 3 sandwiches. I slice and sauté the whole package of tempeh at once and keep the cooked slices in the refrigerator. Use cooked tempeh in rueben sandwiches or add to salads.

Variation: Substitute avocado slices for the cooked tempeh.

APPROXIMATE NUTRITIONAL INFORMATION FOR 1 SERVING: Calories: 460 cal; Protein: 29 g; Carbohydrates: 37 g; Fat: 24 g; Fiber: 5 g; Sodium: 848 mg.

KEY NUTRIENTS: Vitamin A: 71.95 mcg; Thiamine: .29 mg; Riboflavin: .5 mg; Niacin: 4.97 mg; Pantothenic Acid: .74 mg; Vitamin B6: .29 mg; Folate: 47.98 mcg; Vitamin B12: .54 mcg; Vitamin C: 6.59 mg; Vitamin D: 1.25 mcg; Calcium: 416.6 mg; Iron: 4.48 mg; Magnesium: 119.59 mg; Zinc: 3.05 mg.

Veggie Dog and Sauerkraut

This is a really quick and easy lunch. Rinse the sauerkraut to eliminate most of the sodium.

Cook a vegetarian hot dog as directed. Place in toasted bun or slice of bread. Top with mustard and naturally fermented Sauerkraut (page 195).

Makes 1 serving

APPROXIMATE NUTRITIONAL INFORMATION FOR 1 SERVING: Calories: 218 cal; Protein: 16 g; Carbohydrates: 31 g; Fat: 3 g; Fiber: 6 g; Sodium: 1206 mg.

KEY NUTRIENTS: Thiamine: .14 mg; Niacin: 2.38 mg; Vitamin C: 6 mg; Iron: 2.3 mg; Magnesium: 36.55 mg; Zinc: .86 mg.

Breadless Lunches

Stuffed Bell Peppers

Slice off the top (stem side) of a large red or green bell pepper. Remove the seeds. Stuff with one of the following suggestions:

Herbed Cottage Cheese (regular or tofu) (page 274)
Egg or Tofu Salad (page 94)
Tabouli (page 126)
Curried Rice Salad (page 130)
Bean and Rice Salad (page 131)

Makes 1 serving

APPROXIMATE NUTRITIONAL INFORMATION FOR 1 SERVING (using first option): Calories: 164 cal; Protein: 14 g; Carbohydrates: 16 g; Fat: 5 g; Fiber: 3 g; Sodium: 403 mg.

KEY NUTRIENTS: Vitamin A: 934.8 mcg; Thiamine: .11 mg; Riboflavin: .31 mg; Vitamin B6: .41 mg; Folate: 36.08 mcg; Vitamin B12: .48 mcg; Vitamin C: 311.6 mg; Vitamin E: 1.13 mg; Calcium: 94.76 mg.

Baked Potato Lunch

Bake an extra potato or two at dinnertime so you'll be ready to make this easy lunch.

Top a hot baked potato with any of the following suggestions:

Herbed Cottage Cheese (regular or tofu) (page 274)
Egg or Tofu Salad (page 94)
Sunny Cole Slaw (page 125)
Sautéed tempeh and vegetables
Stir-fried tofu and veggies
Cooked beans and minced parsley or shredded cheese
Hummus (page 264)
Quick Bean Dip (page 265)
Steamed vegetables and Light Cheese Sauce (page 277)
Steamed vegetables and No Cheese Sauce (page 278)
Steamed vegetables and Tahini-Miso Sauce (page 276)
Ratatouille (page 160)

Makes 1 serving

APPROXIMATE NUTRITIONAL INFORMATION FOR 1 SERVING (using first option):
Calories: 308 cal; Protein: 17 g; Carbohydrates: 49 g; Fat: 5 g; Fiber: 4 g; Sodium:
414 mg.

KEY NUTRIENTS: Thiamine: .18 mg; Riboflavin: .32 mg; Niacin: 2.84 mg; Pantothenic
Acid: .96 mg; Vitamin B6: .6 mg; Vitamin B12: .48 mcg; Vitamin C: 22.25 mg; Calcium:
97.25 mg; Iron: 2.35 mg; Magnesium 46.58 mg.

Quick Cheesy Rice

This is one of our favorite lunches. Since I usually have leftover rice in the refrigerator, it is easy to make. It also tastes great with a little salsa.

Place 1 cup hot, cooked brown rice (or other grain) in bowl. Sprinkle 1 teaspoon olive oil and 1 ounce shredded cheese on top. Mix until rice is coated. Sprinkle with minced parsley if desired.

Makes 1 serving

Variation: Add 1/4 cup cooked beans.

APPROXIMATE NUTRITIONAL INFORMATION FOR 1 SERVING: Calories: 368 cal; Protein: 12 g; Carbohydrates: 46 g; Fat: 15 g; Fiber: 4 g; Sodium: 212 mg.

KEY NUTRIENTS: Thiamine: .19 mg; Niacin: 3.03 mg; Pantothenic Acid: .57 mg; Vitamin B6: .29 mg; Iron 1.06 mg; Magnesium 85.75 mg; Zinc: 1.27 mg.

Quick Nutritional Yeast Rice

Place 1 cup hot, cooked brown rice (or other grain) in bowl. Sprinkle 1 teaspoon olive oil, 2 teaspoons nutritional yeast flakes, and 1/4 teaspoon soy sauce over top and mix well.

Makes 1 serving

Variation: Add 1/4 cup cooked beans.

APPROXIMATE NUTRITIONAL INFORMATION FOR 1 SERVING: Calories: 284 cal; Protein: 9 g; Carbohydrates: 48 g; Fat: 7 g; Fiber: 5 g; Sodium: 82 mg.

KEY NUTRIENTS: Thiamine: 4.41 mg; Riboflavin: 4.28 mg; Niacin: 27.62 mg; Pantothenic Acid: .56 mg; Vitamin B6: 4.51 mg; Folate: 113.4 mcg; Vitamin B12: 3.51 mcg; Iron: 1.14 mg; Magnesium: 83.85 mg; Zinc: 2.61 mg.

Easy Pasta Lunch

This is really quick if you have leftover cooked pasta from dinner.

4 ounces whole grain pasta, cooked (about 3 cups)
1 tablespoon olive oil
1 tomato, diced
2 tablespoons minced parsley
Sea salt and black pepper to taste
1/4 cup shredded mozzarella cheese (optional)

Toss hot pasta with remaining ingredients.

Makes 2 to 3 servings

APPROXIMATE NUTRITIONAL INFORMATION FOR 1 SERVING: Calories: 312 cal; Protein: 12 g; Carbohydrates: 46 g; Fat: 11 g; Fiber: 1 g; Sodium: 64 mg.

KEY NUTRIENTS: Vitamin A: 91.63 mcg.; Thiamine: .32 mg; Riboflavin: .15 mg; Niacin: 3.37 mg; Pantothenic Acid: .74 mg; Vitamin B6: .19 mg; Folate: 48.47 mcg; Vitamin C: 11.2 mg; Calcium: 103.5 mg; Iron: 2.61 mg; Magnesium: 92.84 mg; Zinc: 1.76 mg.

Quick Asian Noodles

This light, delicious lunch (or dinner) takes literally 10 minutes to make. I love it in the spring with baby spinach and kale from my garden.

2 teaspoons toasted sesame oil or peanut oil
2 cloves garlic, minced
8 ounces firm tofu or Asian-flavored baked tofu, cut into 1-inch cubes
2 cups tender young greens (spinach, kale, chard, etc.)
1 (3.5-ounce) package Bifun Rice Pasta
1 tablespoon chopped cilantro

Sauce:
1 teaspoon toasted sesame oil
2 teaspoons soy sauce
Juice of 1 lime (about 2 tablespoons)

Place 1 1/2 quarts water in pan for pasta. Cover and bring to a boil over high heat. Meanwhile, in small bowl, combine sauce ingredients.

Heat oil in skillet over medium heat. Add garlic and tofu. Sauté until golden (about 5 minutes). Place greens in skillet and cover. Put pasta into boiling water. After two minutes, drain pasta and rinse with cold water. Drain and add to skillet. Remove skillet from heat. Pour sauce over pasta. Toss pasta, tofu, and greens until coated with sauce. Pour into serving dish and top with cilantro.

Makes 3 servings

Note: Start boiling the water for the pasta before you start cooking the tofu and vegetables. The pasta only takes 2 minutes to cook so you want to be able to put it into the water at the same time you start cooking the greens.

APPROXIMATE NUTRITIONAL INFORMATION FOR 1 SERVING: Calories: 279 cal; Protein: 16 g; Carbohydrates: 31 g; Fat: 12 g; Fiber: 2 g; Sodium: 217 mg.

KEY NUTRIENTS: Vitamin A: 149.6 mcg; Thiamine: .14 mg; Riboflavin: .12 mg; Vitamin B6: .14 mg; Folate: 61.81 mcg; Vitamin C: 9.49 mg; Calcium: 540.91 mg; Iron: 9.34 mg; Magnesium: 60.85 mg; Zinc: 1.32 mg.

Salads and Dressings

 This section contains both side- and main-course salads. Raw vegetables and fruit salads are rich in vitamins, minerals, fiber, and enzymes to supplement your entrée. Cooked grains and beans add protein and substance, transforming a salad into a main course. Most of these salads can be made in advance and last several days so they are convenient for a quick snack or meal. Keep plenty of fresh vegetables and fruit, cooked grains and beans, nuts, and seeds on hand. You may even want to wash and chop vegetables in advance or buy them prechopped to save time.

Salads

Greek Salad with Red Wine
  Vinaigrette
Caesar Salad
Pear-Walnut Salad with Balsamic
  Vinaigrette
Fresh Fig and Sunflower Seed Salad
  with Tangy Yogurt Dressing
Orange-Almond Salad
Sunny Cole Slaw
Tabouli
Sweet Potato Salad with Peanut Butter
  Dressing
Roasted Root Vegetable Salad
Tofu and Udon Noodles with Sesame-
  Peanut Dressing
Curried Rice Salad
Bean and Rice Salad with Asian
  Citrus Dressing
Garbanzo Bean Salad with Creamy
  Mint Dressing

Dressings

Quick Herb Dressing
Creamy Herb Dressing
Italian Dressing
Sesame-Orange Dressing
Thousand Island Dressing

Salads

Create your own salad

Start with a base lettuce, such as: romaine, green leaf, red leaf, butterhead, etc. (avoid the nutritional devoid iceberg). You can also use tender, young dark green leafy vegetables, such as: kale, arugula, beet greens, chicory, collards, dandelion greens, escarole, watercress, spinach, turnip greens, etc.

Then choose from these additions:

Artichoke hearts
Beets (shredded raw, cooked, or pickled)
Bell peppers
Broccoli (raw or blanched)
Cauliflower (raw or blanched)
Carrots
Celery
Cheese (dairy or nondairy)
Cottage cheese (dairy or nondairy)
Cooked beans (garbanzo, black, pinto, white, etc.)
Cooked grains (brown rice, barley, millet, quinoa, etc.)
Corn
Cucumbers
Diced tofu, plain or flavored
Green beans (blanched)
Green onions
Fruit (fresh or dried)

Hard-boiled eggs
Nuts or seeds (raw or toasted)
Olives
Onions
Radishes
Peas (pod, snap, or snow)
Pickles
Potatoes
Sauerkraut
Sautéed mushrooms
Sautéed tempeh
Sea vegetables (e.g., soaked arame or toasted nori)
Shredded cabbage
Sprouts (sunflower, buckwheat, alfalfa, etc.)
Summer squash (raw or blanched)
Tomatoes
Whole grain croutons

Top with oil and vinegar or salad dressing of your choice.

Greek Salad with Red Wine Vinaigrette

1/2 head romaine lettuce, coarsely chopped (4 to 5 cups)
1 tomato, cut into wedges
1/2 cucumber, peeled and sliced
1/3 cup crumbled feta cheese or tofu
8 large black or kalamata olives, halved

Red Wine Vinaigrette:
2 teaspoons red wine vinegar
1/2 teaspoon dried oregano (or 1 tablespoon fresh)
1 tablespoon olive oil
Sea salt and black pepper to taste

Place lettuce, tomato, cucumber, feta cheese or tofu, and olives in large bowl. In small bowl or jar, mix dressing ingredients together. Whisk or shake until combined. Sprinkle over salad and toss.

Makes 4 servings

APPROXIMATE NUTRITIONAL INFORMATION FOR 1 SERVING: Calories: 98 cal; Protein: 3 g; Carbohydrates: 5 g; Fat: 8 g; Fiber: 1 g; Sodium: 290 mg.

KEY NUTRIENTS: VITAMIN A: 182.42 MCG; THIAMINE: .1 MG; RIBOFLAVIN: .18 mg; Vitamin B6: .12 mg; Folate: 88.29 mcg; Vitamin B12: .21 mcg; Vitamin C: 22.14 mg.

Caesar Salad

This version omits the raw egg and anchovy paste traditionally used. Good Parmesan cheese makes this salad outstanding. Vegans can use soy or rice Parmesan substitutes, or try Sesame Parmesan (page 285).

1 clove garlic, crushed
1/4 cup olive oil
1 large head romaine lettuce, washed and torn into bite-size pieces (about 8 cups)
1 to 2 cups croutons (optional) (see below)
2 tablespoons lemon juice
1/4 to 1/3 cup grated Parmesan cheese
Sea salt and black pepper to taste

Place garlic in olive oil and let sit while you prepare the lettuce. Place lettuce and croutons in large bowl. Drizzle oil and garlic over top. Sprinkle lemon juice over salad. Add cheese, salt and black pepper. Toss until coated.

Makes 6 servings

Variation: To make this a meal, add diced flavored tofu, chicken-style seitan, or cooked beans. Cooked pasta can also be added.

APPROXIMATE NUTRITIONAL INFORMATION FOR 1 SERVING: Calories: 128 cal; Protein: 3 g; Carbohydrates: 7 g; Fat: 11 g; Fiber: 2 g; Sodium: 127 mg.

KEY NUTRIENTS: Vitamin A: 194.24 mcg; Thiamine: .11 mg; Folate: 108.82 mcg; Vitamin C: 20.41 mg; Iron 1.04 mg.

To make croutons:

Cut dry bread into 3/4-inch cubes. Sprinkle with garlic powder or Spike® All Purpose All Natural Seasoning (available at natural foods stores) and toast on a tray in a toaster oven or conventional oven. You can also sauté them in butter or olive oil over medium heat.

Pear-Walnut Salad with Balsamic Vinaigrette

1 head butter lettuce, washed and torn into bite-sized pieces
1 pear, cored and cut into wedges
2/3 cup coarsely chopped walnuts, toasted
1/4 cup crumbled blue cheese (optional)

Balsamic Vinaigrette:
2 teaspoons balsamic vinegar
1 small clove garlic, crushed
1 teaspoon Dijon mustard
1 tablespoon minced fresh tarragon or (1 teaspoon dried)
1/4 teaspoon sea salt
1/4 cup olive oil

Place lettuce, pear, walnuts, and optional cheese in large bowl. In small bowl or jar, mix dressing ingredients together. Whisk or shake until combined. Pour over salad and toss.

Makes 6 to 8 servings

Note: If your family can't eat the entire salad in one sitting, split the undressed salad into 2 or 3 bowls and just dress the amount you need. Then you'll have a salad ready for another meal. To prevent pears from turning brown, toss them with a little lemon juice.

APPROXIMATE NUTRITIONAL INFORMATION FOR 1 SERVING: Calories: 211 cal; Protein: 4 g; Carbohydrates: 7 g; Fat: 20 g; Fiber: 2 g; Sodium: 168 mg.

KEY NUTRIENTS: Thiamine: .16 mg; Riboflavin: .54 mg; Vitamin B6: .1 mg; Folate: 34.85 mcg.

Fresh Fig and Sunflower Seed Salad with Tangy Yogurt Dressing

This is a wonderful salad in summer when figs are in season. If you can't get fresh figs, you can use dried or substitute an apple, pear, or orange.

1/2 head red leaf lettuce, washed and torn into bite size pieces (4 to 6 cups)
4 fresh figs, cut into wedges
1/2 cup sunflower seeds, toasted

Tangy Yogurt Dressing:
1 tablespoon orange or lemon juice
2 tablespoons yogurt (dairy or nondairy)
Pinch sea salt
Pinch ground cinnamon or cardamom
4 drops liquid stevia, or 1 teaspoon honey or agave nectar

Place lettuce, figs, and sunflower seeds in large bowl. Whisk dressing ingredients together. Pour over salad and toss gently until coated.

Makes 4 servings

APPROXIMATE NUTRITIONAL INFORMATION FOR 1 SERVING: Calories: 153 cal; Protein: 4 g; Carbohydrates: 15 g; Fat: 10 g; Fiber: 4 g; Sodium: 83 mg.

KEY NUTRIENTS: Thiamine: .12 mg; Riboflavin: .11 mg; Niacin: 1.05 mg; Pantothenic Acid: 1.37 mg; Vitamin B6: .23 mg; Folate: 58.44 mcg; Iron: 1.81 mg; Magnesium: 36.09 mg; Zinc: 1.08 mg.

Orange-Almond Salad

This salad supplies iron, and the vitamin C from the cabbage and orange helps it to be absorbed. Try this with walnuts too.

1 head romaine lettuce, washed and cut into bite-sized pieces (about 6 to 8 cups)
1 cup shredded red cabbage
1/2 cucumber, peeled and sliced
2 mandarin oranges or tangerines, peeled and split into sections
1/2 cup almonds, coarsely chopped and toasted

Orange-Sesame Dressing:
6 tablespoons orange juice (1 orange)
1 teaspoon rice or apple cider vinegar.
1 1/2 teaspoons soy sauce
1 tablespoon tahini or almond butter
1 tablespoon toasted sesame oil
1 teaspoon minced fresh ginger

Place lettuce, cabbage, cucumber, orange, and almonds in large bowl. Whisk dressing ingredients together. Pour over salad a little at a time and toss gently until salad is coated. You may not need all the dressing.

Makes 6 servings

APPROXIMATE NUTRITIONAL INFORMATION FOR 1 SERVING: Calories: 119 cal; Protein: 5 g; Carbohydrates: 11 g; Fat: 7 g; Fiber: 4 g; Sodium: 8 mg.

KEY NUTRIENTS: Vitamin A: 157.35 mcg; Thiamine: .17 mg; Riboflavin: .19 mg; Niacin: 1.1 mg; Vitamin B6: .11 mg; Folate: 101.12 mcg; Vitamin C: 45.35 mg; Vitamin E: 3.46 mg; Iron: 1.34 mg; Magnesium: 47.11 mg; Zinc: .73 mg.

Sunny Cole Slaw

Cabbage is a great source of vitamin C and is available year round.

3 cups shredded red or green cabbage (or a mixture)
2 carrots, shredded
1/2 cup sunflower seeds, toasted
2 tablespoons mayonnaise (regular or vegan)
1/4 cup yogurt (dairy or nondairy)
1 tablespoon lemon juice
1 tablespoon fresh dill or 1 teaspoon dried
1/3 teaspoon sea salt
Black pepper to taste

In large bowl, combine all ingredients. Chill for at least one hour before serving.

Makes 6 servings

Note: Mayonnaise can be substituted for yogurt if desired.

APPROXIMATE NUTRITIONAL INFORMATION FOR 1 SERVING: Calories: 128 cal; Protein: 3 g; Carbohydrates: 7 g; Fat: 10 g; Fiber: 3 g; Sodium: 165 mg.

KEY NUTRIENTS: Vitamin A: 574.14 mcg; Pantothenic Acid: .9 mg; Vitamin B6: .19 mg; Folate: 37.24 mcg; Vitamin C: 23.25 mg; Iron: 1.04 mg; Zinc: .71 mg.

Tabouli

2 cups water
1 cup bulgur wheat
Pinch sea salt
1/2 cup chopped green onions
1 stalk celery, minced
2 carrots, shredded
1/2 cup toasted sunflower seeds
1 cup packed fresh parsley, minced
1/2 cup packed fresh peppermint leaves, minced
3 tablespoons lemon juice (1 small lemon)
1/3 cup olive oil
Sea salt and black pepper to taste

In saucepan, bring water to a boil. Add bulgur and salt. Cover and return to boil. Remove from heat and let sit for 20 to 30 minutes, or until water is absorbed. Pour into bowl and mix in remaining ingredients. Refrigerate at least one hour before serving. Serve over salad greens or in pita pockets.

Makes 8 servings

Variation: Add 1 cup cooked navy or garbanzo beans for extra protein.

APPROXIMATE NUTRITIONAL INFORMATION FOR 1 SERVING: Calories: 206 cal; Protein: 4 g; Carbohydrates: 18 g; Fat: 14 g; Fiber: 5 g; Sodium: 88 mg.

KEY NUTRIENTS: Vitamin A: 477.98 mcg; Thiamine: .1 mg; Niacin: 1.57 mg; Pantothenic Acid: .86 mg; Vitamin B6: .17 mg; Folate: 46.16 mcg; Vitamin C: 16.18 mg; Iron: 1.74 mg; Magnesium: 48.96 mg; Zinc: .94 mg.

Sweet Potato Salad with Peanut Butter Dressing

A unique blend of sweet and savory makes this a favorite with all ages.

5 medium sweet potatoes, cooked, peeled, and diced
3 to 4 green onions, thinly sliced
1 stalk celery, diced
1 red bell pepper, seeded and diced
2 tablespoons minced cilantro or parsley
1/2 cup toasted pumpkin seeds or chopped walnuts

Peanut Butter Dressing:
2 tablespoons peanut butter
2 teaspoons brown rice vinegar
1/4 cup orange or pineapple juice
1 teaspoon soy sauce
1 teaspoon toasted sesame oil
1/2 teaspoon powdered ginger

Place sweet potatoes, green onions, celery, bell pepper, cilantro or parsley, and pumpkin seeds or walnuts in large bowl. Place dressing ingredients in blender and puree until smooth. Pour over salad. Toss gently to coat.

Makes 8 servings

Note: Tahini or other nut/seed butter can be substituted for peanut butter if desired.

APPROXIMATE NUTRITIONAL INFORMATION FOR 1 SERVING: Calories: 193 cal; Protein: 5 g; Carbohydrates: 28 g; Fat: 7 g; Fiber: 3 g; Sodium: 56 mg.

KEY NUTRIENTS: Vitamin A: 1703.26 mcg; Riboflavin: .17 mg; Pantothenic Acid: .57 mg; Vitamin B6: .3 mg; Vitamin C: 49.92 mg; Iron: 2.11 mg; Magnesium: 59.87 mg; Zinc: .96 mg.

Roasted Root Vegetable Salad

This salad is great any time of the year. It is full of color and nutrients.

8 cups cubed root vegetables (sweet potatoes, white potatoes, beets, carrots, etc.)
1 large red or yellow onion, cut into large chunks
1/2 teaspoon sea salt
1/4 teaspoon black pepper
Olive oil for roasting
1 1/2 teaspoons balsamic vinegar
2 to 4 tablespoons olive oil
1/2 cup toasted pine nuts or coarsely chopped walnuts
3 tablespoons coarsely chopped basil or parsley

Preheat oven to 450°F. Place cubed root vegetables and onion in large bowl. Sprinkle with salt and pepper and toss in enough olive oil so that every vegetable chunk is well coated. Place in single layer on large baking sheet. Roast for 20 minutes. Turn vegetables. Reduce heat to 350°F and roast for an additional 30 minutes or until vegetables are tender.

Place roasted vegetables in large bowl. Drizzle with balsamic vinegar and olive oil. Start with the lesser amount of oil and add more if you feel it is needed. Sprinkle toasted nuts and chopped basil or parsley over top and toss gently to mix. Serve warm or cold. This salad will keep for several days in the refrigerator.

Makes 8 servings

Variation: For extra protein and calcium, crumble feta, blue cheese, or tofu over salad.

APPROXIMATE NUTRITIONAL INFORMATION FOR 1 SERVING: Calories: 241 cal; Protein: 5 g; Carbohydrates: 35 g; Fat: 10 g; Fiber: 5 g; Sodium: 156 mg.

KEY NUTRIENTS: Vitamin A: 2672.07 mcg; Thiamine: .17 mg; Riboflavin: .22 mg; Niacin: 1.24 mg; Pantothenic Acid: .83 mg; Vitamin B6: .37 mg; Vitamin C: 31.73 mg; Iron: 1.65 mg; Magnesium: 36.02 mg; Zinc: .78 mg.

Tofu and Udon Noodles with Sesame-Peanut Dressing

1 (11-ounce) package udon noodles
1 pound firm tofu, cut into 1/2-inch cubes
3/4 cups thinly sliced green onions (4 to 6)
1 cup frozen peas (optional)
1/4 cup minced fresh cilantro
2 tablespoons toasted sesame oil
3 tablespoons toasted sesame seeds

Sesame-Peanut Dressing:
2 cloves garlic
2 tablespoons minced fresh ginger
2 tablespoons toasted sesame oil or peanut oil
2 tablespoons soy sauce
3 tablespoons brown rice vinegar
1/4 cup peanut butter
3 tablespoons tahini
1 tablespoon honey, brown rice syrup, or agave nectar
Pinch red pepper flakes
1/3 cup boiling water

Cook noodles in boiling water 4 to 6 minutes, or until tender but not mushy. Drain, rinse with cold water, and drain again. Immediately toss noodles with tofu, green onions, frozen peas, cilantro, and oil. Place dressing ingredients in blender and puree until smooth. Pour over noodle mixture. Sprinkle on sesame seeds. Toss gently until noodles are coated with sauce. Chill at least 1 hour before serving.

Makes 8 to 10 servings

APPROXIMATE NUTRITIONAL INFORMATION FOR 1 SERVING: Calories: 410 cal; Protein: 19 g; Carbohydrates: 37 g; Fat: 21 g; Fiber: 6 g; Sodium: 684 mg.

KEY NUTRIENTS: THIAMINE: .2 mg; Riboflavin: .11 mg; Folate: 31.33 mcg; Calcium: 423.53 mg; Iron: 8.03 mg; Magnesium: 51.5 mg; Zinc: 1.51 mg.

Curried Rice Salad

This easy salad will keep in your refrigerator for days so it's handy for lunch or snacks. Try it with other grains like millet or quinoa too.

4 cups cold cooked brown rice
3/4 cup golden raisins
1/2 cup chopped almonds, toasted
3 tablespoons chopped fresh cilantro

Honey-Curry Dressing:
2 tablespoons lemon juice
2 cloves garlic, crushed
2 teaspoons curry powder
1/4 teaspoon ground cumin
1/2 teaspoon ground turmeric
1/4 teaspoon powdered ginger
1 tablespoon honey (or brown rice syrup or agave nectar)
4 tablespoons flavorless oil (grapeseed, canola, safflower, etc.)
1 tablespoon toasted sesame oil

Place rice, raisins, almonds, and cilantro in large bowl. Whisk dressing ingredients together or place in a jar and shake until combined. Pour over rice mixture. Toss until coated. Chill at least one hour before serving.

Makes 8 servings

Note: See the Grain Cooking Chart in the Appendix for instructions on cooking rice.

APPROXIMATE NUTRITIONAL INFORMATION FOR 1 SERVING: Calories: 273 cal; Protein: 4 g; Carbohydrates: 37 g; Fat: 13 g; Fiber: 3 g; Sodium: 7 mg.

KEY NUTRIENTS: Thiamine: .11 mg; Riboflavin: .11 mg; Niacin: 1.92 mg; Vitamin B6: .21 mg; Vitamin E: 2.09 mg; Iron: .96 mg; Magnesium: 65.76 mg; Zinc: .9 mg.

Bean and Rice Salad with Asian Citrus Dressing

2 cups cooked black or kidney beans
2 cups cooked brown rice
1 cup corn kernels (fresh or frozen)
4 green onions, sliced
1 carrot, shredded
1/4 cup chopped fresh cilantro or parsley
Grated peel of 1 orange

Asian Citrus Dressing:
Juice of 1 orange (about 1/3 cup)
Juice of 1 lemon (about 3 tablespoons)
2 tablespoons toasted sesame oil
2 tablespoons olive oil
1 tablespoon soy sauce
2 teaspoons honey, brown rice syrup, or agave nectar

Combine beans, rice, corn, green onions, carrot, cilantro or parsley, and orange peel in large bowl. Whisk together dressing ingredients. Pour over salad and toss gently until coated. Refrigerate at least 1 hour. It's even better if it sits overnight.

Makes 6 to 8 servings

Note: See the Appendix for instructions on cooking brown rice and beans.

APPROXIMATE NUTRITIONAL INFORMATION FOR 1 SERVING: Calories: 280 cal; Protein: 8 g; Carbohydrates: 41 g; Fat: 11 g; Fiber: 6 g; Sodium: 155 mg.

KEY NUTRIENTS: Vitamin A: 298.17 mcg; Thiamine: .28 mg; Niacin: 1.98 mg; Pantothenic Acid: .61 mg; Vitamin B6: .19 mg; Folate: 81.09 mcg; Vitamin C: 15.97 mg; Iron: 2.41 mg; Magnesium: 73.48 mg; Zinc: 1.07 mg.

Garbanzo Bean Salad with Creamy Mint Dressing

This salad will keep in the refrigerator for several days and is perfect for a lunch or snack.

2 cups cooked garbanzo beans
1 large carrot, shredded
2 cups cooked brown rice
1/4 cup minced parsley

Creamy Mint Dressing:
1 tablespoon light miso
1 tablespoon tahini
3 tablespoons lemon juice (1 small lemon)
1/4 cup bean cooking water or plain water
1 clove garlic, peeled and chopped
1/3 cup fresh peppermint leaves

Place garbanzo beans, carrot, brown rice, and parsley in large bowl. Puree dressing ingredients together in blender. Pour over salad and toss until evenly coated. Chill at least one hour before serving.

Makes 6 servings

Note: See the Appendix for instructions on cooking brown rice and garbanzo beans.

APPROXIMATE NUTRITIONAL INFORMATION FOR 1 SERVING: Calories: 192 cal; Protein: 8 g; Carbohydrates: 34 g; Fat: 3 g; Fiber: 6 g; Sodium: 120 mg.

KEY NUTRIENTS: Vitamin A: 358.83 mcg; Thiamine: .18 mg; Niacin: 1.63 mg; Pantothenic Acid: .42 mg; Vitamin B6: .21 mg; Folate: 108.13 mcg; Vitamin C: 9.27 mg; Iron: 2.29 mg; Magnesium: 62.56 mg; Zinc: 1.53 mg.

Salad Dressings

Dressing is what makes a salad taste so good. Many bottled dressings contain chemicals, sugar, and trans-fats. Check the ingredients carefully and avoid those that are high in sugar (especially high-fructose corn syrup), sodium, hydrogenated oils, MSG, chemical flavorings, and preservatives. Look for organic, all natural dressings. Better yet, make dressing yourself using wholesome ingredients. This section contains easy recipes. If you want a bigger batch, double or triple the recipes and keep them refrigerated so you'll always have a dressing on hand. Look back through the salads for additional dressing recipes.

Quick Herb Dressing

This dressing tastes best if it can sit for at least 30 minutes for the herbs and garlic to infuse. Make it first before you cook the meal.

1/3 cup extra virgin olive oil
1 tablespoon lemon juice
1 teaspoon Dijon mustard
1 clove garlic, crushed
1 tablespoon minced fresh herbs (thyme, dill, tarragon, basil, etc.)
Sea salt and pepper to taste

Place all ingredients in a jar. Cover and shake until mixed.

Makes 1/2 cup

Note: When you refrigerate this dressing, the oil may solidify. Leave at room temperature about 15 minutes before serving to liquefy.

APPROXIMATE NUTRITIONAL INFORMATION FOR 1 TABLESPOON: Calories: 82 cal; Protein: 0 g; Carbohydrates: 0 g; Fat: 9 g; Fiber: 0 g; Sodium: 43 mg.

Creamy Herb Dressing

This simple dressing is great over hearty lettuces like romaine and perfect for cole slaw. You can easily double this recipe. It will keep refrigerated for several weeks.

1/2 cup mayonnaise (regular or vegan)
2 tablespoons lemon juice (about 1/2 lemon)
1 teaspoon Dijon mustard
1 tablespoon chopped fresh parsley
1 tablespoon chopped fresh chives
1 tablespoon chopped fresh tarragon

Puree all ingredients in blender until smooth.

Makes about 3/4 cup

APPROXIMATE NUTRITIONAL INFORMATION FOR 1 TABLESPOON: Calories: 72 cal; Protein: 0 g; Carbohydrates: 0 g; Fat: 7 g; Fiber: 0 g; Sodium: 70 mg.

KEY NUTRIENTS: Riboflavin: .25 mg; Vitamin C: 7.22 mg.

Italian Dressing

This delicious dressing keeps well. If the olive oil solidifies in the refrigerator, place dressing at room temperature 15 minutes before serving.

3/4 cup olive oil
1/4 cup wine vinegar
1 clove garlic, crushed
1/2 teaspoon dried basil
1/2 teaspoon dried oregano
2 tablespoons grated Parmesan cheese (dairy or nondairy) (optional)
1 teaspoon nutritional yeast flakes (optional)
1/4 teaspoon sea salt
Black pepper to taste

Place all ingredients in a jar. Cover and shake until combined. Refrigerate at least 1 hour before serving, if possible.

Makes about 1 cup

Note: You may want to increase the nutritional yeast flakes to 2 or 3 teaspoons if you omit the Parmesan cheese.

APPROXIMATE NUTRITIONAL INFORMATION FOR 1 TABLESPOON: Calories: 96 cal; Protein: 0 g; Carbohydrates: 0 g; Fat: 11 g; Fiber: 0 g; Sodium: 47 mg.

KEY NUTRIENTS: Thiamine: .13 mg; Riboflavin: .13 mg.

Sesame-Orange Dressing

Juice of 1 orange (about 1/4 cup)
Grated rind of 1 orange (about 1 teaspoon)
1 tablespoon brown rice vinegar
1/3 cup olive oil
1 tablespoon toasted sesame oil
1 teaspoon soy sauce
1 tablespoon minced fresh ginger or 1/4 teaspoon powdered ginger
1 tablespoon sesame seeds

Place all ingredients in glass jar. Cover tightly and shake to mix.

Makes 3/4 cup

APPROXIMATE NUTRITIONAL INFORMATION FOR 1 TABLESPOON: Calories: 74 cal; Protein: 0 g; Carbohydrates: 1 g; Fat: 8 g; Fiber: 0 g; Sodium: 24 mg.

Thousand Island Dressing

My children love this dressing. We also like it on veggie burgers or as a dip for vegetables or oven fries, too.

2/3 cup mayonnaise (regular or vegan)
2 tablespoons ketchup
2 tablespoons lemon juice
2 tablespoons sweet pickle relish

Mix all ingredients together. Keep refrigerated.

Makes about 1 cup

APPROXIMATE NUTRITIONAL INFORMATION FOR 1 TABLESPOON: Calories: 71 cal; Protein: 0 g; Carbohydrates: 1 g; Fat: 7 g; Fiber: 0 g; Sodium: 79 mg.

Soups and Stews

 Soups and stews are excellent when you're pregnant or lactating because they are so nourishing. They're easy to prepare and there is only one pot to wash. Soups and stews are versatile too. Almost any vegetable, grain, or bean you happen to have will work in a soup. Use these recipes as suggestions or guidelines. If you don't have an ingredient or two, just leave it out or use whatever vegetable or bean you do have. I have included sea vegetables in many of these dishes to provide extra vitamins and minerals. They do not affect the taste of the dish so you don't have to add them if you don't want to.

Make a big batch of soup when you have time so you can heat up a bowl whenever you are hungry. Soup will last up to 5 days in the refrigerator. Soups freeze well too, so make extra before the baby comes and freeze in small containers for postpartum meals.

Stock

Vegetable Stock

Soups

Chunky Vegetable Soup
Miso-Noodle Soup
Soothing Mint Soup
Creamy Parsnip Soup
Thai Pumpkin-Coconut Soup
"Cream" of Watercress Soup
"Cream" of Broccoli Soup
"Cream" of Spinach and Millet Soup
Squash and White Bean Soup
Ginger-Lentil Soup
Herbed Split Pea Soup
Black Bean and Corn Soup
Tortilla Soup
Sea Vegetable Soup

Stews

Garbanzo Stew
Seitan "Chicken" and Barley Stew
Ratatouille
Adzuki-Squash Stew
Coconut-Tempeh Stew
Mild Yellow Curry Stew
Better Than "Beef" Stew

Stock

Homemade stock adds richness, flavor, and nutrients to soups and stews and they are easy to make. Just throw vegetables and herbs in a pot of water and let them simmer. Homemade stock will last about a week in the refrigerator or for months in the freezer. Freeze in 1- or 2-cup-size containers so you can thaw only the amount needed for a recipe. Stock can also be frozen in ice cube trays and then transferred to freezer bag or container.

Alternatives to Stock

Here are some alternatives when you don't have time to make a true vegetable stock.

- Prepared vegetable stock is available at natural foods stores and supermarkets.
- Vegetarian bouillon and powders can be mixed with water to substitute for vegetable stock. They also come in vegetarian chicken- and beef-style flavors.
- Water from steaming, boiling, or blanching vegetables can be refrigerated or frozen and used instead of stock. You can add seaweed-soak water to it also.

Vegetable Stock

Stock can be made from fresh or cooked vegetables and even peels from potatoes. Strong-flavored vegetables like cabbage or broccoli should be used only in small amounts as they may overpower the stock. Fresh herbs can be added for more flavor.

3 onions, cut into thick slices
2 cloves garlic, sliced
5 stalks celery, cut into thirds
6 carrots (about 1 pound), cut into thirds
2 cups potato peels (from organic potatoes only)
1 bunch parsley stems
2 bay leaves
1 strip kombu
3 quarts cold water

Place all ingredients in large soup pot. Cover and bring to a boil over high heat. Reduce heat and simmer for 1 hour.

Remove from heat and let stock sit for 30 minutes. Strain broth through large sieve. Cool stock quickly by placing pot of stock in sink full of ice water. When lukewarm, refrigerate or freeze stock.

Makes about 3 quarts

Variation: Use parsnips or turnips in place of some of the carrots if you have them. You can also use 4 leeks instead of the onions.

APPROXIMATE NUTRITIONAL INFORMATION FOR 1 CUP: Nutritional information unavailable.

Soups

Chunky Vegetable Soup

Don't worry if you don't have every vegetable listed; this soup recipe is very flexible. Use whatever you have on hand. Frozen vegetables are okay too.

1 onion, diced
2 stalks celery, thinly sliced
2 carrots, thinly sliced
2 teaspoons olive oil
8 cups water or vegetable stock
2 cloves garlic, minced
1 sweet potato or rutabaga, diced
1 white potato, diced
1 cup green beans, cut into bite-size pieces
1/4 cup arame, hiziki, or wakame, crushed or 1 tablespoon Sea Veg Mix (page 282)
1/2 cup fresh or frozen peas
1 cup chopped cabbage, kale, collards, or other green
1 tablespoon fresh or 1 teaspoon dried herbs (thyme, rosemary, tarragon, savory, etc.)
1 tablespoon nutritional yeast flakes
1 tablespoon miso
1/2 cup minced fresh parsley
Sea salt and black pepper to taste

Place onion, celery, carrots, and oil in large soup pot. Sauté 5 to 10 minutes over medium heat until onions are soft. Add water or stock, garlic, potatoes, beans, and sea vegetables. Bring to boil. Cover and simmer 20 to 30 minutes until potatoes are tender. Add remaining ingredients except miso, parsley, and seasonings. Simmer 10 minutes until vegetables are tender. Remove from heat. Stir in miso and parsley. Season with sea salt and black pepper.

Makes 6 to 8 servings

Variations

Chunky Vegetable Soup with Tomatoes: Add 2 cups or 1 (15-ounce) can diced tomatoes with peas and greens.

Chunky Vegetable Soup with Protein: Add 2 cups tofu, tempeh, seitan, or cooked beans with peas and greens.

APPROXIMATE NUTRITIONAL INFORMATION FOR 1 SERVING: Calories: 115 cal; Protein: 4 g; Carbohydrates: 21 g; Fat: 2 g; Fiber: 5 g; Sodium: 379 mg.

KEY NUTRIENTS: Vitamin A: 1038.52 mcg; Thiamine: 1.15 mg; Riboflavin: 1.15 mg; Niacin: 7.11 mg; Pantothenic Acid: .39 mg; Vitamin B6: 1.3 mg; Vitamin B12: .89 mcg; Vitamin C: 24.91 mg; Iron: 1.37 mg; Zinc: .84 mg.

Miso-Noodle Soup

This is a soothing soup that is great for upset stomachs or jangled nerves. I especially like it with brown rice pasta.

5 1/2 cups water
2 tablespoons chopped wakame or 1 tablespoon Sea Veg Mix (page 282)
1 carrot, thinly sliced
1 clove garlic, minced
3 green onions, thinly sliced
1 cup chopped kale, cabbage, watercress, or other green
1/2 cup snow or snap peas
1/2 cup small uncooked pasta noodles
8 ounces tofu, diced
2 tablespoons miso
Soy sauce to taste

Place water and sea vegetable in medium-size pan. Cover and bring to a boil over high heat. Add remaining ingredients and simmer uncovered 10 minutes, or until pasta is just cooked. Remove from heat, stir in miso. Season with soy sauce if desired.

Makes 6 servings

APPROXIMATE NUTRITIONAL INFORMATION FOR 1 SERVING: Calories: 118 cal; Protein: 9 g; Carbohydrates: 13 g; Fat: 4 g; Fiber: 3 g; Sodium: 265 mg.

KEY NUTRIENTS: Vitamin A: 400.22 mcg; Thiamine: .14 mg; Riboflavin: .1 mg; Vitamin B6: .1 mg; Vitamin C: 20.34 mg; Calcium: 296 mg; Iron: 5.05 mg; Magnesium: 41.28 mg; Zinc: 1.14 mg.

Soothing Mint Soup

This is a great soup for so many things. It is warming on a cold day. If you have a cold or flu, it will help loosen mucus and promote sweating. I loved it during my first trimester of pregnancy. The mint and ginger help to reduce nausea and the stock and eggs provide nutrients. Best of all, it is quick and easy to make so you can do it even when you aren't feeling your best.

4 cups vegetable stock
1 clove garlic, minced
1 tablespoon peeled and minced fresh ginger
1 cinnamon stick
3 green onions, thinly sliced
1 cup peas, fresh or frozen
1/2 cup tightly packed fresh peppermint leaves, chopped
2 teaspoons soy sauce or to taste
2 eggs, lightly beaten with 1 tablespoon water

In medium pan, heat stock, garlic, ginger, and cinnamon stick over medium heat. When it reaches a boil, stir in green onions, peas, peppermint, and soy sauce. Simmer 2 minutes. Pour egg mixture in a thin stream around edges of pan. Stir a couple of times so eggs form thin streamers. Remove from heat. Discard cinnamon stick.

Makes 4 servings

APPROXIMATE NUTRITIONAL INFORMATION FOR 1 SERVING: Calories: 66 cal; Protein: 4 g; Carbohydrates: 6 g; Fat: 3 g; Fiber: 2 g; Sodium: 186 mg.

KEY NUTRIENTS: Vitamin A: 89.05 mcg; Vitamin B12: .26 mcg; Vitamin C: 6.83 mg; Vitamin D: 1.23 mcg.

Creamy Parsnip Soup

This mellow soup is soothing all year round. The kombu is optional but brings out the sweetness of the parsnips and adds minerals. Don't worry about how neatly the vegetables are chopped as they will be pureed. Only peel the vegetables if the skins look thick or tough, or if they are not organic.

1 small onion, chopped
1 clove garlic, diced
1 stalk celery, cut into chunks
4 parsnips, cut into chunks
4 carrots, cut into chunks
1 bay leaf
1/2 strip kombu (optional)
1/2 teaspoon sea salt
1 tablespoon fresh thyme or 1 teaspoon dried
Pinch ground nutmeg
4 cups water or vegetable stock
1 tablespoon miso
1/4 cup minced fresh parsley or watercress

Place onion, garlic, celery, parsnips, carrots, bay leaf, kombu, sea salt, thyme, nutmeg, and water or stock in large pot. Cover and bring to a boil. Reduce heat and simmer 20 to 30 minutes, or until vegetables are tender. Remove bay leaf. Puree soup with miso in blender or food processor. (You may have to do this in two batches.) Pour into serving dish or return to pot. Sprinkle parsley or watercress over soup.

Makes 6 to 8 servings

APPROXIMATE NUTRITIONAL INFORMATION FOR 1 SERVING: Calories: 118 cal; Protein: 2 g; Carbohydrates: 27 g; Fat: 1 g; Fiber: 6 g; Sodium: 336 mg.

KEY NUTRIENTS: Vitamin A: 1158.08 mcg; Thiamine: .14 mg; Niacin: 1.25 mg; Pantothenic Acid: .75 mg; Vitamin B6: .19 mg; Folate: 76.39 mcg; Vitamin C: 22.19 mg; Vitamin E: 1.34 mg; Iron: 1.11 mg; Magnesium: 45.39 mg.

Thai Pumpkin-Coconut Soup

This tasty soup is so easy you'll want to make it often.

2 cups or 1 (15-ounce) can pureed, cooked pumpkin
1 (14-ounce) can light coconut milk
2 cups vegetable stock
1 tablespoon miso
1/8 to 1/4 teaspoon red curry paste, or to taste
1/4 teaspoon sea salt or to taste
3 tablespoons chopped fresh cilantro

Place pumpkin, coconut milk, and stock in pan. Warm over medium heat until just about to boil. Remove from heat. Mix in miso, curry paste, and sea salt. Sprinkle cilantro over top.

Makes 4 to 6 servings

APPROXIMATE NUTRITIONAL INFORMATION FOR 1 SERVING: Calories: 100 cal; Protein: 1 g; Carbohydrates: 7 g; Fat: 7 g; Fiber: 2 g; Sodium: 296 mg.

KEY NUTRIENTS: Vitamin A: 137.75 mcg; Vitamin C: 13.91 mg; Vitamin E: 1.32 mg.

"Cream" of Watercress Soup

This light, lemony soup is an excellent meal during early labor and postpartum.

2 tablespoons butter or olive oil
2 tablespoons flour (any kind)
2 cups vegetable stock
1 bunch watercress, chopped (about 4 cups)
1/2 cup raw cashews
1 1/2 cups water
1 tablespoon lemon juice
Sea salt and black pepper to taste

Heat butter or olive oil in pan over medium heat. Stir in flour. Add stock and watercress. Cover and cook 5 to 10 minutes, or until watercress is wilted. Place cashews in blender and grind to powder. Add water and lemon juice. Puree until smooth. Add watercress mixture and puree with cashew mixture. You will have to do this in at least two batches. Return soup to pan. Season to taste and reheat if necessary.

Makes 4 to 6 servings

Note: 1 1/2 cups light cream or milk can be substituted for cashews and water.

APPROXIMATE NUTRITIONAL INFORMATION FOR 1 SERVING: Calories: 166 cal; Protein: 4 g; Carbohydrates: 8 g; Fat: 14 g; Fiber: 2 g; Sodium: 213 mg.

KEY NUTRIENTS: Vitamin A: 213.41 mcg; Vitamin C: 16.37 mg; Vitamin D: 3.98 mcg; Iron: 1.35 mg; Magnesium: 74.36 mg; Zinc: 1.13 mg.

"Cream" of Broccoli Soup

1/2 onion, chopped
1 clove garlic
1 stalk celery, sliced
1 large carrot, sliced
3 cups coarsely chopped broccoli
3 cups water
1/2 cup raw cashews
1 tablespoon arrowroot
1/2 teaspoon sea salt or to taste
1 tablespoon miso
1/4 teaspoon black pepper
1 teaspoon dried basil

Place onion, garlic, celery, carrot, broccoli, and water in soup pot. Cover and bring to a boil. Reduce heat to medium-low and simmer 15 to 20 minutes, or until vegetables are tender. Remove 8 to 10 small broccoli florets and set aside.

Place cashews in blender. Grind to powder. Add remaining ingredients to blender along with half of the cooked vegetable/water mixture. Puree until smooth and pour into a pot. Puree remaining vegetables and water, and add it to soup in the pot. Stir in reserved florets. Reheat if necessary but do not boil because it will destroy the beneficial enzymes in the miso.

Makes 4 to 6 servings

APPROXIMATE NUTRITIONAL INFORMATION FOR 1 SERVING: Calories: 149 cal; Protein: 6 g; Carbohydrates: 15 g; Fat: 9 g; Fiber: 4 g; Sodium: 468 mg.

KEY NUTRIENTS: Vitamin A: 609.67 mcg; Riboflavin: .11 mg; Pantothenic Acid: .44 mg; Vitamin B6: .17 mg; Folate: 60.17 mcg; Vitamin C: 65 mg; Vitamin E: 1.23 mg; Iron: 2 mg; Magnesium: 85.41 mg; Zinc: 1.47 mg.

"Cream" of Spinach and Millet Soup

This creamy soup provides a lot of iron. You can replace up to half of the spinach with kale if you like.

4 cups water
2/3 cup millet
1 teaspoon Sea Veg Mix (optional)
8 cups coarsely chopped fresh spinach
2 tablespoons tahini
2 teaspoons nutritional yeast flakes
1/4 teaspoon ground nutmeg
2 cups milk (dairy or nondairy)
1 tablespoon miso
Sea salt and pepper to taste

Bring water to a boil in saucepan. Add millet, sea vegetables, and spinach. When mixture returns to a boil, reduce heat and simmer for 20 minutes. Put cooked spinach mixture in blender along with remaining ingredients and puree until smooth. (You may need to do this in several batches.) Reheat soup if necessary but do not boil because the live enzymes in the miso will be destroyed.

Makes 6 servings

APPROXIMATE NUTRITIONAL INFORMATION FOR 1 SERVING: Calories: 185 cal; Protein: 8 g; Carbohydrates: 24 g; Fat: 7 g; Fiber: 4 g; Sodium: 190 mg.

KEY NUTRIENTS: Vitamin A: 297.44 mcg; Thiamine: .93 mg; Riboflavin: 1.01 mg; Niacin: 5.84 mg; Pantothenic Acid: .51 mg; Vitamin B6: .92 mg; Folate: 124 mcg; Vitamin B12: .88 mcg; Vitamin C: 12.46 mg; Calcium: 165.28 mg; Iron: 2.13 mg; Magnesium: 73.92 mg; Zinc: 1.46 mg.

Squash and White Bean Soup

This simple soup is packed full of vitamins, minerals, and protein. The squash doesn't need to be chopped evenly because the soup will be pureed.

1 small onion, peeled and chopped
2 teaspoons olive oil
2 cloves garlic, chopped
4 cups water or vegetable stock
1 butternut, kabucha, or hubbard squash, peeled and cut into cubes (about 7 cups)
1 tablespoon minced fresh ginger or 1/2 teaspoon powdered ginger
1 teaspoon ground cinnamon
1/4 teaspoon ground nutmeg
1 1/2 tablespoons miso
1 tablespoon tahini
2 cups cooked white beans
1/2 cup minced fresh parsley or watercress
Sea salt and black pepper to taste

In large soup pot over medium-low heat, add onion and oil. Stir gently to spread and then cook about 15 minutes without stirring until onions are brown and caramelized. Stir in garlic. Add water or stock and squash. Cover and bring to boil over high heat. Lower heat and simmer 30 minutes until squash is tender. Puree squash mixture in blender or food processor with spices, miso, and tahini. Add water if soup is too thick. Return to pot and stir in beans and parsley or watercress over low heat. Season with sea salt and black pepper. Garnish with roasted pumpkin or squash seeds if desired.

Makes 6 servings

Note: See the Bean and Legume Cooking Chart in the Appendix for instructions on cooking white beans.

APPROXIMATE NUTRITIONAL INFORMATION FOR 1 SERVING: Calories: 203 cal; Protein: 8 g; Carbohydrates: 38 g; Fat: 4 g; Fiber: 7 g; Sodium: 354 mg.

KEY NUTRIENTS: Vitamin A: 1300.56 mcg; Thiamine: .35 mg; Riboflavin: .1 mg; Niacin: 2.4 mg; Pantothenic Acid: .87 mg; Vitamin B6: .37 mg; Folate: 139.67 mcg; Vitamin C: 42.06 mg; Calcium: 146.52 mg; Iron: 3.38 mg; Magnesium: 104.66 mg; Zinc: 1.24 mg.

Ginger-Lentil Soup

Lentils are a good source of iron and the kale or cabbage supplies vitamin C to aid absorption. Ginger and kombu make the lentils more digestible. Don't worry if you can't finish the whole pot in one meal; this soup tastes even better the second (or third) day.

1 cup lentils
1/2 cup brown rice
1 strip kombu (optional)
1 bay leaf
8 cups water
1 onion, minced (optional)
2 cloves garlic, minced
2 stalks celery, diced
2 carrots, diced
1 cup fresh or frozen corn kernels
1 1/2 cups chopped kale or green cabbage
1/4 cup minced parsley
2 tablespoons ginger juice (page 360) or 1 teaspoon powdered ginger
1 tablespoon soy sauce
1 tablespoon miso

Place lentils, rice, kombu, bay leaf, and water in large soup pot. Cover and bring to a boil while chopping vegetables. Reduce heat to low and simmer 10 minutes. Add onion, garlic, celery, and carrots and continue to simmer (covered) for 30 to 45 minutes, or until lentils are tender. Stir in remaining ingredients and heat 5 to 10 minutes. Do not boil as this will destroy the beneficial enzymes in the miso.

Makes 8 servings

APPROXIMATE NUTRITIONAL INFORMATION FOR 1 SERVING: Calories: 169 cal; Protein: 9 g; Carbohydrates: 32 g; Fat: 1 g; Fiber: 10 g; Sodium: 302 mg.

KEY NUTRIENTS: Vitamin A: 552.99 mcg; Thiamine: .24 mg; Riboflavin: .12 mg; Niacin: 1.91 mg; Pantothenic Acid: .85 mg; Vitamin B6: .29 mg; Folate: 129.84 mcg; Vitamin C: 23.36 mg; Iron: 2.97 mg; Magnesium: 66.21 mg; Zinc: 1.4 mg.

Herbed Split Pea Soup

This soup is very easy to make. Not much chopping is involved and it is ready in an hour. I love this in the spring when my garden is full of fresh herbs. You can use water instead of stock if you like but the soup won't be as flavorful.

4 cups vegetable stock
2 cups water
1 cup green split peas
1 cup long-grain brown rice
1 bay leaf
1/2 strip kombu or wakame (optional)
2 carrots, diced
1/2 cup minced kale, chard, spinach or other leafy green
1 tablespoon fresh thyme
1 tablespoon minced fresh basil
1 tablespoon minced fresh sage
2 tablespoons chopped chives
2 tablespoons minced fresh parsley
2 tablespoons miso dissolved in 2 tablespoons water
Sea salt and black pepper to taste

Put stock, water, split peas, rice, bay leaf, and kombu or wakame in heavy pot. Cover and bring to a boil over high heat. Reduce heat to low and simmer 40 minutes. Add carrots. Cover and simmer 15 minutes, or until carrots are tender. Remove from heat. Remove and discard bay leaf. Stir in remaining ingredients.

Makes 6 servings

APPROXIMATE NUTRITIONAL INFORMATION FOR 1 SERVING: Calories: 253 cal; Protein: 12 g; Carbohydrates: 49 g; Fat: 2 g; Fiber: 11 g; Sodium: 241 mg.

KEY NUTRIENTS: Vitamin A: 642.34 mcg; Thiamine: .4 mg; Riboflavin: .14 mg; Niacin: 2.85 mg; Pantothenic Acid: 1.11 mg; Vitamin B6: .28 mg; Folate: 106.24 mcg; Vitamin C: 12.21 mg; Iron: 2.47 mg; Magnesium: 95.76 mg; Zinc: 1.9 mg.

Black Bean and Corn Soup

1 tablespoon olive oil
1 onion, chopped
2 cloves garlic, chopped
2 jalapeño peppers, seeded and chopped
2 teaspoons ground cumin
4 cups vegetable stock
1 cup water
5 cups cooked black beans
2 large carrots, sliced
1 teaspoon dried oregano
1/2 strip kombu, broken up
Sea salt to taste
2 cups corn kernels
1/4 cup chopped cilantro

Heat oil in soup pot. Stir in onion. Sauté 10 minutes. Stir in garlic, jalapeños, and cumin. Sauté 5 minutes. Stir in stock, water, beans, carrots, oregano, and kombu. Simmer covered 30 minutes, or until carrots are tender. Puree soup in blender or food processor. (You will have to do this in several batches.) Return to pot. Season with sea salt to taste. Stir in corn and cilantro. Heat to desired temperature.

Makes 8 servings

Note: 2 cups dried black beans will cook up to 5 cups for this recipe. See the Bean and Legume Cooking Chart in the Appendix for instructions on cooking the beans.

APPROXIMATE NUTRITIONAL INFORMATION FOR 1 SERVING: Calories: 215 cal; Protein: 11 g; Carbohydrates: 39 g; Fat: 3 g; Fiber: 8 g; Sodium: 166 mg.

KEY NUTRIENTS: Vitamin A: 512.93 mcg; Thiamine: .37 mg; Riboflavin: .11 mg; Niacin: 1.51 mg; Pantothenic Acid: .66 mg; Vitamin B6: .18 mg; Folate: 124.77 mcg; Vitamin C: 7.19 mg; Iron: 3.74 mg; Magnesium: 79.46 mg; Zinc: 1.14 mg.

Tortilla Soup

This hearty, delicious soup is a favorite with my family and friends. Although the ingredient list looks long, this is really a quick soup to make if you have cooked or canned beans on hand. Since my children don't like spicy foods, I leave the Tabasco sauce out of the soup and put the bottle on the table so each person can spice his or her soup.

1 tablespoon olive oil
1 onion, diced
2 cloves garlic, minced
2 cups cooked pinto beans
2 cups cooked white beans
2 cups cooked black beans
4 1/2 cups water
2 cups or 1 (15-ounce) can diced tomatoes
1 tablespoon Sea Veg Mix (page 282) (optional)
1 teaspoon ground cumin
1 teaspoon dried oregano
1 teaspoon chili powder
1 tablespoon miso
1 tablespoon tahini
2 teaspoons nutritional yeast flakes (optional)
1/2 teaspoon Tabasco sauce or to taste
Sea salt, if necessary
Tortilla chips

Optional Toppings:
Minced fresh cilantro
Sliced black olives
Shredded Jack cheese

Heat oil in large soup pot over medium-low heat. Add onion and cook 10 minutes without stirring so they brown. Stir in garlic. Add beans, water, tomatoes, Sea Veg Mix, cumin, oregano, and chili powder. Heat until soup starts to boil. Reduce heat and simmer uncovered about 30 minutes to let flavors combine. Remove 2 cups of soup and place in blender with miso and tahini. Puree and return to soup. Add Tabasco and sea salt to taste.

To serve, ladle soup into bowls. Insert tortilla chips into soup around edges of bowl. Top with cilantro, olives, and/or cheese if desired.

Makes 8 servings

Note: See the Bean and Legume Cooking Chart in the Appendix for instructions on cooking your own beans, or use beans you have cooked and frozen. Canned beans are also work well here; just use one can of each type of bean. You can also use just one or two types of beans or different ones than I suggest. Just make sure they add up to about 6 cups.

APPROXIMATE NUTRITIONAL INFORMATION FOR 1 SERVING: Calories: 288 cal; Protein: 14 g; Carbohydrates: 47 g; Fat: 6 g; Fiber: 12 g; Sodium: 161 mg.

KEY NUTRIENTS: Thiamine: .83 mg; Riboflavin: .66 mg; Niacin: 3.98 mg; Pantothenic Acid: .48 mg; Vitamin B6: .73 mg; Folate: 198.98 mcg; Vitamin B12: .44 mcg; Vitamin C: 10.61 mg; Calcium: 97.67 mg; Iron: 4.24 mg; Magnesium: 91.96 mg; Zinc: 1.98 mg

Sea Vegetable Soup

This nourishing soup is excellent postpartum to replenish your mineral supply. In many Asian countries, this type of soup is traditionally served the first week after childbirth. I have substituted tempeh for the fish that is usually included. The beneficial enzymes and bacteria in the tempeh and miso will help to prevent yeast-related problems like thrush. This soup is excellent during cold and flu season, or anytime you need a vitamin and mineral boost.

8 ounces tempeh, diced
1 clove garlic, minced (optional)
2 carrots, thinly sliced
1/2 cup hiziki, wakame, or arame, crushed, or 1/4 cup Sea Veg Mix
4 cups water or vegetable stock
1 cup chopped kale, spinach, or other leafy green
1 tablespoon minced fresh ginger
1 tablespoon miso
2 tablespoons minced fresh parsley or cilantro

Place tempeh, garlic, carrots, sea vegetables, and water or stock in a soup pot. Cover and bring to a boil over high heat. Reduce heat and simmer 10 minutes, or until carrots are tender. Stir in greens and ginger. Simmer 3 to 5 minutes, or until greens are tender. Remove from heat. Stir in miso. Add a little sea salt or soy sauce if desired. Sprinkle cilantro or parsley over soup.

Makes 4 servings

APPROXIMATE NUTRITIONAL INFORMATION FOR 1 SERVING: Calories: 150 cal; Protein: 12 g; Carbohydrates: 13 g; Fat: 7 g; Fiber: 3 g; Sodium: 221 mg.

KEY NUTRIENTS: Vitamin A: 1017.31 mcg; Thiamine: .1 mg; Riboflavin: .32 mg; Niacin: 2.02 mg; Vitamin B6: .23 mg; Vitamin C: 25.77 mg; Calcium: 125.87 mg; Iron: 2.4 mg; Magnesium: 59.78 mg; Zinc: .96 mg.

Stews

Garbanzo Stew

This hearty, vegetarian stew supplies a lot of iron. Try it with lima beans too.

1 bay leaf
1 onion, peeled and chopped
1 tablespoon olive oil
2 cloves garlic, peeled and chopped
4 to 5 red potatoes, cut into bite-size chunks
3 carrots, sliced
2 stalks celery, sliced
2 cups water or vegetable stock
1 teaspoon sea salt
2 cups cooked garbanzo beans
2 tomatoes, diced or 1 (15-ounce) can chopped tomatoes with juice
1 cup chopped green cabbage
1/2 teaspoon ground cumin
1/4 teaspoon ground turmeric
1 tablespoon miso
1 tablespoon tahini
1 1/2 tablespoons arrowroot powder
1/4 cup water

In large pot over medium heat, sauté bay leaf and onion in olive oil about 5 minutes, or until onion is translucent. Add garlic, potatoes, carrots, celery, and sauté 5 minutes longer. Add water or stock and sea salt. Cover and bring to boil over high heat. Reduce heat and simmer until potatoes are tender. Add garbanzo beans, tomatoes, cabbage, cumin, and turmeric. In small bowl, combine miso, tahini, and arrowroot with 1/4 cup water to form a smooth paste. Stir it into stew and heat for 5 minutes, or until broth thickens. Do not boil as this will destroy the beneficial enzymes in the miso. Remove bay leaf.

Makes 6 servings

APPROXIMATE NUTRITIONAL INFORMATION FOR 1 SERVING: Calories: 214 cal; Protein: 10 g; Carbohydrates: 35 g; Fat: 5 g; Fiber: 11 g; Sodium: 519 mg.

KEY NUTRIENTS: Vitamin A: 900.9 mcg; Thiamine: .28 mg; Riboflavin: .15 mg; Niacin: 3.29 mg; Pantothenic Acid: .99 mg; Vitamin B6: .49 mg; Folate: 164.22 mcg; Vitamin C: 49.63 mg; Iron: 3.75 mg; Magnesium: 79.51 mg; Zinc: 1.72 mg.

Storing Parsley

I like to add fresh parsley to soups and stews for a boost of vitamin C and minerals. To make it more convenient, wash the whole bunch of parsley and dry it well. Mince it in a food processor or by hand. Then transfer to freezer container or bag and store in freezer. You can easily break off chunks as you need them. This method works for cilantro, dill, and other herbs as well.

Seitan "Chicken" and Barley Stew

This soup is very soothing and grounding as well as filling. It is extremely high in protein and iron. Seitan is made from wheat gluten and can replace meat or chicken in any recipe. Find it in the refrigerated section of your natural foods store.

1 cup hulled barley, soaked for at least six hours and drained
8 cups water
2 vegetarian chicken-flavored bouillon cubes
1 tablespoon Sea Veg Mix (optional)
1 large carrot or parsnip, cut into half-moons
1 cup cut green beans (1-inch lengths)
1 pound chicken-style seitan, cut into bite-sized pieces
1 tablespoon fresh thyme or 1 teaspoon dried
1 tablespoon minced fresh rosemary or 1 teaspoon dried
1 cup fresh or frozen peas
2 tablespoons miso dissolved in 1/2 cup water
1/4 cup minced fresh parsley
Black pepper to taste

Place barley, water, bouillon, and Sea Veg Mix in large pot. Cover and bring to a boil over high heat. Reduce heat to low and simmer one hour, or until barley is tender. Add carrot or parsnip, beans, seitan, thyme, and rosemary. Cover and cook 15 minutes, or until vegetables are just tender. Stir in peas. Remove from heat. Stir in miso and parsley. Season with black pepper if desired.

Makes 8 servings

Note: If you substitute pearled barley (which is more refined), you don't need to soak it.

APPROXIMATE NUTRITIONAL INFORMATION FOR 1 SERVING: Calories: 187 cal; Protein: 20 g; Carbohydrates: 25 g; Fat: 1 g; Fiber: 7 g; Sodium: 654 mg.

KEY NUTRIENTS: Vitamin A: 285.47 mcg; Thiamine: .17 mg; Riboflavin: .1 mg; Niacin: 1.22 mg; Vitamin B6: .1 mg; Vitamin C: 6.45 mg; Iron: 11.51 mg; Magnesium: 36.29 mg; Zinc: .84 mg.

Ratatouille

This is a simple stew to make because there are just a few ingredients to chop. It can be made the day before or in the morning if you like. The flavor gets better as it sits. I've added garbanzo beans for extra protein. Serve over brown rice or Polenta Porridge (page 53).

1 tablespoon olive oil
1 onion, coarsely chopped
2 cloves garlic, minced
1 medium eggplant, cut into 1-inch cubes
1 large zucchini, cut into 1-inch cubes
2 red bell peppers, seeded and cut into bite-size pieces
2 tomatoes, diced (about 2 cups) with liquid
2 cups cooked garbanzo beans (optional)
1/2 cup minced kale, collards, or chard
1/2 teaspoon sea salt
1/2 teaspoon dried oregano or 1 tablespoon fresh
3/4 teaspoon dried thyme or 1 tablespoon fresh
Sea salt and black pepper to taste
1/4 cup minced parsley (optional)

Heat oil in large heavy-bottomed pot. Sauté onion about 10 minutes, until soft. Stir in garlic, eggplant, zucchini, and peppers. Sauté 5 minutes. Add tomatoes, garbanzo beans, kale, sea salt, oregano, and thyme. Bring to a boil and simmer covered about 15 minutes, or until vegetables are soft. Stir as little as possible so vegetables retain their shapes. Add additional sea salt and black pepper to taste. Sprinkle with minced parsley before serving. Serve with crumbled chèvre goat cheese, sour cream, or toasted pine nuts if desired.

Makes 6 servings

Note: This stew is delicious without tomatoes too. Just add about 1/4 cup water to keep vegetables from scorching.

Variation: For a spicy stew, substitute 1/2 cup salsa for 1/2 cup of diced tomatoes.

APPROXIMATE NUTRITIONAL INFORMATION FOR 1 SERVING: Calories: 172 cal; Protein: 8 g; Carbohydrates: 29 g; Fat: 4 g; Fiber: 9 g; Sodium: 202 mg.

KEY NUTRIENTS: Vitamin A: 352.04 mcg; Thiamine: .22 mg; Riboflavin: .13 mg; Niacin: 1.66 mg; Pantothenic Acid: .61 mg; Vitamin B6: .39 mg; Folate: 147.03 mcg; Vitamin C: 99.73 mg; Iron: 2.77 mg; Magnesium: 64.57 mg; Zinc: 1.25 mg.

Adzuki-Squash Stew

This traditional macrobiotic dish is a good source of vitamin A and iron.

1 cup adzuki beans
5 1/2 cups water
1 strip kombu (optional)
1 medium kabucha squash, cut into 1-inch cubes (7 to 8 cups)
Sea salt to taste
1/2 cup chopped fresh parsley or watercress

Place beans, water, and kombu in heavy-bottomed pan. Cover and bring to a boil. Reduce heat to low and simmer 45 minutes. Add squash. Cover and simmer 20 minutes, or until squash is tender. Season with sea salt. Stir in parsley.

Makes 6 servings

APPROXIMATE NUTRITIONAL INFORMATION FOR 1 SERVING: Calories: 163 cal; Protein: 9 g; Carbohydrates: 34 g; Fat: 1 g; Fiber: 7 g; Sodium: 224 mg.

KEY NUTRIENTS: Vitamin A: 576.11 mcg; Thiamine: .29 mg; Riboflavin: .11 mg; Niacin: 2.01 mg; Pantothenic Acid: 1.04 mg; Vitamin B6: .23 mg; Folate: 241.6 mcg; Vitamin C: 23.3 mg; Iron:: 2.73 mg; Magnesium: 80.62 mg; Zinc: 1.88 mg.

Coconut-Tempeh Stew

4 cups vegetable stock
1 (14-ounce) can light coconut milk
1 strip wakame, chopped or crushed
1 1/2 pounds tempeh, cut into cubes
6 cups chopped fresh spinach
3 cups cooked brown rice
1/4 to 1/2 teaspoon Tabasco sauce
Juice of 1 lime or lemon (3 to 4 tablespoons)
1 tablespoon minced fresh ginger
6 to 8 basil leaves, chopped
Sea salt to taste
2 tablespoons chopped fresh cilantro

Place stock, coconut milk, and wakame in large pan. Heat until coconut milk melts and steam rises from liquid. Add tempeh. Cover and bring to a boil. Simmer 10 minutes, or until tempeh is heated through. Stir in spinach, rice, Tabasco sauce, juice, ginger, basil, and sea salt. Simmer 5 minutes or until spinach is wilted. Sprinkle cilantro over stew.

Makes 8 servings

Note: See the Grain Cooking Chart in the Appendix for instructions on cooking rice.

APPROXIMATE NUTRITIONAL INFORMATION FOR 1 SERVING: Calories: 293 cal; Protein: 21 g; Carbohydrates: 30 g; Fat: 11 g; Fiber: 9 g; Sodium: 243 mg.

KEY NUTRIENTS: Vitamin A: 164.38 mcg; Thiamine: .1 mg; Niacin: 1.4 mg; Vitamin B6: .15 mg; Folate: 47.43 mcg; Vitamin C: 11.86 mg; Iron: 3.13 mg; Magnesium: 50.2 mg.

Mild Yellow Curry Stew

2 teaspoons olive oil
1 onion, chopped
2 cups diced tofu, tempeh, or seitan (1/2-inch)
1 large sweet potato or two large red potatoes, cut into 1/2-inch cubes
1 clove garlic, minced
1 jalapeño or serrano chili, minced (seeds and membranes removed)
2 tablespoons peeled and minced fresh ginger
1 teaspoon curry powder
Pinch ground cinnamon
1 3/4 cups vegetable stock
1/2 cup light coconut milk
1/2 teaspoon sea salt
1 medium head cauliflower, broken into florets
2 cups or 1 (15-ounce) can diced tomatoes
4 packed cups baby spinach (6 ounces)
1 tablespoon miso
1/4 cup chopped fresh cilantro leaves
1/4 cup chopped fresh peppermint leaves

Heat oil over medium heat in large pan. Add onion and tofu, tempeh, or seitan. Brown 5 minutes, or until golden. Stir in potato, garlic, chili, ginger, curry powder, and cinnamon. Sauté 2 minutes. Add stock, coconut milk, salt, and cauliflower. Cover and bring to a boil. Reduce heat to low and simmer 15 minutes, or until vegetables are tender. Stir in tomatoes and spinach. Simmer 5 minutes. Remove from heat. Mix miso with a little curry broth until you have a smooth paste. Stir miso into curry. Sprinkle cilantro and peppermint over curry. Eat as is or over rice.

Makes 6 to 8 servings

APPROXIMATE NUTRITIONAL INFORMATION FOR 1 SERVING: Calories: 237 cal; Protein: 17 g; Carbohydrates: 23 g; Fat: 11 g; Fiber: 7 g; Sodium: 355 mg.

KEY NUTRIENTS: Vitamin A: 852.2 mcg; Thiamine: .28 mg; Riboflavin: .27 mg; Niacin: 1.65 mg; Pantothenic Acid: 1.14 mg; Vitamin B6: .5 mg; Folate: 141.07 mcg; Vitamin C: 77.82 mg; Calcium: 636.1 mg; Iron: 10.38 mg; Magnesium: 96.99 mg; Zinc: 2 mg.

Better Than "Beef" Stew

This hearty beef-style stew is made with tempeh.

1 tablespoon olive oil
1 onion, chopped
1 pound tempeh, diced
2 stalks celery, sliced
3 carrots, sliced
3 red or new potatoes, cubed
1 teaspoon sea salt
1 teaspoon dried oregano (or 1 tablespoon fresh)
1 teaspoon dried thyme (or 1 tablespoon fresh)
1/2 teaspoon dried rosemary (or 1/2 tablespoon fresh)
1 tablespoon Sea Veg Mix (page 282) or 2 tablespoons crushed arame
1 vegetable bouillon cube, preferably beef-flavored
3 cups water
2 cup chopped cabbage
1 cup cooked brown rice or wild rice
1 cup peas (fresh or frozen)
1 tablespoon vegetarian Worcestershire Sauce
Black pepper to taste
1/4 cup minced parsley

Heat oil in large soup pot over medium-low heat. Add onion and tempeh and sauté until tempeh is golden. Stir in celery, carrots, and potatoes. Sauté 5 minutes. Add salt, herbs, sea vegetables, bouillon, and water. Simmer covered until potatoes are tender but not mushy (15 to 20 minutes). Add cabbage, rice, and peas. Return to boil and cook 5 minutes. Add remaining ingredients.

Makes 6 to 8 servings

Note: See the Grain Cooking Chart in the Appendix for instructions on cooking rice.

APPROXIMATE NUTRITIONAL INFORMATION FOR 1 SERVING: Calories: 290 cal; Protein: 21 g; Carbohydrates: 34 g; Fat: 9 g; Fiber: 13 g; Sodium: 653 mg.
KEY NUTRIENTS: Vitamin A: 898.34 mcg; Thiamine: .17 mg; Riboflavin: .1 mg; Niacin: 2.54 mg; Pantothenic Acid: .64 mg; Vitamin B6: .35 mg; Folate: 59.47 mcg; Vitamin C: 37.61 mg; Iron: 4.13 mg; Magnesium: 53.51 mg; Zinc: .77 mg.

SIDE DISHES

This section contains easy recipes for cooking grains and vegetables. To save time when preparing dinner, keep frozen cooked brown rice, barley, and other grains in your freezer. Millet and quinoa cook quickly so they're a good choice when you're in a hurry. To save time on vegetable preparation, cut your veggies earlier in the day or buy precut or frozen vegetables. I have included sea vegetables, nuts, seeds, etc., to add extra vitamins, minerals, and protein to these dishes but they can be omitted if you don't have them on hand.

Grains

Basic Brown Rice

Basic Baked Brown Rice

Mexican Rice

Fried Rice and Veggies

Fragrant Baked Rice

Brown and Wild Rice Pilaf

Basic Millet

Millet Mashies

Basic Quinoa

Sesame-Carrot Quinoa Pilaf

Basic Kasha

Kasha-Vegetable Casserole

Barley and Oat Groats

Wheat Berry Pilaf

Vegetables

Baked Potatoes

Mashed Potatoes

Oven Fries

Roasted Root Vegetables

Baked Winter Squash

Carrots and Peas with Tarragon

Simple Green Beans

Spinach, Mushrooms, and Pine Nuts

Brussels Sprouts with White Sauce

Cauliflower with Toasted Walnuts

Mixed Vegetables with Tahini-Miso
    Sauce

Cabbage and Zucchini Sauté

Braised Greens with Sesame

Cultured Vegetables

Sauerkraut

Carrot-Wakame Pickles

Biscuits

Whole Wheat Biscuits

Sweet Potato-Spelt Biscuits

Grains

Basic Brown Rice

I cook sea vegetables with my rice for extra protein and minerals. Adding a small amount will not affect the taste of the rice.

1 1/2 cups brown rice
3 1/4 cups water
Pinch sea salt
1 to 3 teaspoons Sea Veg Mix or crushed hiziki (optional)

Place rice in heavy-bottomed pan with remaining ingredients. Cover and bring to boil over high heat. Reduce heat and simmer 35 minutes, or until water is absorbed.

Makes 6 servings

APPROXIMATE NUTRITIONAL INFORMATION FOR 1 SERVING: Calories: 172 cal; Protein: 4 g; Carbohydrates: 36 g; Fat: 1 g; Fiber: 2 g; Sodium: 36 mg.

KEY NUTRIENTS: Thiamine: .19 mg; Niacin: 2.36 mg; Pantothenic Acid: .69 mg; Vitamin B6: .24 mg; Magnesium: 66.55 mg; Zinc: .94 mg.

Add pizzazz and nutrients to plain grains and vegetables with the following toppings:

- Butter or olive oil and minced parsley or watercress
- Toasted nuts or seeds
- Shredded cheese
- Nutritional yeast flakes
- Lemon or lime juice
- Soy sauce
- Miso
- Brown rice vinegar
- Gomashio (page 284)
- Tahini-Miso Sauce (page 276)
- Light Cheese Sauce (page 277)
- No-Cheese Sauce (page 278).
- Parsley-Walnut Pesto (page 269)

Basic Baked Brown Rice

This method produces perfect rice every time and you don't have to worry about the rice scorching or boiling over. It is especially convenient if you are already using the oven for something else like Bean and Nut Loaf (page 226) or Baked Ginger-Orange Tofu (page 258).

1 1/2 cups brown rice
1/2 teaspoon sea salt
2 1/2 cups boiling water
2 teaspoons olive oil

Preheat oven to 375°F. Place rice and sea salt in 1 1/2-quart casserole dish. Pour boiling water and oil over rice. Cover and bake 50 minutes, or until water is absorbed.

Makes 6 servings

Note: The oven temperature is slightly flexible; you could bake this at 350°F if you have something else baking at that temperature. The rice will just take a few minutes longer.

APPROXIMATE NUTRITIONAL INFORMATION FOR 1 SERVING: Calories: 184 cal; Protein: 4 g; Carbohydrates: 36 g; Fat: 3 g; Fiber: 2 g; Sodium: 187 mg.

KEY NUTRIENTS: Thiamine: .19 mg; Niacin: 2.35 mg; Pantothenic Acid: .69 mg; Vitamin B6: .24 mg; Magnesium: 66.14 mg; Zinc: .93 mg.

Mexican Rice

This is delicious with beans, quesadillas, or in a burrito.

1 1/2 tablespoons olive oil
1 1/2 cups brown rice
1/2 onion, minced
2 cloves garlic, minced
2 to 3 teaspoons chili powder
1 teaspoon sea salt or to taste
3 cups water

Heat oil in heavy-bottomed pan over medium-low heat. When oil is hot, add the rice. Cook, stirring occasionally, until rice is golden and smells like popcorn (about 8 minutes). Stir in onion, garlic, and chili powder. Add sea salt and water. Cover and bring to a boil over high heat. Reduce heat to low and simmer 30 to 40 minutes, or until water is absorbed.

Makes 6 to 8 servings

Variation: Add 1 cup pureed tomato (1 large tomato) with onion and garlic if desired.

APPROXIMATE NUTRITIONAL INFORMATION FOR 1 SERVING: Calories: 206 cal; Protein: 4 g; Carbohydrates: 37 g; Fat: 5 g; Fiber: 2 g; Sodium: 374 mg.

KEY NUTRIENTS: Thiamine: .19 mg; Niacin: 2.38 mg; Pantothenic Acid: .71 mg; Vitamin B6: .26 mg; Magnesium: 67.3 mg; Zinc: .96 mg.

Fried Rice and Veggies

This light, flavorful dish is an excellent way to serve leftover rice. Use whatever vegetables you have on hand but be sure to cut them small (or shred them with a food processor if you are in a hurry) so they will cook quickly. Other grains like millet and quinoa can be substituted for the rice.

1 tablespoon toasted sesame oil
1 small onion, diced
1 carrot, diced
1 cup sliced green beans
1 cup chopped broccoli
3 cups cold cooked brown rice
1/4 cup water
1 tablespoon soy sauce or to taste

Heat sesame oil in large skillet over medium heat. Add onion and sauté 2 minutes. Add carrot, green beans, and broccoli. Cover and steam 5 minutes. Add rice, water, and soy sauce. Toss to mix. Cover and steam 5 to 10 more minutes until vegetables are tender and rice is hot.

Makes 6 servings

Variation: Make this a meal by adding 1 to 2 cups diced tofu, tempeh, seitan, or beans with the vegetables.

APPROXIMATE NUTRITIONAL INFORMATION FOR 1 SERVING: Calories: 150 cal; Protein: 4 g; Carbohydrates: 27 g; Fat: 3 g; Fiber: 3 g; Sodium: 156 mg.

KEY NUTRIENTS: Vitamin A: 308.57 mcg; Thiamine: .12 mg; Niacin: 1.7 mg; Pantothenic Acid: .39 mg; Vitamin B6: .19 mg; Vitamin C: 16.16 mg; Magnesium: 48.28 mg; Zinc: .72 mg.

Fragrant Baked Rice

This is a dish impressive enough for company but simple enough to make anytime. We like the leftovers warmed with milk for breakfast.

1 1/2 cups long-grain brown or basmati rice
2 carrots, shredded or finely diced
1/2 cup raisins or currants
1 teaspoon ginger juice (page 360)
1 cinnamon stick
1/2 teaspoon sea salt
3 cups boiling water
1/2 cup pine nuts, toasted

Preheat oven to 350°F. Toast rice in dry skillet over medium heat until aromatic (about 5 minutes). Pour rice into casserole dish. Add carrots, currants or raisins, ginger juice, cinnamon stick, sea salt, and boiling water. Stir to combine. Cover and bake 50 to 60 minutes, or until water is absorbed. Meanwhile, toast pine nuts in skillet until golden. When ready to serve, remove cinnamon stick and stir pine nuts into rice.

Makes 6 to 8 servings

APPROXIMATE NUTRITIONAL INFORMATION FOR 1 SERVING: Calories: 280 cal; Protein: 7 g; Carbohydrates: 49 g; Fat: 7 g; Fiber: 3 g; Sodium: 198 mg.

KEY NUTRIENTS: Vitamin A: 572.44 mcg; Thiamine: .32 mg; Niacin: 3.05 mg; Pantothenic Acid: .76 mg; Vitamin B6: .31 mg; Iron: 2.08 mg; Magnesium: 99.58 mg; Zinc: 1.49 mg.

Brown and Wild Rice Pilaf

2 tablespoons butter or olive oil
1 onion, diced
2 stalks celery, diced
1/2 cup brown rice
1/2 cup wild rice
1 tablespoon minced fresh rosemary
2 1/2 cups boiling water
1/2 teaspoon sea salt
Black pepper to taste
1/2 cup dried cranberries
1/2 cup chopped pecans or walnuts

Heat butter or oil in saucepan. Stir in onion and sauté 5 minutes. Add celery, rice, and rosemary. Sauté 10 minutes. Pour boiling water over rice. Add salt. Cover and simmer 35 to 40 minutes, or until water is absorbed. Season with black pepper. Stir in cranberries and nuts.

Serves 6

Note: This is a great stuffing for winter squash.

APPROXIMATE NUTRITIONAL INFORMATION FOR 1 SERVING: Calories: 247 cal; Protein: 4 g; Carbohydrates: 34 g; Fat: 12 g; Fiber: 3 g; Sodium: 239 mg.

KEY NUTRIENTS: Thiamine: .16 mg; Niacin: 1.97 mg; Pantothenic Acid: .53 mg; Vitamin B6: .18 mg; Magnesium: 61.54 mg; Zinc: 1.61 mg.

Basic Millet

Millet cooks quickly and is similar in texture to couscous. Toasting the millet brings out the flavor and helps to keep grains separate.

1 cup millet
3 cups water
Pinch sea salt

Toast millet in dry pan over medium-low heat until grains begin to pop and give off a nutty aroma. Add water and sea salt. Cover and bring to a boil. Reduce heat to low and simmer 25 minutes, or until water is absorbed.

Makes 6 servings

Note: Leftover millet makes a quick breakfast. Heat with milk (dairy or nondairy) and a little cinnamon. Stir in dried fruit, nuts, and/or a little sweetener if desired.

APPROXIMATE NUTRITIONAL INFORMATION FOR 1 SERVING: Calories: 126 cal; Protein: 4 g; Carbohydrates: 24 g; Fat: 1 g; Fiber: 3 g; Sodium: 27 mg.

KEY NUTRIENTS: Thiamine: .14 mg; Riboflavin: .1 mg; Niacin: 1.57 mg; Vitamin B6: .13 mg; Thiamine: .11 mg; Riboflavin: .14 mg; Niacin: 1.4 mg; Pantothenic Acid: .5 mg; Vitamin B6: .13 mg; Iron: 1 mg; Magnesium: 38 mg.

Millet Mashies

This is a delicious alternative to mashed potatoes. It is a good source of protein and iron and the vitamin C from the cauliflower and parsley help the iron to be absorbed.

1 1/2 cups millet
4 cups cauliflower florets
5 cups water
Pinch sea salt
2 teaspoons miso
Black pepper to taste
1/4 cup minced parsley (optional)

Place millet, cauliflower, water, and sea salt in a pan. Cover and bring to a boil. Reduce heat and simmer 25 minutes, or until water is absorbed. Stir in miso. Puree millet mixture in food processor, using additional water or milk to get a mashed potato consistency. (Food mill can also be used.) Season with black pepper if desired. Sprinkle with parsley.

Makes 8 servings

APPROXIMATE NUTRITIONAL INFORMATION FOR 1 SERVING: Calories: 160 cal; Protein: 5 g; Carbohydrates: 30 g; Fat: 2 g; Fiber: 5 g; Sodium: 82 mg.

KEY NUTRIENTS: Thiamine: .19 mg; Riboflavin: .15 mg; Niacin: 2.06 mg; Pantothenic Acid: .64 mg; Vitamin B6: .26 mg; Folate: 62.48 mcg; Vitamin C: 29.96 mg; Iron: 1.49 mg; Magnesium: 49.87 mg; Zinc: .81 mg.

Basic Quinoa

It's important to rinse quinoa to remove the bitter coating. Quinoa is high in protein, especially lysine. Roasting the quinoa brings out the flavor and helps to keep the grains separate.

1 cup quinoa
1 1/2 cups water
Pinch sea salt

Rinse and drain quinoa. Pour into pan. Toast quinoa over medium-low heat until it begins to pop and give off a nutty aroma. Add water and sea salt. Cover and bring to boil. Reduce heat to low and simmer 20 minutes, or until water is absorbed.

Makes 4 to 6 servings

APPROXIMATE NUTRITIONAL INFORMATION FOR 1 SERVING: Calories: 180 cal; Protein: 7 g; Carbohydrates: 29 g; Fat: 4 g; Fiber: 11 g; Sodium: 45 mg.

KEY NUTRIENTS: Riboflavin: .14 mg; Vitamin E: 2.01 mg; Iron: 2.7 mg; Magnesium: 64 mg; Zinc: 2.25 mg.

Sesame-Carrot Quinoa Pilaf

1 cup quinoa, rinsed and drained
2 cups water
1 carrot, shredded
Pinch sea salt
2 tablespoons toasted sesame seeds
2 teaspoons toasted sesame oil

Place quinoa in pan over medium-low heat. Toast quinoa, stirring constantly, until aromatic, about 5 minutes. Add water, carrot, and salt. Cover and bring to a boil. Reduce heat and simmer 20 minutes, or until water is absorbed. Add sesame seeds and oil and fluff gently with a fork to combine.

Makes 4 to 6 servings

APPROXIMATE NUTRITIONAL INFORMATION FOR 1 SERVING: Calories: 232 cal; Protein: 8 g; Carbohydrates: 32 g; Fat: 8 g; Fiber: 12 g; Sodium: 50 mg.

KEY NUTRIENTS: Vitamin A: 429.03 mcg; Thiamine: .14 mg; Riboflavin: .16 mg; Vitamin E: 2.18 mg; Iron: 3.43 mg; Magnesium: 82.08 mg; Zinc: 2.63 mg.

Basic Kasha

Buckwheat is a hearty and warming grain, making it ideal for damp, cold days. Never rinse buckwheat because it will become sticky.

1 1/2 cups whole buckwheat groats
3 cups boiling water or vegetable stock

Place buckwheat groats in pot. Toast about 5 minutes over medium heat until golden and aromatic. Pour boiling water over buckwheat. Cover and simmer 20 minutes, or until water is absorbed.

Makes 6 servings

Variation

Traditional Kasha: Place a beaten egg in pan with the buckwheat groats and toast until groats are dry and golden. Continue as directed.

APPROXIMATE NUTRITIONAL INFORMATION FOR 1 SERVING: Calories: 142 cal; Protein: 5 g; Carbohydrates: 31 g; Fat: 1 g; Fiber: 4 g; Sodium: 5 mg.

KEY NUTRIENTS: Niacin: 2.11 mg; Pantothenic Acid: .51 mg; Vitamin B6: .14 mg; Iron: 1.01 mg; Magnesium: 90.61 mg; Zinc: .99 mg.

Kasha-Vegetable Casserole

1 1/2 tablespoons olive oil, butter, or ghee
1 small onion, diced
1 clove garlic, minced
1 cup whole buckwheat groats
1 cup corn, fresh or frozen
1 1/2 cups cut green beans (bite-sized pieces), fresh or frozen
2 cups boiling water
1/2 teaspoon sea salt
1/4 cup minced fresh parsley
1/3 cup toasted sunflower seeds

Preheat oven to 350°F. Heat oil, butter, or ghee in pan over medium-low heat. Stir in onion and sauté 5 minutes. Stir in buckwheat and sauté 10 minutes, or until golden. Pour into ovenproof casserole dish. Stir in corn and green beans. Add boiling water and sea salt. Cover and bake 40 minutes, or until liquid is absorbed. Remove from oven and let sit 5 minutes before removing cover. Sprinkle parsley and sunflower seeds evenly over top.

Makes 6 servings

APPROXIMATE NUTRITIONAL INFORMATION FOR 1 SERVING: Calories: 211 cal; Protein: 7 g; Carbohydrates: 30 g; Fat: 9 g; Fiber: 6 g; Sodium: 11 mg.

KEY NUTRIENTS: Thiamine: .11 mg; Riboflavin: .16 mg; Niacin: 2.79 mg; Pantothenic Acid: 1.09 mg; Vitamin B6: .16 mg; Folate: 44.06 mcg; Vitamin C: 7.28 mg; Iron: 1.81 mg; Magnesium: 87.09 mg; Zinc: 1.24 mg.

Barley and Oat Groats

This is a hearty alternative to rice. If you don't have whole oats, you can use all barley.

3/4 cup hulled barley (not pearled)
3/4 cup whole oat groats
4 1/2 cups water
1/2 teaspoon sea salt

Place grains in heavy-bottomed pot with water. Let grains soak 8 to 12 hours. When ready to cook, cover pot and bring to boil over high heat. Reduce heat to lowest setting and simmer 30 to 40 minutes, or until water is absorbed.

Makes 6 servings

APPROXIMATE NUTRITIONAL INFORMATION FOR 1 SERVING: Calories: 157 cal; Protein: 6 g; Carbohydrates: 30 g; Fat: 2 g; Fiber: 6 g; Sodium: 187 mg.

KEY NUTRIENTS: Thiamine: .3 mg; Niacin: 1.25 mg; Vitamin B6: .1 mg; Iron: 1.75 mg; Magnesium: 65.11 mg; Zinc: 1.41 mg.

Wheat Berry Pilaf

This is another favorite of my children. The leftovers are delicious warmed with milk for breakfast.

1 cup wheat berries
3 cups water
Pinch sea salt
1 cinnamon stick
1/3 cup golden raisins
1/3 cup dried cranberries
1/2 cup chopped almonds, toasted
1/2 tablespoon butter or olive oil

Soak wheat berries 8 hours or overnight. Drain. Place in heavy-bottomed pot with water, sea salt, and cinnamon stick. Cover and bring to boil. Reduce heat and simmer 1 1/2 hours until tender. Stir in remaining ingredients. Cover and let sit 10 minutes. Remove cinnamon stick.

Makes 6 servings

Variation: Substitute hulled barley for the wheat berries.

APPROXIMATE NUTRITIONAL INFORMATION FOR 1 SERVING: Calories: 198 cal; Protein: 5 g; Carbohydrates: 34 g; Fat: 6 g; Fiber: 5 g; Sodium: 35 mg.

KEY NUTRIENTS: Thiamine: .14 mg; Riboflavin: .11 mg; Niacin: 1.83 mg; Vitamin B6: .11 mg; Vitamin E: 2.83 mg; Iron: 1.49 mg; Magnesium: 63.05 mg; Zinc: 1.06 mg.

Vegetables

Baked Potatoes

Bake an extra potato or two for a lunch (page 113).

Preheat oven to 400°F. Scrub large russet potatoes. (Allow 1 per person.) Pierce skins with fork to prevent potatoes from bursting. Place potatoes directly on oven rack and bake about 1 hour, or until potatoes are easily pierced by fork. Add one of the following toppings if desired.

Topping Suggestions:
Olive oil or butter and minced parsley
Yogurt or sour cream (dairy or nondairy) and chives
Herbed Cottage Cheese (regular or tofu) (page 274)
Tahini-Miso Sauce (page 276)
Light Cheese Sauce (page 277)
No Cheese Sauce (page 278)
Mushroom Gravy (page 280)

APPROXIMATE NUTRITIONAL INFORMATION FOR 1 POTATO (without topping): Calories: 188 cal; Protein: 4 g; Carbohydrates: 44 g; Fat: 0 g; Fiber: 4 g; Sodium: 14 mg.

KEY NUTRIENTS: Thiamine: .18 mg; Niacin: 2.84 mg; Pantothenic Acid: .96 mg; Vitamin B6: .6 mg; Vitamin C: 22.25 mg; Iron: 2.35 mg; Magnesium: 46.58 mg.

Mashed Potatoes

This is delicious with Mushroom Gravy (page 280).

6 medium russet potatoes, peeled and cubed
Pinch sea salt
1 bay leaf
1/2 strip kombu (optional)
2 to 3 tablespoons milk (dairy or nondairy)
1 tablespoon fresh thyme
1 tablespoon light miso
1 tablespoon butter or olive oil
Sea salt and black pepper to taste

Place potatoes in pan and cover with water. Add salt, bay leaf, and kombu. Cover and bring to a boil. Reduce heat to low and cook 20 minutes, or until potatoes are easily pierced with fork. Drain. (Reserve water if using for gravy.) Remove bay leaf and kombu. Return potatoes to burner and cook a minute or two to eliminate moisture. Place potatoes in large bowl along with remaining ingredients and mash.

Makes 6 servings

Variations

Mashed Potatoes and Carrots: Substitute 4 large carrots for 2 of the potatoes.
Mashed White and Sweet Potatoes: Substitute 3 sweet potatoes for 3 russet potatoes.

APPROXIMATE NUTRITIONAL INFORMATION FOR 1 SERVING: Calories: 171 cal; Protein: 3 g; Carbohydrates: 35 g; Fat: 2 g; Fiber: 3 g; Sodium: 173 mg.

KEY NUTRIENTS: Thiamine: .17 mg; Niacin: 2.22 mg; Pantothenic Acid: .87 mg; Vitamin B6: .46 mg; Vitamin C: 12.4 mg; Magnesium: 39.23 mg.

Oven Fries

These are just as tasty as deep-fried potatoes but much healthier. Yukon Gold potatoes are especially delicious.

6 medium potatoes, cut into strips or bite-size pieces (about 7 cups)
2 tablespoons olive oil
1 teaspoon sea salt or to taste
1 to 2 tablespoons minced herbs (optional)
Black pepper or paprika to taste (optional)

Preheat oven to 375°F. Place potatoes in large bowl and toss with remaining ingredients. Spread on large baking sheet in a single layer. Sprinkle with black pepper or paprika, if desired. Bake 20 to 30 minutes, or until bottoms are brown and crisp. Turn potatoes. Bake another 10 to 20 minutes until bottoms are brown.

Makes 4 servings

APPROXIMATE NUTRITIONAL INFORMATION FOR 1 SERVING: Calories: 342 cal; Protein: 6 g; Carbohydrates: 65 g; Fat: 7 g; Fiber: 6 g; Sodium: 573 mg.

KEY NUTRIENTS: Thiamine: .28 mg; Niacin: 4.26 mg; Pantothenic Acid: 1.44 mg; Vitamin B6: .9 mg; Vitamin C: 33.38 mg; Iron: 3.52 mg; Magnesium: 69.86 mg; Zinc: .83 mg.

Roasted Root Vegetables

Roasting vegetables is so easy. The veggies come out sweet and the whole house smells wonderful. You can peel the vegetables if you like but if they are organic and the skins look good, just scrub them and leave the peels on. Don't skimp on the oil. It gives the vegetables a crisp coating. Use any kind of root vegetables you like (white or sweet potatoes alone are delicious) – just make sure they add up to about 8 cups.

2 sweet or white potatoes, cut into 1-inch cubes
2 rutabagas or beets, peeled and cut into 1-inch cubes
2 large carrots, scrubbed or peeled and thickly sliced
2 parsnips, scrubbed or peeled and thickly sliced
3 to 4 tablespoons olive oil
2 tablespoons chopped fresh herbs or 2 teaspoons dried (thyme, rosemary, tarragon, etc.)
Sea salt and black pepper to taste

Preheat oven to 450°F. Place vegetables in large bowl and toss with remaining ingredients. Spread on large baking sheet to form a single layer. Bake for 10 minutes. Reduce the heat to 400°F and roast an additional 30 minutes, or until vegetables are tender when pierced with a fork.

Makes 8 servings

APPROXIMATE NUTRITIONAL INFORMATION FOR 1 SERVING: Calories: 154 cal; Protein: 2 g; Carbohydrates: 25 g; Fat: 6 g; Fiber: 6 g; Sodium: 103 mg.

KEY NUTRIENTS: Vitamin A: 1214.26 mcg; Thiamine: .16 mg; Riboflavin: .12 mg; Niacin: 1.35 mg; Pantothenic Acid: .62 mg; Vitamin B6: .24 mg; Folate: 50.54 mcg; Vitamin C: 38.38 mg; Iron: 1.02 mg; Magnesium: 39.75 mg.

Baked Winter Squash

This is an easy way to cook squash – no peeling or dicing is involved. Bake an extra to use in Butternut Lasagna (page 252).

1 to 2 butternut, hubbard, acorn, or other winter squash

Optional additions:
Butter or olive oil
Sea salt
Ground cardamom, ground cinnamon, or pumpkin pie spice

Preheat oven to 375°F. Lightly oil baking dish or jelly roll pan. Cut squash in half lengthwise and scoop out seeds and pulp. Place cut side down on prepared pan. Add 1/4 inch of water to pan. Bake 45 to 60 minutes, or until squash is tender. Let cool slightly and scoop squash out of peel into a bowl. Season with butter or olive oil, sea salt, and spice to taste.

1 pound squash yields about 1 cup mashed squash

APPROXIMATE NUTRITIONAL INFORMATION FOR 1 CUP BAKED SQUASH: Calories: 82 cal; Protein: 2 g; Carbohydrates: 22 g; Fat: 0 g; Fiber: 0 g; Sodium: 8 mg.

KEY NUTRIENTS: Vitamin A: 1435 mcg; Thiamine: .15 mg; Niacin: 1.99 mg; Pantothenic Acid: .74 mg; Vitamin B6: .25 mg; Folate: 38.95 mcg; Vitamin C: 30.95 mg; Iron: 1.23 mg; Magnesium: 59.45 mg.

Carrots and Peas with Tarragon

3 1/2 cups sliced carrots
1 cup fresh or frozen peas
2 tablespoons olive oil
1 teaspoons Dijon mustard
2 tablespoons chopped fresh parsley
2 tablespoons chopped fresh tarragon leaves

Steam carrots over high heat until almost tender. Add peas and continue cooking until carrots are tender but not mushy. While vegetables are cooking, whisk together oil and mustard. Place vegetables in bowl. Drizzle sauce over carrots. Sprinkle herbs over carrots. Toss mixture gently until vegetables are coated.

Makes 6 servings

APPROXIMATE NUTRITIONAL INFORMATION FOR 1 SERVING: Calories: 92 cal; Protein: 1 g; Carbohydrates: 10 g; Fat: 5 g; Fiber: 3 g; Sodium: 164 mg.

KEY NUTRIENTS: Vitamin A: 2240.64 mcg; Thiamine: .21 mg; Riboflavin: 1.03 mg; Vitamin B6: .13 mg.

Simple Green Beans

This easy dish is best in the summer with fresh beans from your garden or farmers' market.

4 to 6 cups slender, young green beans, stem ends trimmed
2 to 3 teaspoons butter or olive oil
1/2 cup slivered almonds or sunflower seeds, toasted

Steam beans over boiling water until tender. Toss with butter or oil and almonds.

Makes 4 to 6 servings

Note: Toasting really brings out the flavor of the nuts or seeds. Toast them in a dry skillet while the beans are steaming.

APPROXIMATE NUTRITIONAL INFORMATION FOR 1 SERVING: Calories: 128 cal; Protein: 4 g; Carbohydrates: 8 g; Fat: 9 g; Fiber: 4 g; Sodium: 33 mg.

KEY NUTRIENTS: Vitamin D: .13 mcg; Vitamin E: 3.57 mg; Iron: 1.06 mg; Magnesium: 37.17 mg.

Spinach, Mushrooms, and Pine Nuts

This is a delicious way to eat spinach. If you don't have pine nuts, substitute sunflower seeds.

2 teaspoons olive oil
2 cloves garlic, minced
1 cup sliced mushrooms
8 cups washed and chopped spinach leaves
1/4 cup pine nuts, toasted

Heat oil in large skillet. Stir in garlic and mushrooms. Sauté 5 to 10 minutes or until mushrooms become juicy. Add washed spinach. It's fine if the spinach is a little damp; the water will help it cook. Push spinach around pan about 2 minutes, or until wilted and soft. Remove from pan. Season with salt and pepper if desired. Sprinkle with pine nuts.

Makes 4 servings

Variation: Substitute chard for spinach.

APPROXIMATE NUTRITIONAL INFORMATION FOR 1 SERVING: Calories: 88 cal; Protein: 4 g; Carbohydrates: 5 g; Fat: 7 g; Fiber: 2 g; Sodium: 49 mg.

KEY NUTRIENTS: Vitamin A: 403.46 mcg; Thiamine: .13 mg; Riboflavin: .21 mg; Niacin: 1.45 mg; Vitamin B6: .16 mg; Folate: 123.39 mcg; Vitamin C: 17.89 mg; Vitamin D: 1.33 mcg; Vitamin E: 1.45 mg; Iron: 2.62 mg; Magnesium: 69.33 mg; Zinc: .82 mg.

Brussels Sprouts with White Sauce

This delicious sauce is full of nutrients. Try it over broccoli or cauliflower too.

2 pounds brussels sprouts
2 tablespoons butter
1/2 cup cashews
1 1/2 tablespoons arrowroot powder
1 cup water
1 tablespoon fresh thyme or 1/2 teaspoon dried
Sea salt and black pepper to taste

Wash brussels sprouts, trim stems, and remove any dry or yellow leaves. To help sprouts cook faster, either cut a small x in the stem of each sprout or cut sprouts in half. Steam sprouts over boiling water until tender (15 to 20 minutes).

While vegetables are cooking, melt butter in small saucepan over low heat. Place cashews in blender and grind to powder. Add arrowroot and water and blend until smooth. Add to saucepan. Cook over low heat until sauce thickens. Add thyme and season to taste with sea salt and pepper.

Makes 6 servings

APPROXIMATE NUTRITIONAL INFORMATION FOR 1 SERVING: CALORIES: 165 cal; Protein: 6 g; Carbohydrates: 18 g; Fat: 10 g; Fiber: 4 g; Sodium: 118 mg.

KEY NUTRIENTS: Vitamin A: 144.55 mcg; Thiamine: .16 mg; Riboflavin: .12 mg; Vitamin B6: .27 mg; Folate: 93.9 mcg; Vitamin C: 93.74 mg; Vitamin E: 1.36 mg; Iron: 2.58 mg; Magnesium: 71.51 mg; Zinc: 1.15 mg.

Cauliflower with Toasted Walnuts

1 large head cauliflower, cut into florets
1 tablespoon walnut or olive oil
1/2 cup coarsely chopped walnuts, toasted

Steam florets over boiling water until tender. Toss with oil and nuts. Season with salt and pepper if desired.

Makes 6 servings

APPROXIMATE NUTRITIONAL INFORMATION FOR 1 SERVING: Calories: 120 cal; Protein: 4 g; Carbohydrates: 9 g; Fat: 9 g; Fiber: 4 g; Sodium: 42 mg.

KEY NUTRIENTS: Thiamine: .11 mg; Riboflavin: .1 mg; Pantothenic Acid: .97 mg; Vitamin B6: .36 mg; Folate: 89.6 mcg; Vitamin C: 65.09 mg; Iron: .91 mg; Magnesium: 36.8 mg; Zinc: .7 mg.

Mixed Vegetables with Tahini-Miso Sauce

1 large head broccoli, cut into bite-sized pieces
2 carrots, sliced
1 cup fresh or frozen peas
1 recipe Tahini-Miso Sauce (page 276)
1 tablespoon minced fresh parsley (optional)

Steam broccoli and carrots over boiling water until almost tender. Add peas 1 or 2 minutes before vegetables are done. When vegetables are tender, place in serving bowl and cover with sauce. Sprinkle fresh parsley over sauce.

Makes 4 to 6 servings

APPROXIMATE NUTRITIONAL INFORMATION FOR 1 SERVING: Calories: 169 cal; Protein: 8 g; Carbohydrates: 20 g; Fat: 8 g; Fiber: 6 g; Sodium: 239 mg.

KEY NUTRIENTS: Vitamin A: 1003.73 mcg; Thiamine: .27 mg; Riboflavin: .19 mg; Niacin: 1.67 mg; Pantothenic Acid: .55 mg; Vitamin B6: .18 mg; Folate: 62.81 mcg; Vitamin C: 64.69 mg; Vitamin E: 1.41 mg; Calcium: 114.36 mg; Iron: 1.81 mg; Magnesium: 40.05 mg; Zinc: 1.22 mg.

Cabbage and Zucchini Sauté

2 teaspoons toasted sesame oil
2 cloves garlic, minced
1 large zucchini, sliced into half-moons
2 cups thinly sliced green cabbage
1/4 cup toasted sesame seeds

Warm skillet to medium heat. Add oil and tilt pan to distribute. Add garlic, zucchini, and cabbage, Sauté about 10 minutes, or until vegetables are tender. Sprinkle sesame seeds over the top.

Makes 4 servings

Note: To make half-moon slices of zucchini, trim ends off zucchini. Cut zucchini in half lengthwise. Cut halves into 1/4-inch slices.

APPROXIMATE NUTRITIONAL INFORMATION FOR 1 SERVING: Calories: 90 cal; Protein: 3 g; Carbohydrates: 7 g; Fat: 6 g; Fiber: 3 g; Sodium: 14 mg.

KEY NUTRIENTS: Thiamine: .18 mg; Vitamin B6: .14 mg; Folate: 44.63 mcg; Vitamin C: 22.06 mg; Iron: 1.25 mg; Magnesium: 52.50 mg; Zinc: 1.08 mg.

Braised Greens with Sesame

1 bunch kale, chard, or other leafy green, chopped (about 8 cups)
2 teaspoons toasted sesame oil
Soy sauce to taste
Brown rice vinegar to taste
2 tablespoons toasted sesame seeds

Wash greens well and chop coarsely. Don't dry greens. They should still have water adhering to them to help them steam. Heat large skillet and add oil. Add greens to skillet. Cover and steam until wilted. Remove cover. Season with a little soy sauce and vinegar to taste. Sprinkle sesame seeds over top.

Makes 4 servings

APPROXIMATE NUTRITIONAL INFORMATION FOR 1 SERVING: Calories: 111 cal; Protein: 5 g; Carbohydrates: 14 g; Fat: 5 g; Fiber: 3 g; Sodium: 77 mg.

KEY NUTRIENTS: Vitamin A: 1192.88 mcg; Thiamine: .2 mg; Riboflavin: .19 mg; Niacin: 1.56 mg; Vitamin B6: .37 mg; Folate: 42.7 mcg; Vitamin C: 160.8 mg; Vitamin E: 1.16 mg; Calcium: 186.14 mg; Iron: 2.59 mg; Magnesium: 59.4 mg; Zinc: 1 mg.

Cultured Vegetables

Sauerkraut

Naturally fermented sauerkraut is full of enzymes and nutrients. Eat it on sandwiches, veggie hot dogs, salads, or as a side dish.

1 large head cabbage
2 tablespoons sea salt

Remove outer leaves of cabbage and reserve. Remove core from cabbage. Slice the cabbage very thinly. (I use a food processor.) Toss cabbage and salt together in large bowl. Use a wooden spoon, meat pounder or whatever works to pound cabbage until juices are released and cabbage volume is reduced to about 4 cups. This takes 5 to 10 minutes. Let your children take turns. Even a toddler will enjoy doing this.

Transfer cabbage to quart-size jar. Roll up the reserved cabbage leave and place over cabbage in jar. Press down until liquid rises above cabbage. Cover tightly and place in cool spot (not refrigerator) for 3 to 5 days. Taste it periodically. When it tastes tangy, remove cabbage leaves and transfer jar to refrigerator. Flavor will improve with age. Sauerkraut lasts in the refrigerator for months. Rinse sauerkraut in cold water before eating because it is very salty.

Makes about 1 quart

APPROXIMATE NUTRITIONAL INFORMATION FOR 1/4 CUP: Calories: 20 cal; Protein: 1 g; Carbohydrates: 4 g; Fat: 0 g; Fiber: 2 g; Sodium: 842 mg.

KEY NUTRIENTS: Folate: 33.54 mcg; Vitamin C: 25.12 mg.

Carrot-Wakame Pickles

Cultured vegetables help to ensure that your inner ecosystem is rich in friendly bacteria. These pickles are great on sandwiches, salads, or with meals.

8 cups shredded carrots
1 cup wakame, soaked in water 15 minutes
3 tablespoons sea salt
3 cloves garlic, sliced (optional)
2 tablespoons diced ginger (optional)

Toss all ingredients together in large bowl. Use a wooden spoon, meat pounder, or whatever works to pound carrot mixture until juices are released and volume is reduced to about 4 cups. This takes 5 to 10 minutes. Let your children take turns. Even a toddler will enjoy doing this. Transfer mixture to quart-size jar. Press down mixture until liquid rises above it. Cover tightly and place in cool spot (not refrigerator) for 3 days. Transfer to refrigerator. Flavor will improve with age. Pickles will last in refrigerator for months.

Makes about 1 quart

APPROXIMATE NUTRITIONAL INFORMATION FOR 2 TABLESPOONS: Calories: 14 cal; Protein: 0 g; Carbohydrates: 3 g; Fat: 0 g; Fiber: 1 g; Sodium: 672 mg.

KEY NUTRIENTS: Vitamin A: 778.58 mcg.

Biscuits

Whole Wheat Biscuits

Eat leftovers for a snack with nut/seed butter, or butter and jam. They freeze well too.

2 cups whole wheat flour
2 1/4 teaspoons baking powder
1/2 teaspoon baking soda
3 tablespoons cold unsalted butter or coconut oil
3 tablespoons oil
3/4 cup yogurt (dairy or nondairy) or buttermilk
1 tablespoon milk (dairy or nondairy)

Preheat oven to 450°F. Sift together flour, baking powder, and baking soda. Cut in butter and oil until mixture resembles coarse meal. Add yogurt and mix lightly. Place dough on floured surface and knead just until dough holds together. Roll out to 3/4-inch thickness and cut into 2-inch circles. Place on oiled baking sheet. Brush lightly with milk. Bake 12 to 15 minutes or until golden brown.

Makes about 18

Variation

Herbed Whole Wheat Biscuits: Add 1 tablespoon minced fresh dill or rosemary (or 1 teaspoon dried) to flour mixture.

APPROXIMATE NUTRITIONAL INFORMATION FOR 1 BISCUIT: Calories: 90 cal; Protein: 2 g; Carbohydrates: 10 g; Fat: 5 g; Fiber: 2 g; Sodium: 79 mg.

Sweet Potato-Spelt Biscuits

These muffins are so moist and flaky, they practically melt in your mouth. They're great for breakfast, lunch or dinner. They freeze well too.

1 1/2 cups spelt flour (or whole wheat)
1 tablespoon baking powder
1/4 teaspoon sea salt
4 tablespoons cold unsalted butter or coconut oil
1 cup mashed cooked sweet potato (1 medium)
1/4 cup milk (dairy or nondairy)

Preheat oven to 400°F. Sift flour, baking powder, and sea salt together. Cut in butter or coconut oil until mixture resembles coarse meal. Mix in sweet potato and milk until combined. Scoop out 1/4-cup mounds of dough (an ice cream scoop works well) and flatten to biscuit shape on unoiled baking sheet. Bake 25 to 20 minutes, or until bottoms are golden.

Makes 10 biscuits

APPROXIMATE NUTRITIONAL INFORMATION FOR 1 BISCUIT: Calories: 141 cal; Protein: 3 g; Carbohydrates: 23 g; Fat: 5 g; Fiber: 4 g; Sodium: 150 mg.

KEY NUTRIENTS: Vitamin A: 604.14 mcg; Vitamin C: 5.7 mg.

Main Dishes

 The recipes in this section were designed to nourish the entire family, as well as mom. The meals are easy to prepare and many can be started or prepared in advance. There are also many dishes that can be prepared in 35 minutes or less; they are marked ◑ .

To speed meal preparation, keep precooked beans and grains in your freezer, since they require a long cooking time. Do your chopping ahead of time when possible or buy prechopped vegetables at the market. As you prepare dinner, think about future meals. Cook extra rice or beans to use the next day or freeze them for later. Don't worry if a recipe serves more than your family can eat. Leftovers make great lunches and snacks.

Take some time during the third trimester of pregnancy to prepare and freeze meals for after the baby comes. Recipes suitable for freezing are marked ❋ .

Savory Pies

Tamale Pie ✳
Shepherd's Pie
Tofu-Vegetable Pot Pie ✳
Asparagus Quiche with Brown Rice
    Crust
Potato-Kale Quiche
Yogurt-Spinach Quiche
Sesame-Tofu Quiche with Broccoli and
    Mushrooms
Spanakopitta ✳
Pizza
Pizza Crust ✳

Casseroles

Rice and Bean Casserole
Kale and Rice Casserole
Tempeh-Squash Bake ◑
Tempeh, Apple, Potato, and Kraut
    Casserole
Kasha, Potato, and Carrot Casserole ✳
Broccoli-Noodle Casserole ◑ ✳
Roasted Eggplant and Zucchini
    Parmesan ✳

Main-Course Beans and Legumes

Bean and Nut Loaf ✳
Beanballs ✳

Lentil Puree (Dahl)
Gingery Black Beans ◑
Arame and Black-Eyed Peas ◑

Burgers, Burritos, Enchiladas, and Fajitas

Millet-Veggie Burgers ◑ ✳
Falafel with Tangy Tahini Sauce ✳
Tofu Enchiladas ✳
Black Bean and Sweet Potato
    Enchiladas ✳
Burritos ◑
Fajitas ◑

Main-Course Pasta

Pasta with Vegetables and Pine Nuts ◑
Parsley-Walnut Pesto Pasta ◑
High-Protein Pasta ◑ ✳
Vegan Paht Si-Yu ◑
Garbanzos and Pasta in Tomato-Basil
    Sauce ◑ ✳
Mushroom Stroganoff ◑
Saucy Noodles and Vegetables ◑
Pumpkin Seed Pesto Ravioli ✳
Lima-Vegetable Lasagna ✳
Butternut Lasagna ✳

Stir-Fries and Tofu Dishes

Seitan "Chicken" and Cashews ◐
Kung Pao Tofu ◐
Tofu Vegetable Stir-Fry ◐
Baked Ginger-Orange Tofu ◐
Egg Foo Young ◐

Codes: ✳ = *Can be frozen and reheated*   ◐ = *35 minutes or less to prepare*

Savory Pies

Tamale Pie ✳

You'll be amazed how easy it is to make this impressive and delicious dinner. Although it doesn't qualify as a ◑ dinner because the baking time is 30 minutes, it takes only about 20 minutes of actual hands-on time.

Filling:
1 tablespoon olive oil
1 onion, chopped
1 clove garlic, minced
2 teaspoons chili powder
1/2 teaspoon ground cumin
2 cups cooked pinto, kidney, or black beans, drained
1 cup diced tomatoes with juice (canned is fine)
1/2 cup fresh or frozen corn kernels
Sea salt and black pepper to taste

Crust:
1 1/2 cups cornmeal
3 1/4 cups water
3/4 teaspoon sea salt

Topping:
1/4 cup shredded Monterey Jack cheese (optional)

Preheat oven to 350°F. Oil an 8-inch square baking pan.

Heat oil in medium-size pan. Stir in onion and sauté about 5 minutes. Add garlic, chili powder, and cumin. Sauté 5 minutes more. Add beans, tomatoes, and corn. Season to taste with sea salt and black pepper. Let mixture simmer uncovered while you prepare crust.

Whisk together cornmeal and water in medium-size pan. Cook over medium heat until mixture begins to boil. Reduce heat to low. Stir in sea salt. Cook, stirring constantly, until thickened (about 10 minutes). Spread 2/3 of the mixture over bottom and up sides of the prepared baking pan. Pour bean mixture into crust. Top with remaining cornmeal mixture. (Don't worry if beans are not covered completely.) Sprinkle with shredded cheese if desired. Bake 30 minutes. Let sit 10 minutes before cutting.

Makes 6 servings

❄ **Freezing Instructions:** Assemble pie and freeze unbaked. To reheat, thaw pie in refrigerator. Cover and bake at 350°F for 30 minutes. Remove cover and bake 15 minutes, or until heated through.

APPROXIMATE NUTRITIONAL INFORMATION FOR 1 SERVING: Calories: 250 cal; Protein: 9 g; Carbohydrates: 44 g; Fat: 6 g; Fiber: 8 g; Sodium: 509 mg.

KEY NUTRIENTS: Thiamine: .28 mg; Riboflavin: .14 mg; Niacin: 1.77 mg; Pantothenic Acid: .49 mg; Vitamin B6: .24 mg; Folate: 119.57 mcg; Vitamin C: 11.2 mg; Iron: 2.79 mg; Magnesium: 80.09 mg; Zinc: 1.3 mg.

Shepherd's Pie

This is one of my family's very favorite dinners. Try it with other beans too.

Filling:
1 tablespoon olive oil
1 onion, diced
2 cloves garlic, minced
2 carrots, diced
2 cups cabbage, broccoli, or kale, finely chopped
1/2 cup water, vegetable stock, or lentil cooking water
2 cups cooked lentils
1 cup peas (fresh or frozen)
1 cup corn (fresh or frozen)
1 tablespoon soy sauce

Crust:
4 medium potatoes, peeled and cubed
1/3 to 1/2 cup milk (dairy or nondairy)
1 tablespoon miso
2 tablespoons minced fresh parsley
Paprika

Preheat oven to 400°F. Heat oil in large skillet over medium-low heat. Add onion and sauté 5 minutes until soft. Stir in garlic, carrots, and cabbage, broccoli, or kale. Add water and cover pan. Cook 10 minutes, or until vegetables are tender. Stir in remaining filling ingredients. Cook 5 minutes, or until filling is hot. Pour filling into 2-quart casserole dish.

While filling cooks, prepare mashed potato crust. Place potatoes in medium pan with water just up to top of potatoes. Bring to a boil and cook over medium heat until potatoes are tender (about 15 minutes). Drain potatoes and return them to the pot. Add miso. Begin mashing while adding milk a little at a time until potatoes are smooth. Stir in minced parsley. Spread potatoes evenly over filling. Sprinkle evenly with paprika. Bake uncovered 20 to 30 minutes until potatoes and filling are hot and edges are slightly golden.

Makes 6 servings

Note: 4 cups frozen mixed vegetables can be substituted for vegetables in this recipe.

Variation: Add 1 (15-ounce) can diced tomatoes instead of the liquid in the filling.

APPROXIMATE NUTRITIONAL INFORMATION FOR 1 SERVING: Calories: 257 cal; Protein: 11 g; Carbohydrates: 47 g; Fat: 4 g; Fiber: 10 g; Sodium: 300 mg.

KEY NUTRIENTS: Vitamin A: 603 mcg; Thiamine: .31 mg; Riboflavin: .14 mg; Niacin: 2.81 mg; Pantothenic Acid: 1.25 mg; Vitamin B6: .51 mg; Folate: 163 mcg; Vitamin C: 31.60 mg; Iron: 3.29 mg; Magnesium: 66.39 mg; Zinc: 1.53 mg.

Tofu-Vegetable Pot Pie ❄

This recipe requires a little more labor than most of my recipes but it is just so much better than any frozen pie you can buy. Once you try it, you'll agree it was well worth the work. I've arranged the instructions so you can make it in the shortest amount of time possible.

Crust:
1/2 cup cornmeal
1 cup whole wheat pastry flour
4 tablespoons cold unsalted butter or coconut oil, cut into small pieces
3 to 4 tablespoons cold water

Filling:
2 teaspoons olive oil
1 pound firm or extra firm tofu
1 tablespoon olive oil
3/4 cup diced onion (about 1 small)
1 large clove garlic, minced
2 cups diced potatoes (about 1 large)
1 cup diced carrots (about 2)
1 cup chopped cauliflower
1 cup peas (fresh or frozen)

Sauce:
1 1/2 cups water or vegetable stock
1/4 cup nutritional yeast flakes
3 tablespoons arrowroot powder
2 tablespoons miso
1/2 teaspoon dried sage (or 1 tablespoon minced fresh)
1/2 teaspoon dried thyme (or 1 tablespoon minced fresh)
1/4 teaspoon sea salt
1/4 teaspoon black pepper

Preheat oven to 350°F. Lightly oil a large 10-inch deep-dish pie pan.

Place tofu in shallow dish. Place weighted cutting board over tofu to press out water while you prepare the crust.

To prepare crust, mix cornmeal and flour together in bowl or in food processor with metal blade. Cut in butter or coconut oil until mixture resembles coarse meal. Add water a tablespoon at a time until crust holds together when pressed in your hand. Form crust into ball and place in refrigerator while you prepare the filling and sauce.

To prepare filling, dice tofu into 1/2-inch pieces. Heat 2 teaspoons olive oil in skillet over medium heat. Place tofu in skillet and brown until golden on all sides. Remove and set aside.

Add 1 tablespoon olive oil to skillet over medium-low heat. Add onion and cook 5 minutes until soft. Add potatoes, carrots, and cauliflower. Cover and steam 10 minutes until vegetables are tender. Turn heat to low. Stir in peas and cover.

Place sauce ingredients in blender and puree until smooth. Add tofu and sauce to vegetables, and cook until sauce thickens slightly. Pour into prepared pie pan.

On a floured board or between sheets of wax paper, roll out crust to 1/2 inch wider than the size of your pie pan. Place crust over tofu mixture. Prick holes in the crust with a fork. Bake 40 to 45 minutes, or until crust is golden brown around the edges.

Makes 8 servings

Note: Finely dice the vegetables (about 1/4 inch) so they'll cook quickly.

❄ **Freezing Instructions:** Bake pie for 30 minutes, cool and freeze. To reheat, thaw pie on counter while you preheat oven to 350°F. Bake covered for 40 minutes. Uncover and bake 15 minutes, or until filling is hot all the way through.

APPROXIMATE NUTRITIONAL INFORMATION FOR 1 SERVING: Calories: 309 cal; Protein: 17 g; Carbohydrates: 33 g; Fat: 16 g; Fiber: 8 g; Sodium: 274 mg.

KEY NUTRIENTS: Vitamin A: 528.77 mcg; Thiamine: 3.4 mg; Riboflavin: 3.33 mg; Niacin: 20.92 mg; Pantothenic Acid: .54 mg; Vitamin B6: 3.49 mg; Folate: 133.42 mcg; Vitamin B12: 2.67 mcg; Vitamin C: 22.47 mg; Calcium: 421.46 mg; Iron: 8.04 mg; Magnesium: 67.73 mg; Zinc: 2.57 mg.

Asparagus Quiche with Brown Rice Crust

Brown rice is used to make the crust for this delicious quiche. If using leftover rice, heat it slightly so it will be easier to work with.

2 cups hot cooked brown rice
1 tablespoon olive oil
1 small onion, diced
1 clove garlic, minced
1 pound asparagus, cut into 1-inch slices
1/4 cup shredded cheddar cheese (dairy or nondairy)
1 cup milk (dairy or nondairy)
4 eggs
1/4 teaspoon sea salt
1/4 teaspoon black pepper
1 tablespoon nutritional yeast flakes
1 tablespoon minced fresh parsley
1/4 cup grated Parmesan cheese (dairy or nondairy)
1 teaspoon dried dill

Preheat oven to 375°F. Oil 10-inch deep-dish pie pan. Press brown rice into pan and up sides to form a crust.

In skillet, warm oil over medium heat. Add onion and sauté 5 or 10 minutes until soft. Stir in garlic and asparagus. Cover and steam 5 to 10 minutes, or until asparagus is bright green. Reserve 8 asparagus tips and pour the rest of the vegetable mixture into crust. Sprinkle shredded cheese over vegetables.

Beat milk, eggs, sea salt, pepper, nutritional yeast flakes, and parsley together. Pour over vegetables. Press down rice around the edges so it is level with the egg mixture. This will prevent the rice from getting hard.

Arrange asparagus tips on top of quiche to resemble spokes. Sprinkle Parmesan cheese and dill evenly over top of quiche. Bake 40 minutes, or until center is firm to the touch and edges are golden. Let sit 10 minutes before slicing.

Makes 8 servings

Note: See the Grain Cooking Chart in the Appendix for instructions on cooking rice.

APPROXIMATE NUTRITIONAL INFORMATION FOR 1 SERVING: Calories: 176 cal; Protein: 10 g; Carbohydrates: 17 g; Fat: 8 g; Fiber: 3 g; Sodium: 192 mg.

KEY NUTRIENTS: Vitamin A: 109.27 mcg; Thiamine: .96 mg; Riboflavin: 1.09 mg; Niacin: 6.15 mg; Pantothenic Acid: .69 mg; Vitamin B6: 1.01 mg; Folate: 111.14 mcg; Vitamin B12: 1.09 mcg; Vitamin C: 9.25 mg; Vitamin D: 1.35 mcg; Vitamin E: 1.59 mg; Calcium: 132.55 mg; Iron: 1.24 mg; Magnesium: 41.27 mg; Zinc: 1.46 mg.

Potato-Kale Quiche

This is my husband's favorite quiche. It's hearty and filling, yet doesn't weigh you down. If you don't have kale, try spinach, chard or other dark green leafy vegetable.

1 recipe Basic Pie Crust (page 333) or prepared (9- or 10-inch) deep-dish crust, partially prebaked
1 tablespoon olive oil
1 onion, diced
2 cups peeled, diced potatoes (about 3 medium)
2 packed cups chopped kale
3 eggs
1 1/4 cups milk (dairy or nondairy)
1 teaspoon Dijon mustard
1/4 teaspoon sea salt
1/4 teaspoon black pepper
Pinch ground nutmeg
1 cup shredded Monterey Jack or cheddar cheese (4 ounces)

Preheat oven to 375°F. Prepare pie crust and place in 9- or 10-inch deep-dish pie pan. Partially prebake crust as directed on page 333.

Prepare filling while crust is prebaking. Warm oil in skillet over medium heat. Add onion. Sauté 5 minutes. Stir in potatoes. Cover and cook 5 minutes. Stir in kale. Cover and cook another 5 minutes. Kale and potatoes should be tender but not overcooked.

Whisk eggs, milk, mustard, sea salt, pepper, and nutmeg until frothy. Place 1/2 of the cheese evenly over bottom of crust. Place potato-kale mixture over cheese. Cover with remaining cheese. Pour egg mixture over vegetables and cheese to fill crust.

Bake at 375°F for 40 minutes, or until center is set. Cool 10 minutes before cutting.

Makes 8 servings

APPROXIMATE NUTRITIONAL INFORMATION FOR 1 SERVING: Calories: 291 cal; Protein: 12 g; Carbohydrates: 22 g; Fat: 19 g; Fiber: 5 g; Sodium: 229 mg.

KEY NUTRIENTS: Vitamin A: 323.15 mcg; Thiamine: .18 mg; Riboflavin: .24 mg; Niacin: 2.51 mg; Pantothenic Acid: .86 mg; Vitamin B6: .3 mg; Folate: 47.76 mcg; Vitamin B12: .34 mcg; Vitamin C: 33.85 mg; Vitamin D: .98 mcg; Calcium: 198.6 mg; Iron: 2.09 mg; Magnesium: 57.24 mg; Zinc: 1.25 mg.

Yogurt-Spinach Quiche

This quiche is my children's favorite. The yogurt makes this dish lighter than traditional quiche.

1 (8- or 9-inch) Basic Pie Crust (page 333), partially prebaked
2 teaspoons olive oil
1 onion, minced
2 cups minced spinach (fresh or frozen)
2 eggs
1 cup plain yogurt
1/4 teaspoon sea salt
1/4 teaspoon ground nutmeg
1/2 cup shredded cheese (cheddar, Monterey Jack, etc.)
2 tablespoons grated Parmesan cheese

Preheat oven to 350°F. Prepare and partially prebake pie crust.

Prepare filling while crust is prebaking. Warm oil in skillet over medium heat. Add onions and sauté 5 to 10 minutes until soft. Stir in spinach. Cover and steam about 3 minutes, or until spinach is wilted. Remove cover and cook a minute or two to let water evaporate. In mixing bowl, beat eggs, yogurt, sea salt, and nutmeg together. Fold in cooked spinach and cheeses. Pour into prepared crust. Bake 40 minutes, or until center is set. Wait 10 minutes before slicing.

Serves 6

APPROXIMATE NUTRITIONAL INFORMATION FOR 1 SERVING: Calories: 240 cal; Protein: 9 g; Carbohydrates: 19 g; Fat: 15 g; Fiber: 4 g; Sodium: 209 mg.

KEY NUTRIENTS: Vitamin A: 504.71 mcg; Thiamine: .14 mg; Riboflavin: .27 mg; Niacin: 1.46 mg; Pantothenic Acid: .57 mg; Vitamin B6: .18 mg; Folate: 71.87 mcg; Vitamin B12: .33 mcg; Vitamin C: 6.88 mg; Vitamin D: .75 mcg; Vitamin E: 1.06 mg; Calcium: 192.33 mg; Iron: 1.75 mg; Magnesium: 67.78 mg; Zinc: 1.49 mg.

Sesame-Tofu Quiche with Broccoli and Mushrooms

This quiche supplies lots of calcium and iron. The delicious nondairy filling is rich and creamy.

Sesame-Corn Crust:
1/2 cup cornmeal
1 cup whole wheat pastry flour
2 tablespoons sesame seeds
4 tablespoons cold unsalted butter or coconut oil, cut into small pieces
3 to 4 tablespoons cold water

Filling:
1 tablespoon toasted sesame oil
1 small onion, diced
2 cloves garlic, minced
1 1/2 cups chopped white mushrooms
2 cups chopped broccoli
1 tablespoon minced fresh ginger
1 pound firm tofu
1 tablespoon nutritional yeast flakes
2 tablespoons tahini
1 tablespoon soy sauce
Pinch ground nutmeg

Topping:
1 tablespoon sesame seeds

Preheat oven to 350°F. Mix cornmeal, flour, and sesame seeds together in food processor with metal blade or in a bowl. Cut in butter or coconut oil until mixture resembles coarse meal. Add water a tablespoon at a time until crust holds together when pressed in your hand. Roll out crust on floured board to fit a 9-inch pie pan. Arrange crust in pan and flute edges. Prick all over with fork and prebake 15 minutes.

While crust is baking, heat oil in skillet over medium-low heat. Add onion and sauté 5 minutes or until soft. Add garlic, mushrooms, broccoli, and ginger. Cover and steam 5 to 10 minutes, or until broccoli is tender. Remove from heat.

In food processor or blender, puree tofu, nutritional yeast flakes, tahini, soy sauce, and nutmeg until smooth. Gently fold together broccoli mixture and tofu mixture. (I just do it in the skillet instead of dirtying another dish.) Place filling in prebaked crust. Sprinkle with sesame seeds. Bake 30 minutes, or until edges are golden.

Makes 8 servings

APPROXIMATE NUTRITIONAL INFORMATION FOR 1 SERVING: Calories: 280 cal; Protein: 15 g; Carbohydrates: 23 g; Fat: 18 g; Fiber: 6 g; Sodium: 131 mg.

KEY NUTRIENTS: Vitamin A: 121.26 mcg; Thiamine: 1.03 mg; Riboflavin: 1.02 mg; Niacin: 6.31 mg; Pantothenic Acid: .55 mg; Vitamin B6: 1 mg; Folate: 68.35 mcg; Vitamin B12: .68 mcg; Vitamin C: 30.34 mg; Calcium: 467.42 mg; Iron: 7.76 mg; Magnesium: 70.22 mg; Zinc: 2 mg.

Spanakopitta ❄

This delicious Greek pie will give you your daily dose of greens and more. It is very easy to make so you may want to make an extra to freeze. The Fillo Factory (www.fillofactory.com) makes organic, vegan phyllo dough with no hydrogenated oils. It comes in unbleached white flour, spelt and whole wheat varieties and is available at many natural foods stores and supermarkets.

2 teaspoons olive oil
4 green onions, thinly sliced
1 pound fresh spinach, washed and chopped (about 10 cups)
2 eggs
1 teaspoon dried dill or 1 tablespoon fresh
1 cup crumbled feta cheese (4 ounces)
Black pepper to taste
8 sheets phyllo dough, preferably whole grain
Olive oil for brushing dough

Preheat oven to 375°F. Warm oil in large skillet over medium heat. Add green onions and sauté 2 minutes, or until soft. Add spinach to pan. (It looks like a lot of spinach but just pack it in. It will cook down.) Cover pan and cook 5 to 10 minutes or until spinach is wilted. Transfer to a colander and let it drain.

In bowl, beat eggs and dill. Stir in cheese and spinach. Season with black pepper. You can add sea salt but the salt from the feta is usually enough for me.

Set up your work station. Unwrap phyllo dough and cover it with a damp towel. Pour some olive oil into a bowl and get a pastry brush. Lightly brush a 10-inch pie or tart pan with olive oil. Place a sheet of phyllo in pan. Brush lightly with oil. Place a second sheet over the first but position it so the corners don't match up. Brush with oil. Repeat until you have four layers of phyllo. Spread the spinach filling evenly in pan. Turn the corners of the phyllo dough over filling. Layer 4 more sheets of phyllo over filling, brushing each piece with oil as before. Tuck corners under pie. Bake 40 to 45 minutes, or until golden brown.

Makes 6 servings

Variations

Kale and Spinach Spanakopitta: Substitute kale for up to 1/2 of the spinach.

Zucchini and Spinach Spanakopitta: Finely dice 1 medium zucchini and sauté with spinach.

Vegan Spanakopitta: Substitute 1 1/4 cups Herbed Tofu Cottage Cheese (page 274) for the feta cheese, eggs and dill.

❄ **Freezing Instructions:** Assemble spanakopitta and bake for only 30 minutes. To reheat, thaw slightly. Bake covered in 375°F oven for 30 minutes. Remove cover and bake 10 minutes, or until golden brown.

APPROXIMATE NUTRITIONAL INFORMATION FOR 1 SERVING: Calories: 236 cal; Protein: 10 g; Carbohydrates: 21 g; Fat: 14 g; Fiber: 3 g; Sodium: 459 mg.

KEY NUTRIENTS: Vitamin A: 575.77 mcg; Thiamine: .11 mg; Riboflavin: .45 mg; Niacin: .86 mg; Pantothenic Acid: .51 mg; Vitamin B6: .28 mg; Folate: 168.9 mcg; Vitamin B12: .59 mcg; Vitamin C: 23.12 mg; Vitamin D: .87 mcg; Vitamin E: 1.62 mg; Calcium: 222.35 mg; Iron: 3.4 mg; Magnesium: 68.14 mg; Zinc: 1.34 mg.

Pizza

My children love to help make pizza and homemade is much healthier than takeout.

1. Preheat oven to 400°F. If you have a baking stone, place it in oven.
2. Start with a pizza crust. Make your own (page 217), buy premade dough, or buy a premade crust. (I keep a few frozen crusts in the freezer for convenience.)
3. Spread a sauce over the crust. You can use Easy Marinara Sauce (page 281) or store-bought marinara. We also love using Parsley-Walnut Pesto (page 269) or traditional basil pesto.
4. Add your toppings. Some suggestions are:
   • Artichoke hearts
   • Asparagus
   • Black olives
   • Chopped broccoli or cauliflower
   • Chopped spinach or kale
   • Cooked beans
   • Corn
   • Diced bell peppers
   • Diced onions
   • Diced tomatoes
   • Shredded carrots
   • Sliced mushroom
   • Sliced zucchini
   Also, try sautéing the vegetables in olive oil before putting them on the pizza. It tastes incredible.
5. Sprinkle shredded cheese over the top. It doesn't have to be mozzarella either. Try cheddar, provolone, Monterey Jack, or a mixture of cheeses. I like to sprinkle a little Parmesan too. If you are vegan, use nondairy cheese substitute or just leave the cheese off all together. It will still taste good – especially if you sauté the vegetables. You can also sprinkle some Sesame Parmesan or chopped nuts over the top.
6. Bake 10 to 20 minutes (depending on how thinly you rolled the dough). Pizza is done when cheese is bubbly and crust is golden around the edges.

Pizza Crust ❄

This whole grain crust taste delicious without oil or sweeteners. Plan to start this crust at least two hours before you need to use it.

1 teaspoon active dry yeast
1/2 cup warm water
2 1/4 cups whole wheat or spelt flour
1 teaspoon sea salt
1 teaspoon dried oregano (optional)
1 teaspoon crushed dried rosemary (optional)
3/4 cups warm water

Sprinkle yeast in 1/2 cup warm water. Let sit 5 to10 minutes until it becomes foamy. (If it doesn't foam, the yeast is probably dead.)

In a large bowl, mix flour, sea salt, and herbs. Stir in yeast mixture. Stir in remaining water a little at a time until the dough holds together but is not gooey. With wet hands on a wet surface, knead dough for 10 minutes. When dough is ready, it will not tear when you stretch it.

Rinse out mixing bowl with warm water and leave it damp. Form dough into a ball and place in bowl. Turn dough in bowl until it is moist on all sides. Cover bowl with a plate or damp towel. Let sit in warm place for 1 hour, or until doubled in size. Push down dough and knead a few times. Form dough into a ball. Roll out on floured board to 1/4-inch thickness.

Makes an 11 x 17-inch crust (about 12 slices)

Note: This crust may be refrigerated or frozen. After the first rising, push down dough and gently form into a ball. Place dough in plastic bag and push out all air. When ready to use, unwrap dough and place it in a wet or oiled bowl and cover with a plate or plastic wrap. Thaw in refrigerator or at room temperature until soft. If thawing dough in refrigerator, bring dough to room temperature before rolling it out.

APPROXIMATE NUTRITIONAL INFORMATION FOR 1 SLICE: Calories: 77 cal; Protein: 3 g; Carbohydrates: 16 g; Fat: 0 g; Fiber: 3 g; Sodium: 185 mg.

KEY NUTRIENTS: Thiamine: .11 mg; Niacin: 1.56 mg; Iron: .93 mg.

Casseroles

Rice and Bean Casserole ◗

This dish is so delicious, nobody will believe how simple it was to make. If you have cooked rice and beans in your refrigerator or freezer, you can make this in a snap.

3 cups cooked brown rice
2 cups cooked black or pinto beans
1 cup fresh or frozen corn
1/2 cup chunky salsa
Sea salt or black pepper to taste
1/2 cup shredded Monterey Jack cheese (optional)

Preheat oven to 350°F. Oil casserole dish or baking dish. Mix rice, beans, corn, and salsa together. Season with sea salt and black pepper. Pour into prepared casserole dish or baking dish. Cover with cheese. Cover dish and bake 15 to 20 minutes, or until cheese is melted and mixture is hot.

Makes 6 servings

Note: See the Appendix for instructions on cooking brown rice and beans.

APPROXIMATE NUTRITIONAL INFORMATION FOR 1 SERVING: Calories: 242 cal; Protein: 11 g; Carbohydrates: 42 g; Fat: 5 g; Fiber: 7 g; Sodium: 225 mg.

KEY NUTRIENTS: Thiamine: .28 mg; Riboflavin: .11 mg; Niacin: 2.22 mg; Pantothenic Acid: .61 mg; Vitamin B6: .2 mg; Folate: 101.13 mcg; Iron: 1.75 mg; Magnesium: 91.56 mg; Zinc: 1.67 mg.

Kale and Rice Casserole

Everyone in my family loves greens this way.

4 cups cooked brown rice
1 cup minced kale, collards, chard, or spinach
1 1/4 cups milk (dairy or nondairy)
3 eggs
1 tablespoon nutritional yeast flakes
1/4 teaspoon ground nutmeg
1/2 teaspoon sea salt
1/4 teaspoon black pepper
1/2 cup shredded cheese (optional)

Preheat oven to 375°F. Oil a 2-quart casserole dish. Mix greens into cooked rice, and spread in prepared baking dish. Beat together milk, eggs, nutritional yeast, and seasonings. Pour over rice. Top with shredded cheese if desired. Bake 40 minutes, or until firm.

Makes 6 servings

Note: See the Grain Cooking Chart in the Appendix for instructions on cooking rice.

APPROXIMATE NUTRITIONAL INFORMATION FOR 1 SERVING: Calories: 260 cal; Protein: 11 g; Carbohydrates: 34 g; Fat: 8 g; Fiber: 3 g; Sodium: 309 mg.

KEY NUTRIENTS: Vitamin A: 164.42 mcg; Thiamine: 1.24 mg; Riboflavin: 1.36 mg; Niacin: 8.38 mg; Pantothenic Acid: .85 mg; Vitamin B6: 1.34 mg; Folate: 49.4 mcg; Vitamin B12: 1.32 mcg; Vitamin C: 14.16 mg; Vitamin D: 1.3 mcg; Vitamin E: 1.02 mg; Calcium: 167.48 mg; Iron: 1.2 mg; Magnesium: 68.8 mg; Zinc: 1.99 mg.

Tempeh-Squash Bake 🌓

I love kabucha squash. Not only does it have an intense sweet taste, but it doesn't need to be peeled. You can substitute hubbard or butternut squash but they need to be peeled.

1 onion, peeled and cut into chunks
1 medium kabucha squash, pulp removed, cut into 1-inch chunks (7 to 8 cups)
1 (8-ounce) package tempeh, cut into 1-inch chunks
1/4 cup pine nuts (optional)
1/2 teaspoon sea salt
1/4 teaspoon black pepper
2 tablespoons fresh thyme or 2 teaspoons dried
2 to 3 tablespoons olive oil

Preheat oven to 450°F. Place all ingredients in large bowl and toss. Use enough olive oil so that onion, squash, and tempeh are well coated. Pour mixture into 9 x 13-inch baking pan. Cover loosely with foil. Place in oven. Reduce heat to 375°F. Bake 30 minutes, or until squash is tender.

Makes 6 servings

APPROXIMATE NUTRITIONAL INFORMATION FOR 1 SERVING: Calories: 247 cal; Protein: 12 g; Carbohydrates: 28 g; Fat: 12 g; Fiber: 10 g; Sodium: 187 mg.

KEY NUTRIENTS: Vitamin A: 851.6 mcg; Thiamine: .26 mg; Niacin: 1.91 mg; Pantothenic Acid: .87 mg; Vitamin B6: .2 mg; Folate: 73.68 mcg; Vitamin C: 24.24 mg; Iron: 2.25 mg; Magnesium: 34.17 mg; Zinc: .9 mg.

Tempeh, Apple, Potato, and Kraut Casserole

During my pregnancies, I craved foods from my childhood. This casserole brings together some traditional German favorites. Don't worry if your family doesn't like sauerkraut – my kids don't either – but they love this dish.

1 tablespoon olive oil
1 onion, diced
2 (8-ounce) packages tempeh, diced
1 teaspoon mustard powder
1/8 teaspoon ground cloves
2 cups sauerkraut, rinsed and drained
3 medium cooking apples, sliced (4 to 5 cups)
4 medium russet potatoes, thinly sliced (1/8 inch)
1/2 teaspoon sea salt
1 cup shredded cheddar cheese (dairy or nondairy)

Preheat oven to 375°F. Lightly oil 9 x 13-inch baking dish. Heat oil in large skillet over medium heat. Stir in onion and tempeh. Sauté 10 to 15 minutes until golden brown. Stir in mustard powder, cloves, sauerkraut and apples. In separate bowl, toss potatoes with sea salt.

Arrange 1/2 of the potatoes over bottom of baking dish with slices slightly overlapping. Spread 1/2 of the sauerkraut mixture over potatoes. Arrange another layer using the remaining potatoes. Cover with the rest of the sauerkraut mixture. Cover with cheese. Bake 30 minutes.

Makes 8 servings

Variation: 1 cup coarsely chopped walnuts can be substituted for cheese.

APPROXIMATE NUTRITIONAL INFORMATION FOR 1 SERVING: Calories: 254 cal; Protein: 18 g; Carbohydrates: 24 g; Fat: 11 g; Fiber: 10 g; Sodium: 383 mg.

KEY NUTRIENTS: Thiamine: .11 mg; Riboflavin: .1 mg; Niacin: 2.39 mg; Pantothenic Acid: .54 mg; Vitamin B6: .23 mg; Folate: 33.98 mcg; Vitamin C: 27.3 mg; Calcium: 155.16 mg; Iron: 3.06 mg; Magnesium: 28.48 mg; Zinc: .85 mg.

Kasha, Potato, and Carrot Casserole ✳

This is especially good with Mushroom Gravy (page 280).

1 cup raw whole buckwheat groats
1 tablespoon olive oil or ghee
1 onion, diced
2 potatoes, diced
2 carrots, diced
1 tablespoon minced fresh thyme, or 3/4 teaspoon dried
3/4 teaspoon sea salt
1/4 teaspoon black pepper
1 1/4 cups boiling water
1/4 cup minced fresh parsley

Preheat oven to 350°F. Oil a 2-quart casserole dish. Toast buckwheat in dry skillet until golden. Pour into casserole dish. Heat oil or ghee in skillet over medium-low heat. Add onion and sauté 5 minutes. Stir in potatoes and carrots. Sauté 5 minutes. Pour vegetables into casserole dish. Sprinkle salt and pepper over vegetables. Pour boiling water into dish. Cover and bake 30 minutes or until water is absorbed and potatoes are tender. Fluff with fork. Sprinkle parsley over top.

Makes 6 servings

✳ **Freezing Instructions:** Freeze cooked casserole. To reheat, thaw in refrigerator. Bake covered at 350°F 30 minutes, or until heated through.

APPROXIMATE NUTRITIONAL INFORMATION FOR 1 SERVING: Calories: 152 cal; Protein: 6 g; Carbohydrates: 28 g; Fat: 3 g; Fiber: 6 g; Sodium: 290 mg.

KEY NUTRIENTS: Vitamin A: 584.98 mcg; Thiamine: .1 mg; Riboflavin: .15 mg; Niacin: 3.26 mg; Pantothenic Acid: .68 mg; Vitamin B6: .24 mg; Folate: 38.51 mcg; Vitamin C: 18.03 mg; Iron: 1.62 mg; Magnesium: 87.91 mg; Zinc: 1.02 mg.

Broccoli-Noodle Casserole ◑ ❄

This tastes delicious with Pesto Ribbons made by Eden Organic Pasta Company. If you have a small family, you may want to serve half and freeze half so you'll end up with two meals.

1 pound pasta ribbons, cooked and drained
4 cups bite-sized pieces or broccoli, steamed
1 cup frozen peas

Sauce:
1 pound tofu
1 clove garlic
1 teaspoon dried basil
1 tablespoon miso
1 tablespoon tahini
1 tablespoon nutritional yeast flakes
2/3 cup milk (dairy or nondairy)

Crumb Topping:
1 cup bread crumbs
2 tablespoons olive oil or melted butter

Preheat oven to 400°F. Lightly oil a large casserole dish. While pasta and broccoli are cooking, puree tofu, garlic, basil, miso, tahini, and nutritional yeast flakes with milk in blender until smooth. Add extra milk if sauce seems too thick. Drain pasta and return to pot. Add cooked broccoli and peas. Pour sauce over pasta and toss gently until coated. Pour mixture into casserole dish. Mix breadcrumbs and oil and sprinkle evenly over pasta. Bake uncovered 15 minutes or until crumbs are golden.

Makes 8 servings

Variation: Add 2 cups or 1 (15-ounce) can diced tomatoes to pasta mixture. You can also sprinkle shredded cheese over casserole, with or without the bread crumbs.

❄ **Freezing Instructions:** Assemble casserole and freeze unbaked. To reheat, bake covered at 400°F for 30 minutes. Bake uncovered for 15 minutes, or until crumbs are golden and casserole is heated through.**APPROXIMATE NUTRITIONAL**

INFORMATION FOR 1 SERVING: Calories: 403 cal; Protein: 23 g; Carbohydrates: 54 g; Fat: 12 g; Fiber: 6 g; Sodium: 164 mg.

KEY NUTRIENTS: Vitamin A: 134.67 mcg; Thiamine: 1.19 mg; Riboflavin: 1.03 mg; Niacin: 7.15 mg; Pantothenic Acid: .38 mg; Vitamin B6: .94 mg; Folate: 47.66 mcg; Vitamin B12: .74 mcg; Vitamin C: 35.31 mg; Calcium: 464.15 mg; Iron: 8.28 mg; Magnesium: 94.5 mg; Zinc: 2.6 mg.

Roasted Eggplant and Zucchini Parmesan ✳

I was hesitant to serve eggplant to my children because I didn't think they would like it. This dish was such a hit that now they request it.

1 medium eggplant, cut into 1/4-inch slices
2 medium zucchini, cut into 1/4-inch slices
1 pound firm or silken tofu
2 tablespoons minced parsley
1 teaspoon olive oil
1 cup Easy Marinara Sauce (page 281)
1 cup shredded mozzarella cheese (dairy or nondairy)
2 tablespoons grated Parmesan cheese (dairy or nondairy)

Preheat oven to 400°F. Oil a large baking sheet. Place eggplant slices on prepared baking sheet. Bake 7 to 10 minutes per side, or until tender. Repeat with zucchini. Reduce heat to 375°F. While vegetables are roasting, puree tofu, and parsley with olive oil in food processor or blender.

Cover the bottom of an 8- or 9-inch baking dish with a thin layer of marinara sauce. Arrange a layer of eggplant in pan. Spread a thin layer of tofu mixture, then a thin layer of marinara. Next, arrange a layer of zucchini. Spread a thin layer of tofu mixture over zucchini, then a layer of marinara. Repeat until all vegetables are used. End with sauce layer. Sprinkle mozzarella cheese evenly over top. Sprinkle with Parmesan.

Bake 20 to 25 minutes, or until bubbly around the edges. Remove from oven and let sit 10 minutes before serving.

Makes 6 servings

Note: Ricotta cheese may be substituted for tofu.

❄ **Freezing Instructions:** Assemble casserole and freeze unbaked. To reheat, thaw in refrigerator. Bake covered at 400°F 30 minutes. Uncover and bake 10 minutes, or until cheese is slightly golden.

APPROXIMATE NUTRITIONAL INFORMATION FOR 1 SERVING: Calories: 222 cal; Protein: 19 g; Carbohydrates: 14 g; Fat: 12 g; Fiber: 6 g; Sodium: 221 mg.

KEY NUTRIENTS: Vitamin A: 126.63 mcg; Thiamine: .22 mg; Riboflavin: .19 mg; Niacin: 1.16 mg; Pantothenic Acid: .41 mg; Vitamin B6: .22 mg; Folate: 57.48 mcg; Vitamin C: 11.8 mg; Calcium: 684.93 mg; Iron: 9 mg; Magnesium: 73.64 mg; Zinc: 2.13 mg.

Main-Course Beans and Legumes

Bean and Nut Loaf ❄

My children love this with oven fries. They dip both the loaf and the fries in ketchup.

2 tablespoons flaxseeds
1/4 cup water
1 cup chopped walnuts or pecans
2 cups cooked pinto or kidney beans, drained
2 carrots, shredded or minced
2 tablespoons minced parsley
1 1/2 tablespoons minced fresh herbs or 1 1/2 teaspoons dried (thyme, oregano, basil, etc.)
3/4 cup breadcrumbs (about 1 1/2 slices of bread)
1/2 cup tomato sauce
1 1/4 teaspoons sea salt

Preheat oven to 375°F. Oil a loaf pan. Grind flaxseeds in coffee grinder or blender. Mix with water. Combine all ingredients (including flax mixture) together, mashing the beans as you mix. (A food processor works really well.) Press mixture into loaf pan. Bake for 70 minutes, or until dry and firm.

Makes 8 servings

Note: Oven Fries (page 185), Roasted Root Vegetables (page 186), Baked Potatoes (page 183), or Basic Baked Brown Rice (page 170) can be cooked along with the loaf.

❄ **Freezing Instructions:** To freeze this loaf, cook it for about 55 minutes and then freeze. To reheat, thaw in refrigerator. Bake covered at 375°F for 30 minutes. Uncover and bake 15 minutes, or until loaf is heated through.

APPROXIMATE NUTRITIONAL INFORMATION FOR 1 SERVING: Calories: 196 cal; Protein: 7 g; Carbohydrates: 19 g; Fat: 11 g; Fiber: 7 g; Sodium: 388 mg.

KEY NUTRIENTS: Vitamin A: 434.52 mcg; Thiamine: .17 mg; Vitamin B6: .21 mg; Folate: 101.98 mcg; Vitamin E: 1.13 mg; Iron: 2.23 mg; Magnesium: 65.38 mg; Zinc: 1.19 mg.

Beanballs ❄

These are a great substitute for meatballs in any dish. They are simple to make and kids love them.

1 carrot
1/4 cup parsley
1 slice whole grain bread or 1/2 cup breadcrumbs
1 3/4 cups cooked kidney or pinto beans, well drained
Sea salt and black pepper to taste

Preheat oven to 375°F. Oil baking sheet. Mince carrot and parsley in food processor or by hand. Add bread or breadcrumbs and beans. Puree or mash until combined. Season with sea salt and pepper to taste. This step can be done ahead of time and batter kept refrigerated until ready to cook. (Cold mixture is easier to roll, too.)

Roll bean mixture into 1-inch balls and place on baking sheet. Bake 10 minutes, or until bottoms are browned. Turn balls and bake 5 to 10 more minutes, or until bottoms are golden. Toss with sauce or gravy and serve.

Makes 4 servings

Variations

Swedish-Style Beanballs: Make Beanballs as directed above, adding a pinch of nutmeg to bean mixture. Prepare Tahini-Miso Sauce (page 276) as directed. Add cooked Beanballs to hot sauce. Cover and let sit 10 minutes to absorb sauce.

Italian-Style Beanballs: Make Beanballs as directed above adding 1/2 teaspoon dried oregano and 1/2 teaspoon dried basil to bean mixture. Heat 2 cups Easy Marinara Sauce (page 281) in pan. Add cooked Beanballs to sauce. Cover and let sit 10 minutes to absorb sauce. Serve with grated Parmesan if desired.

❄ **Freezing Instructions:** Beanballs can be frozen after cooking. To reheat: Warm frozen or thawed beanballs in sauce or oven.

APPROXIMATE NUTRITIONAL INFORMATION FOR 1 SERVING: Calories: 123 cal; Protein: 8 g; Carbohydrates: 23 g; Fat: 1 g; Fiber: 6 g; Sodium: 184 mg.

KEY NUTRIENTS: Vitamin A: 448.48 mcg; Thiamine: .17 mg; Vitamin B6: .13 mg; Folate: 112 mcg; Vitamin C: 7.34 mg; Iron: 2.82 mg; Magnesium: 45.03 mg; Zinc: 1.03 mg.

Lentil Puree (Dahl)

We love this version of Indian dahl. It's a delicious way to get lots of iron. If you want to be authentic, serve it with naan (Indian flatbread), but tortillas, lavash, and chaptis also work well.

1 cup lentils
1/2 strip kombu (optional)
3 cups water
1 tablespoon oil or ghee
1 onion, diced
1/2 teaspoon chili powder
1/4 teaspoon ground turmeric
1/4 teaspoon ground cumin
1/4 teaspoon powdered ginger
1 cup diced tomatoes
1/2 teaspoon sea salt

Place lentils, kombu, and water in heavy-bottomed pan. Cover and bring to a boil. Reduce heat to low and simmer 45 to 60 minutes, or until lentils are tender. While lentils are cooking, heat skillet. Add oil or ghee, onion, chili powder, turmeric, cumin, and ginger. Sauté 10 minutes, or until onion is soft. Stir in tomatoes. Cook about 5 minutes. Pour cooked lentils and tomato mixture into food processor or blender and pulse to puree, leaving some texture. Serve with millet, quinoa, or brown rice, and/or flatbread.

Makes 6 servings

APPROXIMATE NUTRITIONAL INFORMATION FOR 1 SERVING: Calories: 143 cal; Protein: 9 g; Carbohydrates: 22 g; Fat: 3 g; Fiber: 11 g; Sodium: 205 mg.

KEY NUTRIENTS: Thiamine: .18 mg; Riboflavin: .1 mg; Niacin: 1.05 mg; Pantothenic Acid: .69 mg; Vitamin B6: .22 mg; Folate: 146.54 mcg; Vitamin C: 10.96 mg; Iron: 3.06 mg; Magnesium: 43.37 mg; Zinc: 1.22 mg.

Gingery Black Beans ◐

This is a deliciously simple way to eat beans. I keep cooked beans in my freezer to make this but you can use canned, too. We love this with Roasted Root Vegetables (page 186) or Baked Winter Squash (page 187).

1 tablespoon olive oil
1 onion, peeled and diced
3 cloves garlic, minced
4 cups cooked black beans with a little cooking water
1/2 teaspoon ground ginger or 2 tablespoons ginger juice (page 360)
1/8 teaspoon ground cumin
Sea salt to taste

Warm pan over low heat and add oil. Add onion and garlic. Let onion cook 10 to 15 minutes to caramelize. Stir only if it looks like onion is burning. Add remaining ingredients. Heat about 10 minutes or until hot. Add additional water if necessary to keep beans from scorching.

Makes 6 servings

Note: See the Bean and Legume Cooking Chart in the Appendix for instructions on cooking black beans. If using canned beans, do not use the liquid. Drain and rinse canned beans. Use a little water to prevent beans from scorching.

APPROXIMATE NUTRITIONAL INFORMATION FOR 1 SERVING: Calories: 181 cal; Protein: 10 g; Carbohydrates: 29 g; Fat: 3 g; Fiber: 10 g; Sodium: 94 mg.

KEY NUTRIENTS: Thiamine: .29 mg; Vitamin B6: .12 mg; Folate: 174.38 mcg; Iron: 2.47 mg; Magnesium: 82.47 mg; Zinc: 1.34 mg.

Arame and Black-Eyed Peas ◑

This meal takes just over 30 minutes to cook, as long as you remember to soak the beans ahead of time. The hands-on time is only about 5 minutes.

2 cups dried black-eyed peas
4 cups water
2/3 cup arame
3 tablespoons soy sauce
2 tablespoons maple syrup, brown rice syrup, or agave nectar
1/2 tablespoon minced fresh ginger
1 teaspoon brown rice vinegar
1/4 cup chopped fresh cilantro or parsley

Soak peas in plenty of water for 4 hours or overnight. Drain. Place peas, water, and arame in heavy-bottomed pan. Cover and bring to a boil. Reduce heat and simmer 30 minutes, or until peas are tender. Stir in soy sauce, syrup, ginger, and vinegar. Sprinkle cilantro or parsley over peas.

Makes 6 to 8 servings

APPROXIMATE NUTRITIONAL INFORMATION FOR 1 SERVING: Calories: 223 cal; Protein: 14 g; Carbohydrates: 39 g; Fat: 1 g; Fiber: 8 g; Sodium: 480 mg.

KEY NUTRIENTS: Thiamine: .38 mg; Riboflavin: .11 mg; Niacin: 1.57 mg; Pantothenic Acid: .85 mg; Vitamin B6: .2 mg; Folate: 356.18 mcg; Iron: 5.79 mg; Magnesium: 200.03 mg; Zinc: 3.88 mg.

Burgers, Burritos, Enchiladas, and Fajitas

Millet-Veggie Burgers 🕐 ❄

These are great on a bun or in a pita pocket. My kids love them spread with Thousand Island Dressing (page 136).

1/2 zucchini, grated or minced
1 carrot, grated or minced
1/2 cup packed greens (kale, chard, collards), minced
3 cups cooked millet
1/4 cup Toasted Seed Mix (page 283) or toasted sesame seeds
1 egg or 1 tablespoon olive oil
2 teaspoons soy sauce
1 teaspoon dried oregano

Preheat oven to 400°F. Oil a baking sheet. Combine all ingredients by hand or in a food processor. Scoop out 1/3 cup at a time (an ice cream scoop works well) and shape into patties. Place on prepared baking sheet. Bake 10 to 15 minutes on each side, or until brown and crisp.

Makes 9 burgers

Note: You can make these in seconds with a food processor. Mince the vegetables in the food processor with the metal blade. Add the remaining ingredients, and pulse to mix.

Variation: Substitute cooked brown rice or quinoa for the millet.

❄ **Freezing Instructions:** Freeze cooked patties. To reheat, thaw slightly. Heat in toaster oven or conventional oven at 400°F 5 to 10 minutes, or until hot and crisp.

APPROXIMATE NUTRITIONAL INFORMATION FOR 1 BURGER: Calories: 107 cal; Protein: 4 g; Carbohydrates: 16 g; Fat: 3 g; Fiber: 2 g; Sodium: 75 mg.

KEY NUTRIENTS: Vitamin A: 238.69 mcg; Thiamine: .1 mg; Riboflavin: .1 mg; Niacin: 1.03 mg; Pantothenic Acid: .31 mg; Vitamin B6: .12 mg; Vitamin C: 6.13 mg; Vitamin D: .29 mcg; Iron: 1.01 mg; Magnesium: 44.21 mg; Zinc: .89 mg.

Falafel with Tangy Tahini Sauce ❄

These vegetarian patties are surprisingly easy to make from scratch and so much tastier than using a prepackaged mix. The batter lasts up to 3 days in the refrigerator so you can make it ahead of time. Leftover patties can be refrigerated or frozen for a quick lunch or snack.

4 cups cooked garbanzo beans, drained
3 cloves garlic, minced
2 teaspoons ground cumin
1 teaspoon ground turmeric
1 teaspoon ground coriander
1 teaspoon sea salt
1/3 cup minced onion
1/4 cup minced parsley
1/3 cup water
1 tablespoon lemon juice
1/4 teaspoon black pepper
1/3 cup flour (any kind)

Tangy Tahini Sauce:
1/4 cup plain yogurt (dairy or nondairy)
1/4 cup tahini
1 tablespoon lemon juice
1/4 teaspoon sea salt
1/4 to 1/3 cup water

Puree falafel ingredients in food processor until smooth. Add a little more water if necessary to get a smooth consistency. If possible, let batter sit for 1 hour before cooking to thicken batter and intensify flavor.

   Use your hands to form patties approximately 3 inches in diameter and 1/2 inch thick. Cook patties using either of the two methods below.

1. **Oven Method:** (This method is best if you are cooking the whole batch of falafel batter at once. The oven method also requires less oil.)
   Preheat oven to 450°F. Place patties on oiled baking sheet and bake for 10 minutes on each side, or until brown and crisp.

2. **Pan Method:** (This method is best if you are just cooking a few patties and don't want to heat the oven.)

Warm a skillet to medium heat. Pour in just enough oil to coat pan. Drop in patties and grill 10 minutes on each side, or until brown and crisp. Add additional oil if needed during cooking process. Keep cooked falafels in warm oven until ready to serve.

Make sauce as follows: Puree yogurt, tahini, lemon juice, and sea salt in blender or bowl. While blending, add water a little at a time until desired thickness is achieved.

Serve falafels with sauce. Or serve them the traditional way – in warmed pita pockets with lettuce, tomato slices, cucumber slices, and Tangy Tahini Sauce.

Makes 6 to 8 servings

Note: Yogurt can be replaced with additional tahini if desired.

❄ **Freezing Instructions:** Freeze cooked patties. To reheat, thaw slightly. Heat in toaster oven or conventional oven at 400°F 5 to 10 minutes, or until hot and crisp.

APPROXIMATE NUTRITIONAL INFORMATION FOR 1 SERVING: Calories: 273 cal; Protein: 13 g; Carbohydrates: 40 g; Fat: 8 g; Fiber: 10 g; Sodium: 482 mg.

KEY NUTRIENTS: Thiamine: .3 mg; Riboflavin: .16 mg; Niacin: .1.66 mg; Pantothenic Acid: .52 mg; Vitamin B6: .23 mg; Folate: 207.7 mcg; Vitamin C: 8.17 mg; Calcium: 118.46 mg; Iron: 3.88 mg; Magnesium: 75.32 mg; Zinc: 2.46 mg.

Tofu Enchiladas ✳

I like to use mountain bread (available at most natural foods stores) to make enchiladas because the square shape makes them easy to roll. Tortillas work fine too, of course.

1 tablespoon oil
1/2 onion, finely diced
12 ounces firm tofu, finely diced
2 medium zucchini, diced (about 2 cups)
1 cup fresh or frozen corn kernels
1 tablespoon water
2 tablespoons minced fresh cilantro or parsley
3 cups Enchilada Sauce (page 279)
8 large whole grain flour tortillas or slices mountain bread, or 10 to 12 corn tortillas

Preheat oven to 400°F. Make filling: Place oil, onion, and tofu in hot skillet over medium heat. Sauté 10 minutes, or until tofu is golden brown. Add zucchini, corn, and water. Cover and steam 10 minutes until vegetables are bright and just tender. Remove from heat. Stir in cilantro or parsley.

Pour 1/3 of the enchilada sauce in bottom of baking dish. Roll enchiladas as follows. Place tortilla or mountain bread on flat surface. Place a line of filling across the width of tortilla or mountain bread about 2 inches from the bottom. Roll up and place in pan, seam side down. Repeat with the rest of tortillas or bread. Pour remaining sauce over top of enchiladas to cover them completely. Bake 20 minutes. Serve with guacamole or sour cream if desired.

Makes 8 servings

✳ **Freezing Instructions:** Assemble enchiladas in pan as directed. Cover and freeze. To reheat, bake covered at 375°F about 45 minutes, or until heated through.

APPROXIMATE NUTRITIONAL INFORMATION FOR 1 SERVING: Calories: 321 cal; Protein: 14 g; Carbohydrates: 43 g; Fat: 11 g; Fiber: 6 g; Sodium: 362 mg.

KEY NUTRIENTS: Vitamin A: 128.43 mcg; Thiamine: .2 mg; Riboflavin: .12 mg; Niacin: 2.09 mg; Pantothenic Acid: .62 mg; Vitamin B6: .24 mg; Folate: 43.71 mcg; Vitamin C: 15.35 mg; Vitamin E: 2.13 mg; Calcium: 316.05 mg; Iron: 7.13 mg; Magnesium: 63.52 mg; Zinc: 1.07 mg.

Black Bean and Sweet Potato Enchiladas ❅

This delicious meal is high in protein, vitamin A, and iron. If you're in a hurry, you can use prepared enchilada sauce instead of making your own.

2 teaspoons oil
1 small onion, diced
2 sweet potatoes, diced (about 2 1/2 cups)
2 cups cooked black beans with a little cooking water
2 cups chopped greens (kale, spinach, etc.)
Sea salt and black pepper to taste
2 cups Enchilada Sauce (page 279)
8 large whole grain flour tortillas or slices mountain bread, or 10 to 12 corn tortillas
8 ounces sour cream, yogurt cheese (page 273), or crème fraîche.

Preheat oven to 375°F. Heat oil in large skillet. Add onion and sauté 5 to 10 minutes or until soft. Add sweet potatoes. Cover and cook about 10 minutes or until tender. Stir in beans and greens. Cover and heat about 5 minutes until greens are wilted. Add a little water if necessary to prevent scorching. Season with sea salt and pepper to taste.

Cover bottom of 9 x 13-inch baking dish with about 1/3 cup of enchilada sauce. Place tortilla or mountain bread on flat surface. Scoop a line of filling across the width of tortilla or mountain bread about 2 inches from the bottom. Spoon sour cream, yogurt, or crème fraîche across filling. Roll enchilada up and place in pan, seam side down. Repeat until all filling has been used. Cover enchiladas with remaining sauce. Cover pan and bake 20 minutes.

Makes 8 servings

Variations

Black Bean and Squash Enchiladas: Substitute 2 3/4 cups diced squash for sweet potatoes.
Black Bean and Carrot Enchiladas: Substitute 2 3/4 cups diced carrots for sweet potatoes.
Black Bean and Brown Rice Enchiladas: Substitute 2 3/4 cups cooked brown rice for sweet potatoes but add them at the same time as the beans and greens.

✽ **Freezing Instructions:** Assemble enchiladas in pan as directed. Cover and freeze. To reheat, bake covered at 375°F about 45 minutes, or until heated through.

APPROXIMATE NUTRITIONAL INFORMATION FOR 1 SERVING: Calories: 374 cal; Protein: 12 g; Carbohydrates: 54 g; Fat: 12 g; Fiber: 9 g; Sodium: 398 mg.

KEY NUTRIENTS: Vitamin A: 870.03 mcg; Thiamine: .19 mg; Riboflavin: .13 mg; Niacin: 1.55 mg; Pantothenic Acid: .56 mg; Vitamin B6: .26 mg; Folate: 82 mcg; Vitamin C: 34.06 mg; Vitamin E: 1.59 mg; Iron: 3.41 mg; Magnesium: 53.38 mg; Zinc: .8 mg.

Burritos

This is another one of our favorite meals. Not only are burritos delicious, they are also one of the quickest dinners to make. Burritos can be made entirely with leftovers, with fresh ingredients, or a combination. Keep a package or two of whole grain tortillas in your freezer.

Large whole grain tortillas
Shredded cheese (optional)
Cooked brown rice or Mexican Rice (page 171)
Cooked black or pinto beans
Steamed or sautéed mixed vegetables (Diced onions, zucchini, carrots, broccoli, bell peppers, corn, etc.)
Diced avocado
Salsa
Minced cilantro (optional)
Sour cream (optional)

Warm tortillas (optionally topped with shredded cheese) in oven for a minute or two until soft, but not crisp. Place hot rice, beans, and vegetables on tortilla. Top with avocado, salsa, minced cilantro, and sour cream if desired. Fold tortilla like an envelope by folding bottom flap up over filling, then folding sides in over filling and bottom flap, and turning top flap down. Place burrito on plate, seam side down.

Note: See the Appendix for instructions on cooking brown rice and beans.

Fajitas 🌓

We like to eat these with Mexican Rice (page 171).

1 pound tofu
1 tablespoon oil
1 small onion, peeled and sliced
1 cup sliced mushrooms
1 bell pepper, seeded and cut into thin wedges
2 small zucchini, sliced
1 large carrot, sliced
2 cups bite-sized broccoli or cauliflower florets
8 medium whole grain tortillas (flour or corn)

Fajita Sauce:
2 cloves garlic, crushed
1 teaspoon sea salt
1 teaspoon cumin
1/2 teaspoon chili powder
1 teaspoon Tabasco sauce
3 tablespoons lemon juice (about one lemon)
2 tablespoons water
2 tablespoons oil

Place tofu in shallow dish with weighted cutting board on top. Let sit 10 to 15 minutes to expel water. (Chop the vegetables and make the sauce while tofu drains.) Whisk sauce ingredients together and set aside. Drain tofu and cut into 1/2-inch cubes.

Preheat oven to 350°F. Heat oil in large skillet over medium-high heat. Add tofu and brown on all sides. Add onion, mushrooms, pepper, zucchini, carrot, and broccoli. Cover and steam 10 minutes, or until vegetables are slightly tender but still crisp. Pour sauce over vegetable mixture in pan. Cook and stir about 3 minutes. Warm tortillas on baking sheet (it's okay to overlap them) just a minute or two until soft and warm. Wrap in a cloth napkin or dish towel. Place tortillas and filling on table and let everyone make his or her own fajita. Serve with guacamole or sour cream if desired.

Makes 8 servings

APPROXIMATE NUTRITIONAL INFORMATION FOR 1 SERVING: Calories: 293 cal; Protein: 14 g; Carbohydrates: 30 g; Fat: 13 g; Fiber: 4 g; Sodium: 468 mg.

KEY NUTRIENTS: Vitamin A: 335.57 mcg; Thiamine: .16 mg; Riboflavin: .14 mg; Niacin: .98 mg; Vitamin B6: .19 mg; Folate: 43.55 mcg; Vitamin C: 37.06 mg; Vitamin D: .67 mcg; Calcium: 407.92 mg; Iron: 7.55 mg; Magnesium: 48.93 mg; Zinc: 1.15 mg.

Main-Course Pasta

Pasta with Vegetables and Pine Nuts ☽

This is a lovely light dinner full of colorful vegetables. The leftovers are great for lunch the next day.

1 pound penne pasta, cooked and drained
2 cloves garlic, minced
1 tablespoon olive oil
1 large carrot, sliced (1/4 inch)
1 cup cauliflower florets
1 cup broccoli florets
1 cup chopped kale
1/2 cup pine nuts, toasted
2 teaspoons dried basil or 2 tablespoons minced fresh
2 tablespoons olive oil
Sea salt and black pepper to taste

While pasta is cooking, place 1 tablespoon olive oil in large skillet with garlic, carrot, cauliflower, broccoli, and kale. Stir gently and cover pan. Steam 10 to 15 minutes, or until vegetables are just tender. Add a little water if necessary to prevent vegetables from scorching.

Drain pasta and place in large bowl. Add cooked vegetables, pine nuts, basil, 2 tablespoons olive oil, sea salt and pepper. Toss gently. Serve with grated Parmesan cheese if desired.

Makes 8 servings

Note: You can use any combination of vegetables for this or even just two or three, as long as you use a total of 4 cups vegetables.

Variation: Add 2 cups diced tofu, tempeh, or seitan with vegetables.

APPROXIMATE NUTRITIONAL INFORMATION FOR 1 SERVING: Calories: 298 cal;

Protein: 12 g; Carbohydrates: 38 g; Fat: 11 g; Fiber: 7 g; Sodium: 92 mg.

KEY NUTRIENTS: Vitamin A: 354.84 mcg; Thiamine: .4 mg; Riboflavin: .12 mg; Niacin: 2.6 mg; Vitamin B6: .1 mg; Vitamin C: 25.35 mg; Iron: 4.12 mg; Magnesium: 28.28 mg.

Parsley-Walnut Pesto Pasta ◑

This dish is quick, easy, and delicious. Use your favorite kind of pasta — penne, rotelle, linguine, etc. You can whip up the pesto while the pasta cooks.

1 pound pasta, cooked and drained
1 cup Parsley-Walnut Pesto (page 269)
1 cup frozen peas (thawed)

Toss hot pasta with pesto and peas. Serve with grated Parmesan cheese if desired.

Serves 6 to 8

APPROXIMATE NUTRITIONAL INFORMATION FOR 1 SERVING: Calories: 384 cal; Protein: 13 g; Carbohydrates: 38 g; Fat: 20 g; Fiber: 8 g; Sodium: 96 mg.

KEY NUTRIENTS: Vitamin A: 94.95 mcg; Thiamine: .34 mg; Riboflavin: .1 mg; Niacin: 2.33 mg; Vitamin C: 21.84 mg; Calcium: 90.5 mg; Iron: 4.28 mg.

Pasta Cooking Tips

- Use plenty of water when cooking pasta (about 8 quarts per 1 pound pasta).
- Wait until water comes to a full boil before adding pasta.
- Add pasta a little at a time to keep the boil going.
- Start testing pasta for doneness after about 5 minutes.
- As soon as pasta is tender but not mushy (al dente), pour it into a colander to drain.
- To keep pasta from sticking, toss immediately with sauce. If no sauce, toss with a little olive oil.
- To reheat pasta, immerse in boiling water. Cook 30 to 60 seconds and drain.

High-Protein Pasta ◷ ❋

The pureed tofu adds protein, calcium, and iron and tastes like ricotta cheese. If you don't have time to make your own marinara sauce, you can use store-bought. Don't worry if you don't finish all the pasta. The leftovers are great too.

1 pound penne pasta, cooked and drained
2 1/2 cups Easy Marinara Sauce (page 281), heated
1 pound firm tofu
1 tablespoon olive oil
2 tablespoons minced parsley

While pasta is cooking and marinara is warming, blend tofu, olive oil, and parsley in food processor or blender until smooth. When pasta is cooked, drain and return to pot. Pour hot marinara sauce over pasta. Add tofu mixture and toss gently until combined.

Makes 8 servings

❋ **Freezing Instructions:** Freeze leftovers in individual containers. Reheat in a small pan or in the microwave.

APPROXIMATE NUTRITIONAL INFORMATION FOR 1 SERVING: Calories: 324 cal; Protein: 19 g; Carbohydrates: 43 g; Fat: 9 g; Fiber: 9 g; Sodium: 139 mg.

KEY NUTRIENTS: Vitamin A: 154.8 mcg; Thiamine: .4 mg; Riboflavin: .13 mg; Niacin: 2.3 mg; Vitamin C: 6.13 mg; Calcium: 413.65 mg; Iron: 9.88 mg; Magnesium: 35.51 mg; Zinc: .94 mg.

Vegan Paht Si-Yu ◑

This dish is made without the traditional fish sauce and egg. Just about any vegetable you have on hand can be used instead of the broccoli and carrots. Spaghetti or fettuccini can be used instead of rice noodles.

12 ounces flat rice noodles, cooked and drained
2 teaspoons toasted sesame oil
12 ounces firm tofu
2 cloves garlic, minced
2 cups broccoli florets
2 carrots, sliced
1 tablespoon water

Sauce:
2 tablespoons soy sauce
1 tablespoon blackstrap molasses
3 tablespoons toasted sesame oil
1/4 teaspoon black pepper

While noodles are cooking, heat 2 teaspoons sesame oil in large skillet over medium heat. Add tofu and brown on each side. Add garlic, broccoli, carrots, and water. Cover and cook until vegetables are tender. Add more water if necessary to keep mixture from scorching.

In small bowl, mix soy sauce, molasses, sesame oil, and black pepper together. Add noodles to tofu mixture in skillet. Drizzle with sauce. Toss together until everything is hot and coated with sauce.

Makes 6 servings

APPROXIMATE NUTRITIONAL INFORMATION FOR 1 SERVING: Calories: 390 cal; Protein: 12 g; Carbohydrates: 55 g; Fat: 14 g; Fiber: 3 g; Sodium: 407 mg.

KEY NUTRIENTS: Vitamin A: 652.62 mcg; Thiamine: .15 mg; Riboflavin: .11 mg; Niacin: .72 mg; Vitamin B6: .16 mg; Folate: 37.86 mcg; Vitamin C: 24.37 mg; Calcium: 444.79 mg; Iron: 7.24 mg; Magnesium: 56.07 mg; Zinc: 1.49 mg.

Garbanzos and Pasta in Tomato-Basil Sauce ◑ ✲

This makes a big batch but the leftovers are delicious. You can freeze half too.

2 teaspoons oil
2 carrots, cut into half-moon slices
1 medium zucchini, cut into quarter moon slices
1 recipe Tomato-Basil Sauce (page 275)
2 cups cooked garbanzo beans, drained
2 cups coarsely chopped fresh spinach
1 pound rotelle pasta, cooked and drained

Warm oil in large saucepan over medium-low heat. Stir in carrots and zucchini. Cover and steam 10 minutes while you prepare the Tomato-Basil Sauce. Pour sauce over vegetables. Stir in garbanzo beans. Bring to a slow boil and simmer over low heat about 10 minutes. Stir in spinach. Gently toss sauce with hot pasta.

Makes 8 servings

Note: See the Bean and Legume Cooking Chart in the Appendix for instructions on cooking garbanzo beans, or use beans you have cooked and frozen. Canned beans also work fine.

✲ **Freezing Instructions:** Leftovers can be frozen. To reheat, warm in microwave or oven until heated through.

APPROXIMATE NUTRITIONAL INFORMATION FOR 1 SERVING: Calories: 359 cal; Protein: 17 g; Carbohydrates: 60 g; Fat: 6 g; Fiber: 13 g; Sodium: 203 mg.

KEY NUTRIENTS: Vitamin A: 625.97 mcg; Thiamine: 1.33 mg; Riboflavin: 1.01 mg; Niacin: 9.29 mg; Pantothenic Acid: .67 mg; Vitamin B6: 1.09 mg; Folate: 130.28 mcg; Vitamin B12: .67 mcg; Vitamin C: 17.42 mg; Vitamin E: 2.98 mg; Calcium: 99.8 mg; Iron: 6.1 mg; Magnesium: 64.6 mg; Zinc: 1.52 mg.

Mushroom Stroganoff ◑

I especially like this with a mixture of mushrooms like white, crimini, portabella, etc.

1 tablespoon olive oil
1 tablespoon butter (optional)
1 onion, chopped
1 large clove garlic, minced
8 ounces diced tempeh or tofu (optional)
3 cups sliced mushrooms (about 1/2 pound)
2 tablespoons flour
1 1/2 cups water or vegetable stock
2 tablespoons tahini
1 tablespoon fresh tarragon or 1 teaspoon dried
1 tablespoon miso
Black pepper to taste
8 ounces egg noodles or ribbon noodles, cooked and drained
1/4 cup chopped fresh parsley

Heat olive oil and optional butter in large skillet. Add onion, garlic, and tempeh or tofu. Brown over medium-low heat. Stir in mushrooms. Cook several minutes until mushrooms become soft and juicy. Sprinkle flour over mushrooms and stir to coat. In small bowl, mix together water or stock, tahini, and tarragon until smooth. Pour over mushrooms and stir. Bring sauce to a simmer and cook 5 to 10 minutes, or until sauce is thickened. Remove from heat. Mash miso with a little water to form a paste and stir into sauce. Season with black pepper to taste.

Pour hot noodles into a serving bowl or platter. Pour sauce over top. Sprinkle with parsley. You can serve this with grated Parmesan cheese too if you like.

Makes 4 to 6 servings

APPROXIMATE NUTRITIONAL INFORMATION FOR 1 SERVING: Calories: 455 cal; Protein: 26 g; Carbohydrates: 52 g; Fat: 17 g; Fiber: 11 g; Sodium: 217 mg.

KEY NUTRIENTS: Thiamine: .32 mg; Riboflavin: 1.03 mg; Niacin: 4.95 mg; Pantothenic Acid: .92 mg; Vitamin B6: .13 mg; Vitamin C: 8.19 mg; Vitamin D: 4.19 mcg; Iron: 4.67 mg; Zinc: 1.09 mg.

Saucy Noodles and Vegetables ◑

10 ounces pasta ribbons, cooked and drained
2 cups cauliflower florets
2 carrots, sliced
2 cups chopped dinosaur kale
1 cup frozen peas
1 batch Light Cheese Sauce (page 277) or No Cheese Sauce (page 278)

While pasta is cooking, steam cauliflower and carrots over boiling water until almost tender. Add kale and peas and steam a couple of minutes, or until kale is bright green. Gently toss vegetables and sauce with pasta until combined.

Makes 6 servings

Note: Frozen mixed vegetables can be substituted for cauliflower, carrots, kale, and peas.

APPROXIMATE NUTRITIONAL INFORMATION FOR 1 SERVING: Calories: 387 cal; Protein: 20 g; Carbohydrates: 44 g; Fat: 15 g; Fiber: 8 g; Sodium: 271 mg.

KEY NUTRIENTS: Vitamin A: 706.66 mcg; Thiamine: 1.15 mg; Riboflavin: 1.34 mg; Niacin: 6.78 mg; Pantothenic Acid: .63 mg; Vitamin B6: 1.29 mg; Folate: 61.8 mcg; Vitamin B12: 1.37 mcg; Vitamin C: 48.94 mg; Vitamin D: .46 mcg; Calcium: 315.51 mg; Iron: 2.74 mg; Magnesium: 30.19 mg; Zinc: 1.57 mg.

Pumpkin Seed Pesto Ravioli ✻

Using prepared wonton wrappers (available in the deli section of most markets) makes it easy to make ravioli. This is a little more work than most of the recipes in this book but they are so good, you'll want to make them every now and then for a treat. If you get your family to help wrap up the raviolis, it won't take any time at all.

1 cup pumpkin seeds, lightly toasted
1 cup packed parsley leaves
2 cloves garlic
2 teaspoon miso
1/4 teaspoon sea salt
8 ounces firm tofu
1/4 cup olive oil
1 (50-piece) package round or square wonton/dumpling wrappers

Mince pumpkin seeds, parsley, and garlic together in food processor with metal blade. Add sea salt and tofu, and process until mixed. While processor is running, drizzle oil through the top.

Flour a tray or board for prepared ravioli, and flour a small work surface for their preparation. Place a cup of water next to your work station. Form ravioli as follows: Place a wrapper on floured work surface and put about 1 teaspoon of pesto filling in center. Dip finger in water and wet edges of wrapper. Fold wrapper over diagonally to form half-moon (round wraps) or triangle (square wraps). Press to seal. Place ravioli on floured tray or board. Continue with remaining wraps and filling. Ravioli can be frozen at this point (see freezing instructions).

When ready to serve, drop ravioli into a large pot of boiling water. Cook 2 to 4 minutes, or until they float to the top. Remove to serving platter with slotted spoon. If cooking all the ravioli at once, do it in several batches.

You can serve the ravioli with traditional marinara sauce; however, I prefer it tossed with just olive oil, salt, and pepper (and maybe a little Parmesan cheese) so I can taste the delicious flavor of the pesto.

Makes 8 servings

❋ **Freezing Instructions:** Place uncooked ravioli on a tray or baking sheet lined with parchment paper. Place tray in freezer for several hours, or until ravioli are frozen. Transfer ravioli to freezer container or bag. Cook as directed above; however, increase cooking time by a couple of minutes. Do not thaw before cooking.

Leftover cooked ravioli and sauce can be frozen in individual-size containers. To reheat, warm in pan or microwave until heated through.

APPROXIMATE NUTRITIONAL INFORMATION FOR 1 SERVING: Calories: 347 cal; Protein: 14 g; Carbohydrates: 34 g; Fat: 18 g; Fiber: 3 g; Sodium: 419 mg.

KEY NUTRIENTS: Thiamine: .35 mg; Riboflavin: .28 mg; Niacin: 3.24 mg; Vitamin B6: .1 mg; Folate: 73.12 mcg; Vitamin C: 10.59 mg; Calcium: 237.2 mg; Iron: 7.75 mg; Magnesium: 123.27 mg; Zinc: 2.22 mg.

Lima-Vegetable Lasagna ❄

This delicious dish is made without dairy or soy products. You don't need to precook the noodles either. Although there are several steps involved, they don't all need to be done at the same time. The lima beans and marinara sauce can be made the day before or in the morning. The Sesame Parmesan can be made ahead of time as well. Then, at dinnertime, you'll just need to assemble and bake. (You can also use store-bought marinara sauce and canned lima beans to make this really easy.) Freeze any leftovers in individual-size containers for quick meals after the baby comes.

9 to 11 uncooked lasagna noodles, preferably whole grain
1 batch (4 cups) Easy Marina Sauce (page 281)
1 zucchini, thinly sliced
1 cup chopped spinach or watercress
1 batch (1/2 cup) Sesame Parmesan (page 285)

Lima Bean "Cheese" Sauce:
3 1/2 cups cooked dried lima beans
2 to 4 tablespoons bean cooking water
3/4 teaspoon sea salt
1 teaspoon dried basil
Black pepper to taste

Preheat oven to 350°F. Make Lima Bean "Cheese" Sauce as follows: Mash sauce ingredients together using a potato masher or in a food processor, using just enough liquid to get a smooth mixture.

To assemble lasagna, cover bottom of 9 x 13-inch pan with thin layer of marinara sauce. Place a single layer of lasagna noodles in bottom of pan. Leave a little space between noodles because they will expand when cooked. Spread 1/3 of the "Cheese" Sauce over noodles. Arrange zucchini slices evenly over sauce. Cover with 1/3 of the remaining marinara sauce. Place a layer of noodles over sauce. Cover with a layer of "Cheese"Sauce, then spread the spinach or watercress in an even layer. Cover with marinara. Repeat with "Cheese" Sauce, zucchini, and marinara. Press noodles down gently to make sure they are covered with liquid. Sprinkle Sesame Parmesan evenly over the top.

Bake 50 to 55 minutes, or until noodles are tender. Let lasagna sit about 10 minutes before cutting. Refrigerate or freeze leftovers.

Serves 9

Note: 1/2 cup grated Parmesan cheese (dairy or nondairy) can be substituted for Sesame Parmesan if desired.

❄ **Freezing Instructions:** Assemble lasagna and bake as directed but only for 45 minutes. Cool and freeze. To reheat, thaw in refrigerator. Bake covered at 350°F for 30 minutes. Uncover and bake 10 minutes, or until heated through.

Leftovers can be frozen in individual-size containers. To reheat, warm in microwave or oven until heated through.

APPROXIMATE NUTRITIONAL INFORMATION FOR 1 SERVING: Calories: 302 cal; Protein: 14 g; Carbohydrates: 51 g; Fat: 6 g; Fiber: 10 g; Sodium: 274 mg.

KEY NUTRIENTS: Vitamin A: 345.78 mcg; Thiamine: 1.97 mg; Riboflavin: 1.72 mg; Niacin: 12.59 mg; Pantothenic Acid: .88 mg; Vitamin B6: 1.83 mg; Folate: 130.11 mcg; Vitamin B12: 1.19 mcg; Vitamin C: 25.22 mg; Vitamin D: .59 mcg; Vitamin E: 2.7 mg; Calcium: 117.14 mg; Iron: 5.42 mg; Magnesium: 92.15 mg; Zinc: 2.14 mg.

Butternut Lasagna ❄

Sweet winter squash and lasagna are both favorites of mine. Together, they are even better. If you are using a food processor, chop the nuts first before you make the fillings to save you having to wash and dry between steps. The filling and sauce can be made ahead of time, and you don't need to precook the noodles.

9 to 11 lasagna noodles, preferably whole grain
1/2 onion, minced
2 teaspoons olive oil
2 cloves garlic, minced
8 cups chopped spinach, kale, chard, or other dark green leafy vegetable
3/4 cup chopped walnuts or pecans
1/2 cup boiling water

Tofu Filling:
1 1/2 pounds firm or silken tofu
2 eggs or 2 tablespoons olive oil
2 teaspoons dried basil
1/2 teaspoon sea salt
1/4 teaspoon black pepper

Sauce:
3 cups mashed cooked butternut squash
3/4 cup milk (dairy or nondairy)
1/2 teaspoon sea salt
1 tablespoon miso
1/4 teaspoon ground nutmeg

Preheat oven to 375°F. Sauté onion in olive oil until soft. Stir in garlic and greens. If greens are dry, add a little water. Cover and steam 5 minutes or until soft. Set aside.

Place tofu filling ingredients in food processor or blender. Puree until smooth. Remove to bowl and set aside. Place sauce ingredients in food processor or blender. Puree until smooth.

Assemble lasagna as follows: Cover bottom of 9 x 13-inch pan with thin layer of sauce. Place a single layer of lasagna noodles in bottom of pan. Leave a little space between the noodles because they will expand when cooked. Spread 1/2 of the tofu filling over noodles. Sprinkle 1/2 of the cooked greens over tofu. Spread 1/3 of the butternut sauce over the greens. Repeat for one more layer. Place noodle layer on top and cover with butternut sauce. Sprinkle chopped nuts evenly over squash. Pour boiling water in corners and around edges of lasagna. Cover pan with foil and bake for 35 minute. Remove cover and bake 10 minutes. Allow to stand 5 to 10 minutes before serving.

Makes 8 servings

Note: To save time, you can buy frozen pureed squash. Many markets also carry fresh or frozen peeled and cut squash that can be quickly steamed.

Variation: Ricotta cheese can be substituted for tofu. Only use 1 egg or 1 tablespoon olive oil if using ricotta cheese.

❋ **Freezing Instructions:** Assemble lasagna and bake as directed but only for 30 minutes. Cool and freeze. To reheat, thaw in refrigerator. Bake covered at 350°F for 30 minutes. Uncover and bake 10 minutes, or until heated through.
   Leftovers can be frozen in individual-size containers. To reheat, warm in microwave or oven until heated through.

APPROXIMATE NUTRITIONAL INFORMATION FOR 1 SERVING: Calories: 410 cal; Protein: 24 g; Carbohydrates: 41 g; Fat: 19 g; Fiber: 5 g; Sodium: 421 mg.

KEY NUTRIENTS: Vitamin A: 247.67 mcg; Thiamine: .52 mg; Riboflavin: .42 mg; Niacin: 2.51 mg; Pantothenic Acid: .44 mg; Vitamin B6: .25 mg; Folate: 102.95 mcg; Vitamin B12: .21 mcg; Vitamin C: 20.88 mg; Vitamin D: 1.57 mcg; Vitamin E: 1.06 mg; Calcium: 689.11 mg; Iron: 11.88 mg; Magnesium: 96.81 mg; Zinc: 2.16 mg.

Stir-fries and Tofu Dishes

Seitan "Chicken" and Cashews 🕐

Look for chicken-style seitan near the tofu in the refrigerated section of your natural foods store. If you don't have cashews, toasted walnuts or almonds are delicious in this dish too. If you have nut allergies, try sunflower or pumpkins seeds.

2 teaspoons oil
1 small onion, coarsely chopped
1 pound chicken-style seitan, cut into bite-size pieces
1 bell pepper, seeded and cut into bite-size pieces
2 carrots, sliced
1 cup chopped green cabbage
1 cup corn kernels (fresh or frozen)
1/2 cup toasted (or dry-roasted) cashews

Sauce:
1/2 cup seitan broth, vegetable stock, or water
2 tablespoons soy sauce
2 teaspoons arrowroot powder
1/4 to 1/2 teaspoon crushed red pepper flakes (optional)

Warm oil in large skillet over medium heat. Add onion and cook 5 minutes, or until soft. Add seitan and brown on all sides. Add pepper and carrots. Reduce heat to medium-low and steam 5 minutes. Add cabbage and corn. Whisk sauce ingredients together and pour into skillet. Cover and cook 5 minutes, or until vegetables are tender. Remove from heat. Stir in cashews. Serve with brown rice or other cooked grain.

Makes 6 servings

APPROXIMATE NUTRITIONAL INFORMATION FOR 1 SERVING: Calories: 223 cal; Protein: 24 g; Carbohydrates: 17 g; Fat: 7 g; Fiber: 3 g; Sodium: 455 mg.

KEY NUTRIENTS: Vitamin A: 586.5 mcg; Thiamine: .1 mg; Vitamin B6: .12 mg; Vitamin C: 26.87 mg; Iron: 14.32 mg; Magnesium: 59.07 mg; Zinc: .88 mg.

Kung Pao Tofu

Pressing the water out of the tofu is optional but it helps the tofu to brown better. To save time, set up the tofu, then get out all the rest of the ingredients and chop the vegetables.

1 pound tofu
1 tablespoon oil
4 cups bite-sized broccoli florets
1/4 cup minced green onions (white part only)
2 tablespoons minced fresh ginger
2 cloves garlic, minced

Sauce:
3/4 cup water
1 teaspoon chili powder
1 tablespoon soy sauce
1 tablespoon brown rice vinegar
1 tablespoon vegetarian Worcestershire sauce
1 teaspoon toasted sesame oil
1 tablespoon honey, brown rice syrup, or agave nectar
1 tablespoon arrowroot powder
Red chili paste, to taste (optional)

3/4 cup toasted almonds, cashews, or peanuts

Place tofu in shallow dish with weighted cutting board on top. Let sit 10 to 15 minutes to expel water. Drain tofu. Cut horizontally into 1/2-inch slices.

Heat oil in large skillet over medium-high heat. Add a single layer of tofu. Brown on both sides. Remove and brown remaining tofu. Set tofu aside. Add broccoli and sauté until seared. Add green onions, ginger, and garlic. Cover and cook 5 to 10 minutes until broccoli is bright green and slightly tender.

Meanwhile, whisk sauce ingredients together. Reduce heat to low. Add tofu and sauce. Stir and simmer until sauce is thickened and tofu and broccoli are coated. Stir in nuts. Serve with brown rice or other cooked grain.

Makes 6 servings

APPROXIMATE NUTRITIONAL INFORMATION FOR 1 SERVING: Calories: 255 cal; Protein: 17 g; Carbohydrates: 14 g; Fat: 17 g; Fiber: 4 g; Sodium: 192 mg.

KEY NUTRIENTS: Vitamin A: 156.61 mcg; Thiamine: .19 mg; Riboflavin: .25 mg; Niacin: 1.16 mg; Pantothenic Acid: .42 mg; Vitamin B6: .18 mg; Folate: 62.46 mcg; Vitamin C: 45.46 mg; Vitamin E: 4.33 mg; Calcium: 578.25 mg; Iron: 9.01 mg; Magnesium: 94.79 mg; Zinc: 1.87 mg.

Tofu Vegetable Stir-Fry ◐

Pressing the water out of the tofu helps it to brown better. To save time, set up the tofu, then get out all the rest of the ingredients and chop the vegetables.

1 pound firm tofu
1 tablespoon toasted sesame oil
1/2 onion, chopped
1 clove garlic, minced
1 tablespoon minced fresh ginger
2 carrots, sliced
2 cups broccoli florets
1 bell pepper, cut into bite-size pieces
1 cup snow or snap peas

Sauce:
3 to 4 tablespoon soy sauce
2 tablespoons toasted sesame oil
1 tablespoon arrowroot powder
3 tablespoons water
1/4 teaspoon crushed red pepper flakes (optional)

Place tofu in shallow dish with weighted cutting board on top. Let sit about 15 minutes to expel water. Drain. Cut tofu into 3/4-inch cubes.

Heat oil in a large skillet over medium heat. Add tofu and brown on all sides. Add onion, garlic, ginger, carrots, and broccoli. Cover and cook 5 to 10 minutes, or until vegetables are slightly tender. Add bell pepper and snow or snap peas. Cover and cook 5 minutes, or until vegetables are tender but still crisp. Mix sauce ingredients together and pour over vegetables. Reduce heat to low and sauté until tofu and vegetables are coated. Serve with brown rice, millet, quinoa, or rice noodles.

Makes 6 servings

APPROXIMATE NUTRITIONAL INFORMATION FOR 1 SERVING: Calories: 210 cal; Protein: 13 g; Carbohydrates: 11 g; Fat: 14 g; Fiber: 3 g; Sodium: 445 mg.

KEY NUTRIENTS: Vitamin A: 669.79 mcg; Thiamine: .19 mg; Riboflavin: .13 mg; Vitamin B6: .22 mg; Folate: 52.31 mcg; Vitamin C: 48.9 mg; Calcium: 542.95 mg; Iron: 8.57 mg; Magnesium: 58.83 mg; Zinc: 1.4 mg.

Baked Ginger-Orange Tofu ●

1 pound firm tofu
1/4 cup orange marmalade
1/4 cup boiling water
1 tablespoon soy sauce
1 tablespoon orange juice, lemon juice, or brown rice vinegar
1 tablespoon minced fresh ginger or 1/2 teaspoon powdered
1 tablespoon sesame seeds

Preheat oven to 400°F. Oil 9-inch square baking dish. Place tofu in shallow dish. Place weighted cutting board over tofu to press out water while you prepare the sauce. Mix marmalade with boiling water until smooth. Add soy sauce, juice or vinegar, and ginger. Stir well.

Drain tofu. Cut it in half lengthwise, then cut horizontally into 1/2-inch slices. Place in bowl. Cover with sauce and toss gently until coated. Arrange slices in prepared baking dish. Sprinkle sesame seeds over top. Bake 30 minutes. Serve with brown rice, millet, quinoa, or rice noodles.

Makes 6 servings

APPROXIMATE NUTRITIONAL INFORMATION FOR 1 SERVING: Calories: 155 cal; Protein: 12 g; Carbohydrates: 13 g; Fat: 7 g; Fiber: 2 g; Sodium: 158 mg.

KEY NUTRIENTS: Thiamine: .13 mg; Calcium: 536.5 mg; Iron: 8.16 mg; Magnesium: 50.09 mg; Zinc: 1.31 mg.

Need an entrée in a hurry?

Cut tofu into 1/2-inch cubes (allow 4 to 6 ounces per person). Toss with soy sauce. Preheat skillet to medium heat. Coat pan with oil and sauté tofu about 5 minutes, or until heated through.

Egg Foo Young ◑

This is by no means authentic but delicious all the same. Light and full of yummy veggies, this makes a great dinner or brunch dish.

2 teaspoons toasted sesame oil
6 green onions, sliced
1 carrot, shredded
1 head bok choy, finely chopped (about 4 cups)
8 eggs
2 tablespoons water
2 teaspoons soy sauce
1/8 teaspoon black pepper

Heat oil in large skillet over medium heat. Add green onions, carrot, and bok choy. Cover and cook about 5 minutes, or until vegetables are soft.

Beat eggs, water, soy sauce, and black pepper together. Pour over vegetables. Cover and cook until firm and golden on bottom. Turn and cook 2 or 3 minutes to brown other side.

Makes 6 servings

APPROXIMATE NUTRITIONAL INFORMATION FOR 1 SERVING: Calories: 130 cal; Protein: 10 g; Carbohydrates: 4 g; Fat: 8 g; Fiber: 1 g; Sodium: 214 mg.

KEY NUTRIENTS: Vitamin A: 419.17 mcg; Folate: 42.36 mcg; Vitamin B12: .67 mcg; Vitamin C: 25.1 mg; Vitamin D: 3.47 mcg; Iron: 1.23 mg; Zinc: .81 mg.

DIPS, SPREADS, SAUCES, AND CONDIMENTS

 Salsas, dips, and spreads are a tasty way to add protein and fat to a snack of crackers or chips. These nutritious recipes are fast and easy. You'll also find recipes for sauces and gravies that are delicious over pasta, grains, or vegetables. This section also provides methods to make your own nut butters, yogurt, tofu cottage cheese, seasonings, and breadcrumbs.

Salsa and Dips

Zucchini-Avocado Salsa
Hummus
Easy Bean Dip
Creamy Watercress Dip or Spread

Spreads, Yogurt, and Cottage Cheese

Nut or Seed Butter
20-Minute Apricot Jam
Parsley-Walnut Pesto
Yogurt
Cashew Yogurt
Yogurt Cheese
Tofu Cottage Cheese
Herbed Cottage Cheese
Pineapple Cottage Cheese

Sauces and Gravies

Tomato-Basil Sauce
Tahini-Miso Sauce
Light Cheese Sauce
No Cheese Sauce
Enchilada Sauce
Mushroom Gravy
Easy Marinara Sauce

Seasonings, Condiments, and Breadcrumbs

Sea Veg Mix
Toasted Seed Mix
Toasted Nut and Seed Mix
Gomashio
Sesame Parmesan
Breadcrumbs

Salsa and Dips

Zucchini-Avocado Salsa

This a delicious alternative to regular salsa. It is great with chips or as a topping for burritos, tacos, or quesadillas.

2 small zucchini, diced (about 2 cups)
1 cup fresh or frozen corn kernels
3 green onions, thinly sliced
2 medium avocados, peeled, pitted, and diced
2 tablespoons fresh lime juice (about 1 lime)
1/4 cup olive oil
1 clove garlic, crushed
3 tablespoons minced fresh cilantro
Dash Tabasco sauce
Sea salt and black pepper to taste

Steam zucchini and corn together for 2 or 3 minutes until colors are bright. Place in a bowl with remaining ingredients. Stir together and chill for at least one hour.

Makes about 3 cups

Variation: Add 1 to 2 cups diced tomatoes

APPROXIMATE NUTRITIONAL INFORMATION FOR 1/4 CUP: Calories: 110 cal; Protein: 1 g; Carbohydrates: 6 g; Fat: 10 g; Fiber: 2 g; Sodium: 53 mg.

KEY NUTRIENTS: Folate: 33.77 mcg; Vitamin C: 6.89 mg.

Hummus

This dip is delicious with raw vegetables or pita triangles. Try it as a spread on sandwiches or bagels.

2 cups cooked garbanzo beans
1/4 cup tahini
1 teaspoon sea salt
1 clove garlic
Juice of 1 lemon (about 3 tablespoons)
Liquid from cooking beans or water
1/3 cup minced fresh parsley

Place beans, tahini, salt, garlic and lemon juice in blender or food processor. While blending, add bean water, a little at a time, until smooth, creamy texture is achieved. Stir in parsley and adjust seasonings.

Makes about 2 cups

Variation: Add 1/4 cup minced green onion or chives.

APPROXIMATE NUTRITIONAL INFORMATION FOR 1/4 CUP: Calories: 123 cal; Protein: 6 g; Carbohydrates: 12 g; Fat: 6 g; Fiber: 3 g; Sodium: 280 mg.

KEY NUTRIENTS: Folate: 75.1 mcg; Vitamin C: 6.68 mg; Iron: 1.8 mg.

Easy Bean Dip

This is a great dip for tortilla chips or raw veggies. It also makes a wonderful spread for sandwiches or tortillas.

2 cups cooked pinto or black beans
1 tablespoon olive oil
1 tablespoon nutritional yeast flakes
3/4 teaspoon chili powder
2 tablespoons minced fresh cilantro or parsley
Sea salt to taste

Place all ingredients in food processor or blender and puree until smooth.

Makes about 2 cups

APPROXIMATE NUTRITIONAL INFORMATION FOR 1/4 CUP: Calories: 79 cal; Protein: 4 g; Carbohydrates: 12 g; Fat: 2 g; Fiber: 4 g; Sodium: 38 mg.

KEY NUTRIENTS: Thiamine: .88 mg; Riboflavin: .84 mg; Niacin: 4.86 mg; Vitamin B6: .87 mg; Folate: 93.93 mcg; Vitamin B12: .67 mcg; Iron: 1.21 mg; Zinc: .73 mg.

Creamy Watercress Dip or Spread

I add whatever herbs happen to be plentiful in my garden to create this flavorful dip. It's delicious with raw vegetables, crackers, or pita triangles. Use it as a sandwich spread, too.

2 green onions, cut into pieces
1/2 cup (packed) watercress
2 tablespoons fresh herbs or 2 teaspoons dried
8 ounces tofu
1 tablespoon lemon juice
2 tablespoons mayonnaise (regular or vegan)
Sea salt and black pepper to taste

Place green onions, watercress, and herbs in food processor with metal blade. Pulse until coarsely chopped. Add tofu, lemon juice, and mayonnaise and puree mixture until smooth. Add salt and pepper to taste. Chill before serving if desired.

Makes about 1 cup

Note: 8 ounces cottage cheese can be substituted for the tofu and lemon juice.

APPROXIMATE NUTRITIONAL INFORMATION FOR 1/4 CUP: Calories: 136 cal; Protein: 9 g; Carbohydrates: 3 g; Fat: 10 g; Fiber: 2 g; Sodium: 118 mg.

KEY NUTRIENTS: Thiamine: .1 mg; Vitamin C: 5.34 mg; Calcium: 398.61 mg; Iron: 6.08 mg; Magnesium: 35.66 mg; Zinc: .93 mg.

Spreads

Nut or Seed Butter

It is easy to make your own nut or seed butters. If you are allergic to peanuts, it is also the safest way because commercial butters may contain traces of peanuts. Use any nut or seed, or a combination. One of our favorites is half almonds and half walnuts.

2 cups nuts or seeds (almonds, cashews, peanuts, sunflower seeds, sesame seeds, etc.)
Pinch sea salt (optional)
1/4 to 1/3 cup oil

Toast nuts or seeds in dry skillet, stirring occasionally until they begin to pop and turn golden. Pour into food processor. Grind to powder. Add sea salt if desired. With processor running, drizzle oil in, a little at a time, until desired consistency. Store in covered jar and keep in cool place or refrigerator.

Makes about 1 1/3 cups

APPROXIMATE NUTRITIONAL INFORMATION FOR 1 TABLESPOON: Calories: 100 cal; Protein: 3 g; Carbohydrates: 3 g; Fat: 9 g; Fiber: 2 g; Sodium: 7 mg.

KEY NUTRIENTS: Vitamin E: 3.49 mg; Magnesium: 36.7 mg.

20-Minute Apricot Jam

This easy spread is delicious on toast, English muffins, or Oat Nut Scones (page 303). It's also wonderful stirred into oatmeal or plain yogurt.

2 cups dried apricots
1 3/4 cups apple juice (divided)
2 teaspoons arrowroot powder
Pinch sea salt

Place apricots in small pan with 3/4 cup apple juice. Simmer about 15 minutes, or until soft and most of the liquid is absorbed. Puree in food processor or mash well with a spoon. Pour remaining 1 cup apple juice into pan. Add arrowroot and stir until dissolved. Turn heat to medium-low. Stir in apricot puree. Simmer 2 to 3 minutes, or until mixture is thickened. Cool and store in covered jar in refrigerator.

Makes 2 cups

APPROXIMATE NUTRITIONAL INFORMATION FOR 1 TABLESPOON: Calories: 26 cal; Protein: 0 g; Carbohydrates: 7 g; Fat: 0 g; Fiber: 1 g; Sodium: 6 mg.

KEY NUTRIENTS: Vitamin A: 58.83 mcg.

Parsley-Walnut Pesto

This is more nutritious than traditional basil pesto. Parsley supplies iron and vitamin C, the walnuts and olive oil are rich in omega-3 fatty acids for brain and nervous system.

1/2 cup walnuts, preferably toasted
1 clove garlic
2 cups packed fresh parsley
1/2 cup olive oil
1/4 cup grated Parmesan cheese (optional)

Place walnuts, garlic, and parsley in food processor with metal blade. Process until parsley is finely chopped. Add remaining ingredient and pulse until smooth.

Makes 1 cup

Note: Freeze leftover pesto in ice cube trays. Add to sauces, dressings, pasta, or grains.

APPROXIMATE NUTRITIONAL INFORMATION FOR 1 TABLESPOON: Calories: 91 cal; Protein: 1 g; Carbohydrates: 1 g; Fat: 10 g; Fiber: 0 g; Sodium: 33 mg.

KEY NUTRIENTS: Vitamin C: 10.07 mg.

Yogurt

Homemade yogurt contains more vigorous cultures than store-bought. It can be made without special equipment, using cow's milk, goat's milk, or soy milk. Homemade yogurt may be slightly thinner than store-bought yogurt. You can add dried milk powder if you want firmer yogurt (see variation). Although I have specified temperatures in the instructions, a thermometer is not necessary when making yogurt. Methods for determining if ingredients are at the correct temperature are explained as well.

3 1/2 cups milk
1/2 cup plain yogurt with live cultures or 1 packet freeze-dried culture

Pour milk into a heavy-bottomed pan. Warm over medium heat until milk just starts to boil (about 180°F). Remove from heat. Cool milk to approximately 105°F to 120°F. At that temperature, you should comfortably be able to immerse your finger in it. To help the milk cool, you can fill your sink with cold water to below the level of the top of the pan. Place pan in sink and stir milk with a whisk. When milk is at correct temperature, whisk in yogurt or culture. Pour into very clean quart-size jar and cover tightly.

Yogurt must incubate in a warm place, undisturbed, for five to ten hours. Possible places include an oven with a pilot light, on a heating pad, wrapped in an electric blanket, or in a thermos. I have found a cooler to be very reliable. Partially fill a cooler with water that is warm but in which you can comfortably immerse your hand (about 120°F). Place jar in cooler. Water should come to just below the top of the jar. Close cooler.

No matter which incubation method you choose, let the yogurt sit undisturbed for about 5 hours. Then check the yogurt periodically. Make sure the temperature is not too hot (which will kill the cultures) or too cold (yogurt won't set). Check the firmness of the yogurt. When it feels firm to the touch, it is done. Refrigerate yogurt for at least 12 hours before you try it. Don't despair if your first batch does not set completely. Drinking liquid yogurt (kefir) is just as beneficial as firm yogurt. Be sure to save enough yogurt to start your next batch. Homemade yogurt lasts at least a week in the refrigerator.

Makes 1 quart

Note: If you prefer sweetened yogurt, add fruit, jam, stevia extract, agave nectar, honey, or maple syrup to prepared yogurt.

Variation: For firmer yogurt, add 2 tablespoons dried nonfat milk powder with yogurt.

APPROXIMATE NUTRITIONAL INFORMATION FOR 1 CUP: Calories: 155 cal; Protein: 8 g; Carbohydrates: 11 g; Fat: 9 g; Fiber: 0 g; Sodium: 119 mg.

KEY NUTRIENTS: Vitamin A: 81.78 mcg; Vitamin B12: .88 mcg; Calcium: 291.12 mg; Magnesium: 31.43 mg; Zinc: .99 mg.

Cashew Yogurt

This creamy, nondairy yogurt just takes a few seconds to mix up. The incubation period is 8 to 24 hours depending how warm you keep it.

1 cup raw cashews
1 cup water

Place cashews in blender and grind to a coarse powder. Add water and blend until smooth. It should have a consistency of heavy cream. Pour mixture into a jar and place in warm location (70°F to 100°F). Cover with a light towel or napkin. Start checking the yogurt after 6 hours. First you should notice bubbles forming. When it has formed thick curd with a layer of liquid (whey) on the bottom, cover and transfer to refrigerator. Chill for at least one hour. When ready to eat, stir the whey and yogurt together. Add a little honey, agave nectar, maple syrup, molasses, fruit, or jam if desired. Yogurt will keep refrigerated up to a week.

Makes 2 cups

Note: Choose a place where the temperature will remain constant to incubate your yogurt. I like to fill a small cooler with warm water and place the jar in the water (make sure the water is below the level of the jar). Another good place is on top of the pilot light in a gas stove. As long as the temperature in your house is at least 70°F, you can place the jar anywhere. Keep in mind, the lower the temperature, the longer the incubation. At 70°F, it will take about 20 hours.

APPROXIMATE NUTRITIONAL INFORMATION FOR 1/2 CUP: Calories: 196 cal; Protein: 6 g; Carbohydrates: 10 g; Fat: 16 g; Fiber: 1 g; Sodium: 4 mg.

KEY NUTRIENTS: Iron: 2.25 mg; Magnesium: 123.36 mg; Zinc: 1.96 mg.

Yogurt Cheese

When the liquid (whey) is drained from yogurt, it becomes firm, like cream cheese.

Line a colander with several layers of cheesecloth. Place a dish underneath to catch drippings. Pour desired amount of yogurt into center of colander. Let sit in refrigerator overnight. It will become quite thick. Discard the whey or use it for Soaked Oatmeal (page 46).

APPROXIMATE NUTRITIONAL INFORMATION FOR 1 CUP: Nutritional information unavailable.

Tofu Cottage Cheese

This is really quick and easy to make. It's a great way to get protein and calcium.

1 pound firm tofu
1 tablespoon olive oil
4 tablespoons fresh lemon juice (1 large lemon)
1 tablespoon tahini (optional)
1/2 teaspoon sea salt

Divide tofu in half. Place 1/2 in blender or food processor with remaining ingredients. Puree until smooth. Place other half of tofu in bowl and mash with fork. Pour blended tofu mixture into bowl and stir to mix.

Makes 2 cups

APPROXIMATE NUTRITIONAL INFORMATION FOR 1/2 CUP: Calories: 220 cal; Protein: 19 g; Carbohydrates: 7 g; Fat: 15 g; Fiber: 3 g; Sodium: 295 mg.

KEY NUTRIENTS: Thiamine: .23 mg; Riboflavin: .14 mg; Vitamin B6: .12 mg; Folate: 38.54 mcg; Vitamin C: 7.24 mg; Calcium: 791.34 mg; Iron: 11.97 mg; Magnesium: 70.29 mg; Zinc: 1.96 mg.

Herbed Cottage Cheese

This is delicious on toast or with Breakfast Potatoes and Veggies (page 84).

2 cups cottage cheese (regular or tofu)
2 tablespoons minced chives
1 tablespoon minced fresh herbs (dill, tarragon, thyme, parsley, etc.)
Sea salt and black pepper to taste

Mix all ingredients together. Keep refrigerated.

Makes about 2 cups

APPROXIMATE NUTRITIONAL INFORMATION FOR 1/2 CUP: Calories: 121 cal; Protein: 13 g; Carbohydrates: 5 g; Fat: 5 g; Fiber: 0 g; Sodium: 400 mg.

KEY NUTRIENTS: Riboflavin: .26 mg; Vitamin B12: .48 mcg.

Pineapple Cottage Cheese

This is delicious with fruit salad, as a spread on bagels, or on its own for a high protein snack.

Stir 1/2 cup crushed pineapple into 2 cups cottage cheese (regular or tofu). Keep refrigerated.

Makes about 2 cups

APPROXIMATE NUTRITIONAL INFORMATION FOR 1 SERVING: Calories: 138 cal; Protein: 13 g; Carbohydrates: 9 g; Fat: 5 g; Fiber: 0 g; Sodium: 403 mg.

KEY NUTRIENTS: Riboflavin: .26 mg; Vitamin B12: .48 mcg.

Sauces and Gravies

Tomato-Basil Sauce

This light sauce is great over pasta. The tahini provides creaminess without dairy or soy.

1 (29-ounce) can pureed tomatoes
3 tablespoons tahini
1 tablespoon nutritional yeast flakes
2 cloves garlic
1/4 cup fresh basil leaves (or 2 teaspoons dried basil)
1 teaspoon oregano (or 1 tablespoon fresh)
1/2 teaspoon sea salt
Black pepper to taste

Puree all ingredients together in blender. Simmer over low heat 5 to 10 minutes.

Makes about 4 cups

APPROXIMATE NUTRITIONAL INFORMATION FOR 1/2 CUP: Calories: 80 cal; Protein: 4 g; Carbohydrates: 12 g; Fat: 3 g; Fiber: 3 g; Sodium: 178 mg.

KEY NUTRIENTS: Vitamin A: 137.03 mcg; Thiamine: .95 mg; Riboflavin: .89 mg; Niacin: 6.78 mg; Pantothenic Acid: .5 mg; Vitamin B6: .98 mg; Folate: 37.69 mcg; Vitamin B12: .67 mcg; Vitamin C: 11.16 mg; Vitamin E: 2.59 mg; Iron: 1.53 mg; Magnesium: 31.32 mg; Zinc: .77 mg.

Tahini-Miso Sauce

This white sauce is great over tempeh, vegetables, grains, or pasta.

1 cup water
2 tablespoons arrowroot powder
1/4 cup tahini
1 tablespoons miso
Pinch ground nutmeg
1/4 cup minced fresh parsley (optional)
Black pepper to taste

Whisk or blend all ingredients together. Pour into saucepan. Heat over low heat until thickened.

Makes about 1 cup

APPROXIMATE NUTRITIONAL INFORMATION FOR 1/4 CUP: Calories: 110 cal; Protein: 3 g; Carbohydrates: 9 g; Fat: 7 g; Fiber: 2 g; Sodium: 170 mg.

KEY NUTRIENTS: Thiamine: .2 mg; Zinc: .88 mg.

Light Cheese Sauce

This sauce is delicious over rice, pasta, or vegetables.

1 1/2 tablespoons butter or olive oil
2 tablespoons arrowroot powder
2 cups milk (dairy or nondairy)
1 cup shredded cheddar (or other) cheese
1 tablespoon nutritional yeast flakes (optional)
1/2 teaspoon mustard powder
Sea salt to taste

In saucepan, heat butter or olive oil over low heat. Stir in arrowroot. Add milk and bring to boil. Simmer 1 to 2 minutes until sauce thickens slightly. Add cheese, nutritional yeast, and mustard powder. Stir until cheese is melted. Salt to taste.

Makes about 2 cups

APPROXIMATE NUTRITIONAL INFORMATION FOR 1/4 CUP: Calories: 137 cal; Protein: 7 g; Carbohydrates: 5 g; Fat: 10 g; Fiber: 0 g; Sodium: 155 mg.

KEY NUTRIENTS: Vitamin A: 86.69 mcg; Thiamine: .83 mg; Riboflavin: .96 mg; Niacin: 4.73 mg; Vitamin B6: .84 mg; Vitamin B12: 1.02 mcg; Vitamin D: .35 mcg; Calcium: 192.99 mg; Zinc: 1.01 mg.

No-Cheese Sauce

This nondairy sauce is great over rice, pasta, or vegetables.

1 3/4 cups water
1/4 cup flour
2 tablespoons nutritional yeast flakes
2 tablespoons tahini
1/4 teaspoon turmeric
2 teaspoons soy sauce
1/2 teaspoon dried oregano
1 teaspoon dried basil
Sea salt and black pepper to taste

Blend or whisk all ingredients together. Pour into saucepan and warm over low heat until thickened.

Makes about 1 1/2 cups

APPROXIMATE NUTRITIONAL INFORMATION FOR 1/4 CUP: Calories: 61 cal; Protein: 3 g; Carbohydrates: 7 g; Fat: 3 g; Fiber: 2 g; Sodium: 99 mg.

KEY NUTRIENTS: Thiamine: 2.22 mg; Riboflavin: 2.17 mg; Niacin: 13.06 mg; Vitamin B6: 2.16 mg; Folate: 60.43 mcg; Vitamin B12: 1.77 mcg; Zinc: 1.08 mg.

Enchilada Sauce

This may not be totally authentic but it is easy and it tastes great.

1 small onion, minced
1 tablespoon olive oil
2 teaspoons chili powder
1 teaspoon ground cumin
2 teaspoons dried oregano
2 cloves garlic, minced
3 cups tomato puree
1/2 cup water
1/2 teaspoon sea salt

Heat oil in medium pan over medium-low heat. Add onion and sauté 5 to 7 minutes, or until onion is golden brown. Stir in chili powder, cumin, oregano, and garlic. Sauté 1 minute. Add remaining ingredients. Bring to a boil and simmer 15 minutes.

Makes 3 1/2 cups

APPROXIMATE NUTRITIONAL INFORMATION FOR 1/4 CUP: Calories: 33 cal; Protein: 1 g; Carbohydrates: 6 g; Fat: 1 g; Fiber: 1 g; Sodium: 97 mg.

KEY NUTRIENTS: Vitamin A: 68.57 mcg; Vitamin C: 6.03 mg; Vitamin E: 1.36 mg.

Mushroom Gravy

1 tablespoon olive oil
1 small onion, diced
1 cup sliced mushrooms
1 clove garlic, minced
1 tablespoon nutritional yeast flakes
1 tablespoon flour
1 cube vegetable bouillon or vegetarian chicken-flavored bouillon
1 1/2 cups potato cooking water or water
Sea salt and black pepper to taste

Heat oil in saucepan. Stir in onion, mushrooms, and garlic. Sauté 10 minutes over medium-low heat until mushrooms are juicy and onion is soft. Stir in nutritional yeast and flour until mushrooms are coated. Add bouillon and liquid. Bring to boil and simmer, stirring occasionally, until gravy thickens (about 10 minutes). Season to taste.

Makes 2 cups

APPROXIMATE NUTRITIONAL INFORMATION FOR 1/4 CUP: Calories: 30 cal; Protein: 1 g; Carbohydrates: 3 g; Fat: 2 g; Fiber: 1 g; Sodium: 124 mg.

KEY NUTRIENTS: Thiamine: .82 mg; Riboflavin: .84 mg; Niacin: 5.1 mg; Vitamin B6: .83 mg; Vitamin B12: .67 mcg; Vitamin D: .67 mcg.

Easy Marinara Sauce

This sauce is even better if it gets a chance to sit, so you can make it the night before you plan to use it. It freezes well so I often make a double batch and freeze extra in meal-size portions.

1 small onion, diced
2 cloves garlic, minced
1 tablespoon olive oil
1 carrot, grated or minced
2 (15-ounce) cans tomato sauce
2 tablespoons minced fresh basil or 1 teaspoon dried
1 tablespoon minced fresh oregano or 1/2 teaspoon dried
3 tablespoons minced fresh parsley
Sea salt and black pepper to taste

Sauté onion and garlic in olive oil until soft. Stir in carrot. Sauté 2 or 3 minutes. Add tomato sauce, basil, and oregano. Simmer 30 minutes. Stir in parsley and season with salt and pepper.

Makes 4 cups (enough for about 1 pound of pasta)

Variation: Brown 12 to 16 ounces diced tofu or tempeh with the onion and garlic.

APPROXIMATE NUTRITIONAL INFORMATION FOR 1/4 CUP: Calories: 29 cal; Protein: 1 g; Carbohydrates: 5 g; Fat: 1 g; Fiber: 1 g; Sodium: 97 mg.

KEY NUTRIENTS: Vitamin A: 112.18 mcg.

Seasonings, Condiments, and Breadcrumbs

Sea Veg Mix

Sea vegetables provide vitamins and minerals. This mixture can be cooked with soup, grains, and vegetables. Don't worry if you can't find every ingredient listed. Just use whichever you can find.

1/2 cup hiziki
1/2 cup arame
1/4 cup dulse
1/4 cup broken up wakame
2 tablespoons granulated kelp

Place sea vegetables in blender. Grind until coarse powder. Store in covered jar.

Makes about 1/2 cup

APPROXIMATE NUTRITIONAL INFORMATION FOR 1 TABLESPOON: Calories: 20 cal; Protein: 0 g; Carbohydrates: 4 g; Fat: 0 g; Fiber: 2 g; Sodium: 170 mg.

KEY NUTRIENTS: Iron: 1.4 mg.

Toasted Seed Mix

Use this as a topping for cereals, salads, or grains to add protein, minerals, essential fatty acids, and delicious nutty flavor.

1/2 cup raw sunflower seeds
1/2 cup raw pumpkin seeds
2 tablespoons raw sesame seeds
2 tablespoons raw flaxseeds

Place seeds in dry skillet over medium heat. Toast, stirring occasionally, 5 to 10 minutes, or until seeds are aromatic and begin to pop. Cool completely. Store in covered jar.

Makes 1 1/4 cups

APPROXIMATE NUTRITIONAL INFORMATION FOR 2 TABLESPOONS: Calories: 101 cal; Protein: 4 g; Carbohydrates: 4 g; Fat: 9 g; Fiber: 2 g; Sodium: 2 mg.

KEY NUTRIENTS: Pantothenic Acid: .53 mg; Vitamin B6: .11 mg; Iron: 1.9 mg; Magnesium: 60.56 mg; Zinc: 1.11 mg.

Toasted Nut and Seed Mix

Use as a topping for cereals, salads, or grains to add protein, minerals, essential fatty acids, and delicious nutty flavor.

1/3 cup coarsely chopped raw almonds
1/3 cup coarsely chopped raw walnuts
1/3 cup raw sunflower seeds
1/3 cup raw pumpkin seeds

Place seeds in dry skillet over medium heat. Toast, stirring occasionally, 5 to 10 minutes, or until seeds are aromatic and begin to pop. Cool completely. Store in covered jar.

Makes 1 1/3 cups

APPROXIMATE NUTRITIONAL INFORMATION FOR 2 TABLESPOONS: Calories: 93 cal; Protein: 3 g; Carbohydrates: 3 g; Fat: 9 g; Fiber: 1 g; Sodium: 1 mg.

KEY NUTRIENTS: Vitamin E: 1.04 mg; Iron: 1.19 mg; Magnesium: 43.71 mg; Zinc: .77 mg.

Gomashio

Use this mineral-rich seasoning to flavor grains, vegetables, and even breakfast porridge.

1 cup sesame seeds
2 tablespoons sea salt

Toast sesame seeds in dry skillet about 5 minutes, or until they begin to pop. If salt is moist, stir it in and let it toast a little too. Cool. Grind seeds and salt in coffee grinder, blender, or with mortar and pestle to coarse powder. Store in covered jar in the refrigerator.

Makes about 1 cup

APPROXIMATE NUTRITIONAL INFORMATION FOR 1 TEASPOON: Calories: 17 cal; Protein: 1 g; Carbohydrates: 1 g; Fat: 1 g; Fiber: 0 g; Sodium: 276 mg.

Sesame Parmesan

This is a delicious vegan substitute for Parmesan cheese.

1/2 cup sesame seeds, toasted and cooled
2 tablespoons nutritional yeast flakes
1/4 teaspoon sea salt

Coarsely grind ingredients together in blender.

Makes about 1/2 cup

APPROXIMATE NUTRITIONAL INFORMATION FOR 1 TABLESPOON: Calories: 62 cal; Protein: 3 g; Carbohydrates: 3 g; Fat: 5 g; Fiber: 2 g; Sodium: 71 mg.

KEY NUTRIENTS: Thiamine: 1.67 mg; Riboflavin: 1.62 mg; Niacin: 9.74 mg; Vitamin B6: 1.67 mg; Folate: 48.73 mcg; Vitamin B12: 1.33 mcg; Iron: 1.43 mg; Magnesium: 31.59 mg; Zinc: 1.22 mg.

Breadcrumbs

Keep a bag of bread heels in the freezer for making breadcrumbs. Whenever you have a heel, add it to the bag.

Place slightly toasted or dry bread slices (bread heels work great) in food processor. Process with metal blade until desired texture is achieved.

One slice makes approximately 1/2 cup breadcrumbs

APPROXIMATE NUTRITIONAL INFORMATION FOR 1/2 CUP: Calories: 69 cal; Protein: 3 g; Carbohydrates: 13 g; Fat: 1 g; Fiber: 2 g; Sodium: 148 mg.

KEY NUTRIENTS: Thiamine: .1 mg; Niacin: 1.07 mg.

Snacks

 Try to keep food in your stomach at all times while pregnant and lactating. An empty stomach and low blood sugar may cause you to feel lightheaded, dizzy, or queasy. Plan for a morning, afternoon, and evening snack. Always bring some Trail Mix or Energy Bars when you go out. Snacks don't mean junk food. Snacks should contain protein, complex carbohydrates, and fat, just like your meals.

Home-baked goodies are my weakness. I especially craved them while I was breastfeeding but I found sugary treats led to mood swings and energy crashes. All of the sweets in this book are made with unrefined sweeteners and grains. I packed as many nutrients into these treats as possible while still making sure they tasted good. For those on special diets, there are wheat-free, gluten-free, egg-free, and dairy-free options.

It is still possible to bake, even with a newborn in the house. Baking can be done in stages as you have time. First, get out the ingredients. Later, measure and mix the dry ingredients. Then prepare the liquid ingredients (keep refrigerated if not using immediately). When you are ready, preheat the oven, combine liquid and dry ingredients and bake. Cookies and bars freeze well so make an extra batch to store in your freezer. They thaw in minutes when you want a treat.

Savory Snacks

Perfect Popcorn
Popcorn Snack Mix
Sabzi
Deviled Eggs
Garbanzo Crunchies
Trail Mix
Spicy Trail Mix
Nori Rice Balls

Quick Breads, Muffins, Doughnuts, and Scones

Barley Soda Bread
Apricot-Nut Bread
Banana-Molasses Muffins
Cranberry-Orange Muffins
Carrot-Bran Muffins
Leftover Oatmeal-Raisin Muffins
Baked Carob Crullers
Oat-Nut Scones
Pumpkin Scones

Crackers, Bars, and Cookies

Raw Seed Wafers
Brown Rice Crackers
Rye-Corn Crackers
Cinnamon Graham Crackers
Gingerbread Bars
Cranberry-Date Bars
Granola Bars
Carob Brownies
Pumpkin Cheesecake Bars
Energy Bars
Carob-Nut Balls
Coconut-Almond Shortbread
Flourless Sesame-Almond Cookies
Sunflower-Sesame Molasses Cookies
Cranberry-Pumpkin Cookies
Everything Cookies

Savory Snacks

Perfect Popcorn

Popcorn is a healthy, inexpensive snack when you make it from scratch. This recipe will fill a two-quart pot to the top. Try one of the variations to add protein.

1/4 cup oil
1/2 cup corn for popping

Pour oil into heavy-bottomed 2-quart pot. Pour corn into oil and tilt pan until it is evenly distributed in one layer. Cover pot and place over high heat. After a minute or two, corn will begin to pop furiously. As soon as popping slows, remove pot from heat. Pour popcorn into serving bowls. Sprinkle popcorn with sea salt and melted butter if desired.

Makes 2 quarts

Note: If you follow this recipe exactly, you should end up with almost no unpopped kernels and a pot full of fluffy popcorn. Do not open the cover during the popping process and there is no need to shake pot. Also, popcorn should be fairly fresh and should not be cold. If popcorn was refrigerated, set it out at room temperature for at least one hour before popping.

> A hot-air popper is also a great way to cook popcorn. Kids will enjoy seeing the corn come out as it pops and older kids can do it themselves.

Variations

Cheesy Popcorn: Sprinkle hot popcorn with grated Parmesan or other cheese and toss to evenly distribute.

Nutritional Yeast Popcorn: Sprinkle or spray hot popcorn with olive oil (optional) and nutritional yeast flakes and toss to evenly distribute.

APPROXIMATE NUTRITIONAL INFORMATION FOR 2 CUPS: Calories: 110 cal; Protein: 2 g; Carbohydrates: 13 g; Fat: 6 g; Fiber: 2 g; Sodium: 194 mg.

Popcorn Snack Mix

4 cups popped corn
1 cup raisins
1/2 cup toasted almonds or peanuts
1 teaspoon ground cinnamon
Sea salt to taste

Mix popcorn with raisins and nuts. Sprinkle with cinnamon and sea salt.

Makes 5 1/2 cups

APPROXIMATE NUTRITIONAL INFORMATION FOR 1 CUP: Calories: 194 cal; Protein: 4 g; Carbohydrates: 28 g; Fat: 9 g; Fiber: 3 g; Sodium: 174 mg.

KEY NUTRIENTS: Riboflavin: .17 mg; Vitamin B6: .12 mg; Vitamin E: 3.57 mg; Iron: 1.25 mg; Magnesium: 53.37 mg; Zinc: .73 mg.

Sabzi

This delicious snack was introduced to me by my friend Christine Crosby. She serves this at every gathering and it is always a hit. Sabzi is a bit dry so I make sure to have a tall glass of Iced Herbal Tea (page 356) or Lemonade (357) to drink with it. If you like, you can add a little Tangy Tahini Sauce (in the Falafel recipe on page 234).

Whole grain lavash or flatbread, cut into quarters
Fresh mint leaves
Fresh herbs (parsley, cilantro, basil, dill, tarragon, chives, etc.)
Crumbled feta cheese

Set out a plate of lavash quarters. Mix the mint and herbs together and place in another dish. Set out the feta cheese. Assemble sabzi as follows: Take a quarter slice of lavash bread and place a handful of mint and herbs on it. Sprinkle on some feta cheese, fold together, and eat.

Deviled Eggs

Keep a batch in your refrigerator for a handy high-protein snack. I replaced some of the mayonnaise with yogurt to provide extra protein and calcium but you can use mayonnaise if you prefer.

8 hard-boiled eggs
1/4 cup plain yogurt
1 tablespoon mayonnaise (regular or vegan)
1 teaspoon Dijon mustard
1 teaspoon nutritional yeast
1/8 teaspoon ground turmeric
1/4 teaspoon ground cumin
1/8 teaspoon sea salt or to taste
Black pepper to taste
2 tablespoons minced fresh parsley

Peel eggs and cut in half lengthwise. Scoop out yolks and place in bowl with remaining ingredients. Mash and mix until smooth. Arrange eggs on plate with cut side up. Place a dollop of yolk mixture in each half. Sprinkle with additional parsley or paprika if desired. Keep eggs covered in the refrigerator up to 5 days.

Makes 8 servings

APPROXIMATE NUTRITIONAL INFORMATION FOR 1 SERVING: Calories: 97 cal; Protein: 7 g; Carbohydrates: 1 g; Fat: 7 g; Fiber: 0 g; Sodium: 118 mg.

KEY NUTRIENTS: Vitamin A: 91.07 mcg; Thiamine: .3 mg; Riboflavin: .53 mg; Niacin: 1.59 mg; Pantothenic Acid: .73 mg; Vitamin B6: .33 mg; Vitamin B12: .8 mcg.

Garbanzo Crunchies

Even nonbean-lovers will like this nutritious snack. These are best eaten the day they are made.

2 cups cooked garbanzo beans, well drained
1 tablespoon olive oil
Sea salt to taste
Paprika or chili powder to taste

Preheat oven to 350°F. Toss garbanzo beans with olive oil. Spread on a baking sheet. Sprinkle sea salt and spice over beans. Bake 30 minutes or until golden. Eat warm or at room temperature.

Makes 2 cups

APPROXIMATE NUTRITIONAL INFORMATION FOR 1/2 CUP: Calories: 164 cal; Protein: 7 g; Carbohydrates: 22 g; Fat: 6 g; Fiber: 6 g; Sodium: 144 mg.

KEY NUTRIENTS: Thiamine: .1 mg; Vitamin B6: .11 mg; Folate: 141.04 mcg; Iron: 2.37 mg; Magnesium: 39.36 mg; Zinc: 1.25 mg.

Trail Mix

Keep a bag of trail mix in your purse or car so you will always have a snack available when you're out.

Choose any or all of the following:

Almonds	Pecans
Cashews	Prunes
Dried apricots	Pumpkin seeds
Dried cherries	Raisins
Dried cranberries	Sunflower seeds
Dried figs	Unsweetened carob chips
Dried mango, chopped	Unsweetened shredded coconut
Dried papaya, chopped	Walnuts

Mix together and keep in covered container. To keep longer than one week, store in refrigerator.

Spicy Trail Mix

This is a high-protein, mineral-rich snack. Soaking and roasting the nuts and seeds makes them more digestible. Although it takes a day to make this, there is almost no work involved and you don't have to be around to monitor it, either.

1 cup raw pumpkin seeds
3/4 cup raw sunflower seeds
1 heaping cup raw almonds
1 heaping cup raw walnuts or pecans
1 tablespoon sea salt
Chili powder or paprika

Place seeds, nuts, and salt in medium-size bowl. Stir to distribute salt. Fill bowl with water to about an inch above nut mixture. Let sit 7 hours to 12 hours. Rinse and drain well. Preheat oven to 150°F. Spread nuts and seeds in an even layer on baking sheet. Sprinkle chili powder or paprika evenly over mixture. Roast 8 to 12 hours. Keep in covered jar.

Makes 4 cups

Variation: Add 2 cups dried fruit to cooked mixture.

APPROXIMATE NUTRITIONAL INFORMATION FOR 1/4 CUP: Calories: 188 cal; Protein: 7 g; Carbohydrates: 6 g; Fat: 17 g; Fiber: 3 g; Sodium: 36 mg.

KEY NUTRIENTS: Thiamine: .22 mg; Riboflavin: .14 mg; Pantothenic Acid: .56 mg; Vitamin B6: .12 mg; Folate: 30.07 mcg; Vitamin E: 6.29 mg; Iron: 2.38 mg; Magnesium: 108.43 mg; Zinc: 1.54 mg.

Nori Rice Balls

Nori is extremely rich in vitamins and minerals. Make a batch and keep in the refrigerator for a quick snack. They are easy to take along for a picnic or lunch on the go.

1 3/4 cups brown rice
3 1/2 cups water
1 package nori (10 sheets)
1/4 cup sesame seeds, toasted
1/4 cup flaxseeds, toasted
3 tablespoons soy sauce
1 tablespoon rice vinegar
1/4 teaspoon ground ginger

Place rice and water in pot. Cover and bring to boil. Reduce heat to low and simmer 40 minutes, or until water is absorbed. Combine sesame and flaxseeds in small bowl.

Set up work station. You will need a gas burner flame or candle to toast nori sheets as you go, or you can separate nori sheets and place them on a baking sheet in 250°oven for 2 to 3 minutes, until lightly toasted. Get a board or use a clean countertop with enough space for one sheet of nori. Also set up a bowl of water for wetting hands and nori. Place rice and toasted seeds within reach.

If you haven't pretoasted the nori, wave a sheet over a candle or gas burner flame until it becomes uniformly light green. Place approximately 1/3 cup hot rice in center of toasted nori sheet. Sprinkle 1 tablespoon seed mixture over rice. Moisten edges of nori. With moist hands, fold nori around rice to form a ball. Press and smooth with moist hands. Repeat for each sheet of nori.

Stir together soy sauce, vinegar, and ginger. Use as dipping sauce for rice balls if desired

Makes 10 rice balls

Note: Pre-toasted nori is available at some natural foods stores.

APPROXIMATE NUTRITIONAL INFORMATION FOR 1 RICE BALL: Calories: 176 cal; Protein: 5 g; Carbohydrates: 28 g; Fat: 4 g; Fiber: 4 g; Sodium: 261 mg.

KEY NUTRIENTS: Thiamine: .16 mg; Riboflavin: .12 mg; Niacin: 1.86 mg; Pantothenic Acid: .54 mg; Vitamin B6: .23 mg; Iron: 1.24 mg; Magnesium: 80.96 mg; Zinc: 1.09 mg.

Quick Snack Ideas

- Whole grain toast with tahini or cream cheese and banana slices
- Toasted English muffins with cottage cheese and fresh fruit slices
- Whole grain bagel with almond butter, mashed avocado, or cream cheese
- Crackers with nut/seed butter or cheese
- Hard-boiled egg with crackers or bread
- Cottage cheese (dairy or nondairy) with fresh fruit or vegetables
- Cottage cheese (dairy or nondairy) and applesauce
- Fresh fruit or raw vegetables and cheese
- Fresh fruit and nuts or seeds
- Raw vegetables with nut/seed butter or cream cheese
- Hummus (page 264) with raw vegetables, pita triangles, or crackers
- Easy Bean Dip (page 265) with raw vegetables, pita triangles, or crackers
- Creamy Watercress Dip (page 266) with raw vegetables, pita triangles, or crackers
- Yogurt with Millet Crunch Granola (page 62)
- Müesli (page 58)
- Cold or hot cereal with fruit and nuts/seeds
- Leftovers from breakfast or dinner
- Leftover salad
- Leftover soup or stew
- Smoothies (pages 362–373)
- Half sandwich
- Apple or pear slices with nut or seed butter for dipping
- Oranges or strawberries with yogurt for dipping
- Fruit salad topped with yogurt, cottage cheese, nuts, or seeds
- Bread chunks dipped in olive or flaxseed oil

Quick Breads, Muffins, Doughnuts, and Scones

Barley Soda Bread

This bread is delicious plain but I especially like it with butter, cream cheese, or nut/seed butter.

3/4 cup rolled oats or rolled barley
1 cup regular or golden raisins
1 1/2 cups plain yogurt (dairy or nondairy)
1/4 cup water or milk
1/4 cup blackstrap molasses
2 tablespoons oil
1 tablespoon maple syrup, brown rice syrup, agave nectar, or honey (optional)
3 1/4 cups barley or other whole grain flour
1/2 cup chopped walnuts (optional)
1 teaspoon sea salt
1 teaspoon baking soda
1 teaspoon baking powder

Preheat oven to 400°F. Oil a large baking sheet. In medium-size bowl, mix together oats, raisins, yogurt, water or milk, molasses, oil, and optional sweetener. In separate large bowl, whisk together flour, nuts, sea salt, baking soda, and baking powder. Add oat mixture to flour mixture. Stir until dough holds together.

Turn out onto a floured board and knead gently for 45 to 60 seconds. Divide dough in half. Shape each half into an oval ball. Place on prepared baking sheet, leaving plenty of room between loaves. Use a sharp knife to make 2 slashes on each loaf about 1/2 inch deep.

Bake for 15 minutes. Reduce heat to 375°F and bake 20 to 25 minutes more, or until loaves are golden. The bottom should sound hollow when tapped. Cool completely on wire rack before slicing.

Makes 2 loaves

APPROXIMATE NUTRITIONAL INFORMATION FOR 1/8 LOAF: Calories: 121 cal; Protein: 3 g; Carbohydrates: 18 g; Fat: 5 g; Fiber: 1 g; Sodium: 249 mg.

KEY NUTRIENTS: Iron: 1.39 mg; Magnesium: 28.11 mg.

Apricot-Nut Bread

This moist, delicious bread supplies vitamin A and iron.

1 cup chopped dried apricots
1 1/2 cups boiling water
1/4 cup maple syrup, brown rice syrup, agave nectar, or honey
1/4 cup oil
1 cup apricot soak water
1/4 cup orange juice
1 teaspoon vanilla extract
1 cup whole wheat pastry flour
1 cup whole wheat flour
1 tablespoon baking powder
1/2 teaspoon baking soda
1/2 teaspoon sea salt
1/2 cup wheat germ
1 cup walnuts, chopped

Place apricots in heatproof bowl. Pour boiling water over apricots and let sit about 15 minutes. Drain apricots, reserving 1 cup of the soak water.

Preheat oven to 350°F. Oil a loaf pan. Beat together sweetener, oil, apricot soak water, orange juice, and vanilla. In separate bowl, sift together flours, baking powder, baking soda, and sea salt. Stir in wheat germ. Stir in liquid ingredients until just mixed. Gently fold in apricots and nuts. Pour into prepared loaf pan. Bake 45 to 55 minutes, or until tester inserted in center of loaf comes out dry. Remove from pan and cool completely on wire rack. For added flavor and moistness, wrap loaf and let sit overnight.

Makes 1 loaf

Variation

Apricot-Nut Muffins: Prepare batter as directed. Pour into oiled muffin tins. Bake about 20 minutes or until tester inserted in center comes out dry.

APPROXIMATE NUTRITIONAL INFORMATION FOR 1/2-INCH SLICE: Calories: 178 cal; Protein: 4 g; Carbohydrates: 23 g; Fat: 10 g; Fiber: 4 g; Sodium: 165 mg.

KEY NUTRIENTS: Vitamin A: 74.61 mcg; Thiamine: .14 mg; Niacin: 1.2 mg; Vitamin E: 1.97 mg; Iron: 1.54 mg; Magnesium: 37.43 mg.

Banana-Molasses Muffins

Yogurt, molasses, and almonds add vitamins and minerals to these moist, flavorful muffins. They're really good spread with Yogurt Cheese (page 273).

1 cup rolled oats
1/4 cup almonds
1 cup whole wheat, spelt, or barley flour
1/2 teaspoon baking soda
1/2 teaspoon baking powder
1/2 teaspoon ground cinnamon
1/4 cup raisins
1 cup mashed ripe bananas (2 to 3 bananas)
1 egg
1/3 cup oil
3 tablespoons blackstrap molasses
1/4 cup plain yogurt (dairy or nondairy)

Preheat oven to 375°F. Lightly oil muffin tins. In food processor or blender, grind oats and nuts to a coarse meal. Transfer to mixing bowl and whisk in flour, baking soda, baking powder, and cinnamon. Stir in raisins. Beat remaining ingredients together until smooth. Add to oat mixture and stir just until mixed. Pour batter into prepared tins. Bake 20 minutes, or until tops are firm to the touch.

Makes 1 dozen

Note: For quick preparation, puree liquid ingredients in food processor or blender after removing oat/nut mixture.

APPROXIMATE NUTRITIONAL INFORMATION FOR 1 MUFFIN: Calories: 178 cal; Protein: 4 g; Carbohydrates: 23 g; Fat: 9 g; Fiber: 3 g; Sodium: 76 mg.

KEY NUTRIENTS: Thiamine: .12 mg; Riboflavin: .11 mg; Vitamin B6: .2 mg; Vitamin D: .22 mcg; Vitamin E: 1.06 mg; Iron: 1.86 mg; Magnesium: 50.14 mg; Zinc: .76 mg.

Cranberry-Orange Muffins

These tangy, eggless muffins are made with flaxseeds to supply omega-3 essential fatty acids that are important for your baby's brain and nervous system development.

1 cup orange juice
1 tablespoon grated orange peel
3 tablespoons honey, brown rice syrup, agave nectar, or maple syrup
1 cup dried cranberries
1/4 cup oil
1 1/2 cups whole wheat pastry flour
1/2 cup whole wheat flour
2 teaspoons baking powder
1/2 teaspoon baking soda
1/4 teaspoon sea salt
3 tablespoons flaxseeds, ground

Preheat oven to 375°F. Oil muffin tins. Place juice, grated orange peel, sweetener, and cranberries in small saucepan over medium-low heat. Heat until steam begins to rise. Remove from heat. Stir in oil.

In separate bowl, sift flours, baking powder, baking soda, and sea salt together. Stir in ground flaxseeds. Mix cranberry mixture into flour mixture. Stir just until combined. Pour batter into prepared muffin tins. Bake 18 to 20 minutes, or until tester inserted in center comes out dry.

Makes 1 dozen

Note: Use a coffee grinder, seed grinder, or blender to grind the flaxseeds.

APPROXIMATE NUTRITIONAL INFORMATION FOR 1 MUFFIN: Calories: 166 cal; Protein: 3 g; Carbohydrates: 28 g; Fat: 8 g; Fiber: 3 g; Sodium: 149 mg.

KEY NUTRIENTS: Vitamin C: 11.08 mg.

Carrot-Bran Muffins

These easy muffins are full of fiber and vitamin A. When you have time, make a batch (or two) and store them in your freezer. They thaw quickly when you need a snack. They can be made gluten-free, too.

2 tablespoons oil
3 tablespoons blackstrap molasses, or 2 tablespoons maple syrup, honey, or agave nectar
1 egg or egg replacer
1 cup plain yogurt (dairy or nondairy)
1/4 cup unsweetened applesauce
1 cup brown rice, barley, or whole wheat flour
1 teaspoon baking soda
1/4 teaspoon sea salt
1/2 teaspoon ground cinnamon
1/4 teaspoon ground nutmeg
1 cup wheat, oat, or rice bran
2 carrots, shredded
1/2 cup sunflower seeds or chopped nuts
1/2 cup raisins, optional

Preheat oven to 350°F. Oil muffin tins. Beat together oil, sweetener, egg, yogurt, and applesauce until smooth. In separate bowl, sift flour, baking soda, salt, and spices. Stir in bran. Add liquid ingredients along with carrots, seeds or nuts, and raisins to flour mixture. Stir gently until combined. Fill prepared muffin tins. Bake 25 minutes, or until tester inserted in center comes out dry.

Makes 1 dozen

APPROXIMATE NUTRITIONAL INFORMATION FOR 1 MUFFIN: Calories: 168 cal; Protein: 5 g; Carbohydrates: 25 g; Fat: 7 g; Fiber: 4 g; Sodium: 174 mg.

KEY NUTRIENTS: Vitamin A: 300.58 mcg; Thiamine: .25 mg; Riboflavin: .12 mg; Niacin: 1.99 mg; Pantothenic Acid: .92 mg; Vitamin B6: .28 mg; Vitamin D: .22 mcg; Vitamin E: 3.37 mg; Iron: 2.31 mg; Magnesium: 82.81 mg; Zinc: 1.23 mg.

Leftover Oatmeal-Raisin Muffins

I always seem to have a little oatmeal leftover from breakfast, but not quite enough to save for another meal. Hence, the creation of these muffins.

3 tablespoons oil
2 tablespoons blackstrap molasses
1 egg or egg replacer
2/3 cup milk (dairy or nondairy)
1/2 cup cooked oatmeal
1/2 cup raisins
1 cup whole wheat, brown rice, or barley flour
1 1/2 teaspoons baking powder
Pinch sea salt
1/2 teaspoon ground cinnamon

Preheat oven to 375°F. Oil muffin tins. Beat together oil, molasses, egg, and milk until completely combined. Stir in oatmeal and raisins. In separate bowl, sift flour, baking powder, salt, and cinnamon together. Add liquid ingredients to flour mixture. Stir gently until combined. Fill prepared muffin tins about 3/4 of the way full. Bake 15 to 20 minutes, or until knife inserted in center comes out dry. Cool muffins 5 minutes before removing from tin. Serve warm or at room temperature.

Makes 8 muffins

Variation

Leftover Oatmeal Surprise Muffins: Omit raisins and prepare batter as directed. Fill muffin tins half full with batter. Place 1 teaspoon jam in the center of each muffin. Top with remaining batter to full tins a little over 3/4 full. Bake as directed.

APPROXIMATE NUTRITIONAL INFORMATION FOR 1 MUFFIN: Calories: 167 cal; Protein: 4 g; Carbohydrates: 24 g; Fat: 7 g; Fiber: 2 g; Sodium: 94 mg.

KEY NUTRIENTS: Thiamine: .11 mg; Riboflavin: .11 mg; Niacin: 1.12 mg; Vitamin B6: .13 mg; Vitamin D: .33 mcg; Iron: 1.85 mg; Magnesium: 41.22 mg; Zinc: .73 mg.

Baked Carob Crullers

I craved doughnuts when I was pregnant even though I hadn't eaten one in years. Your kids will enjoy helping you make (and eat) these.

3/4 cup milk (dairy or nondairy)
1/4 cup honey, brown rice syrup, or agave nectar
1 package (2 teaspoons) dry active yeast
1 egg or egg replacer equivalent
1/4 cup oil
2 1/4 cups whole wheat pastry flour, divided
2 tablespoons carob powder
1/2 teaspoon ground nutmeg
1/2 teaspoon ground cinnamon
2 tablespoons melted butter or corn oil
Ground cinnamon or shredded coconut for topping

In saucepan over low heat, warm milk and sweetener together until sweetener is dissolved. Cool milk until you can comfortably immerse your finger in it. Pour into mixing bowl and stir in yeast. Beat in egg and oil. On low speed, beat in 1 cup of flour, along with carob powder, nutmeg, and cinnamon. Beat on low speed until combined, then beat on medium speed for 2 minutes. Scrape sides of bowl occasionally. Add remaining flour and stir until smooth. Use your hands when dough gets too stiff to stir. Form dough into a ball and place in a bowl. Cover with a damp towel and let dough rise in a warm place until doubled in size (about 50 minutes).

Preheat oven to 400°F. Oil a large cookie sheet. Place dough on floured board. Coat rolling pin with flour and roll out dough to a 12 x 7-inch rectangle, about 1/2 inch thick. Use a sharp knife to cut the dough into 12 (1-inch wide) strips. Twist each strip to a cruller shape. Place on prepared baking sheet. Bake for 10 minutes, or until firm. Immediately brush with melted butter or oil. Sprinkle with cinnamon or shredded coconut.

Makes 1 dozen

APPROXIMATE NUTRITIONAL INFORMATION FOR 1 DOUGHNUT: Calories: 153 cal; Protein: 4 g; Carbohydrates: 20 g; Fat: 10 g; Fiber: 2 g; Sodium: 33 mg.

KEY NUTRIENTS: Vitamin D: .35 mcg.

Oat-Nut Scones

These vegan treats take just seconds to whip up. For breakfast or tea, try them with fruit-sweetened jam. They're also delicious with soup or salad.

2 1/2 cups rolled oats
1 cup whole wheat flour
1 teaspoon baking powder
1/2 teaspoon ground cinnamon
1/4 teaspoon ground cardamom
1/4 teaspoon powdered ginger
1/4 teaspoon sea salt
1/2 cup chopped walnuts or almonds
1/4 cup oil
3/4 cup apple juice

Preheat oven to 325°F. Flour a medium-size baking sheet. In large mixing bowl, stir together oats, flour, baking powder, cinnamon, cardamom, ginger, sea salt, and nuts. Add oil and juice. Mix until combined. Form dough into a ball and place on floured baking sheet. Press into a circle about 1/2-inch thick. Cut dough into 8 wedges but don't separate them. Bake 35 minutes. These are best eaten warm.

Makes 8

Note: These freeze well. To reheat, thaw slightly. Wrap scones in foil and warm in 350°F about 15 minutes, or until heated through.

APPROXIMATE NUTRITIONAL INFORMATION FOR 1 SCONE: Calories: 268 cal; Protein: 7 g; Carbohydrates: 32 g; Fat: 14 g; Fiber: 5 g; Sodium: 110 mg.

KEY NUTRIENTS: Thiamine: .28 mg; Niacin: 1.3 mg; Pantothenic Acid: .51 mg; Vitamin B6: .12 mg; Iron: 1.86 mg; Magnesium: 70.01 mg; Zinc: 1.45 mg.

Pumpkin Scones

My friend Karen Toll is known for her delicious pumpkin scones. I slightly altered her recipe to eliminate the refined sugar and flour. These moist, flavorful scones have very little fat so go ahead and slather on some butter, almond butter, or cream cheese.

1 tablespoon oil or softened unsalted butter
2 tablespoons maple syrup, brown rice syrup, agave nectar, or honey
1 egg
1 cup mashed cooked pumpkin (canned is fine)
1 cup whole wheat or barley flour
1 cup whole wheat pastry flour
1 tablespoon baking powder
1/4 teaspoon sea salt
3/4 teaspoon pumpkin pie spice

Preheat oven to 425°F. Lightly oil a small baking sheet. Beat oil or butter, sweetener, and egg together until smooth. Beat in pumpkin until smooth. In separate bowl, whisk together remaining ingredients. Add flour mixture to pumpkin mixture and stir just until combined. Turn dough onto floured board and knead lightly until dough holds together. Form dough into a ball. Place in center of prepared baking sheet and flatten to a circle about 1 inch high. Cut dough into 8 wedges but don't separate them. Bake 15 to 20 minutes. To test for doneness, insert toothpick in a scone to see if it comes out dry. Transfer to rack to cool.

Makes 8

Note: If you don't have pumpkin pie spice, use 1/2 teaspoon ground cinnamon, 1/4 teaspoon ground nutmeg, and 1/4 teaspoon ground cardamom.

APPROXIMATE NUTRITIONAL INFORMATION FOR 1 SCONE: Calories: 147 cal; Protein: 5 g; Carbohydrates: 27 g; Fat: 3 g; Fiber: 4 g; Sodium: 188 mg.

KEY NUTRIENTS: Thiamine: .15 mg; Riboflavin: .12 mg; Niacin: 2.04 mg; Pantothenic Acid: .44 mg; Vitamin B6: .12 mg; Vitamin D: .33 mcg; Iron: 1.52 mg; Magnesium: 44.78 mg; Zinc: 1.02 mg.

Crackers, Bars, and Cookies

Raw Seed Wafers

A friend of mine during her first trimester of pregnancy asked me why no one sold a cracker that contained all the nutrients she needed since crackers were the only thing she could keep down. Here is that cracker! It provides protein, essential fatty acids, vitamins, and minerals. These are actually dehydrated rather than baked to keep from destroying enzymes and nutrients. Feel free to substitute any grain, bean, nut, or seed you have on hand.

1/3 cup lentils
1/3 cup whole buckwheat groats
1/3 cup sunflower or pumpkin seeds
1/4 cup sesame seeds
1/4 cup flaxseeds

Place lentils, buckwheat, and seeds in a quart-size jar or bowl. Fill bowl with water (about 3 1/2 cups) and let soak overnight.

Preheat oven to 250°F. Line a large baking sheet with parchment paper. Drain seeds. Place soaked seeds in blender with just enough water to allow mixture to puree. Blend until smooth. Spread mixture on prepared baking sheet about 1/4 inch thick. Bake for an hour or two. When mixture is stiff enough, remove the wafer with parchment paper from baking sheet and place it directly on oven rack. Bake until crispy (about 4 to 7 more hours). Break into pieces. Eat plain, or with butter, nut or seed butter, or cream cheese.

Makes about 2 1/2 dozen

APPROXIMATE NUTRITIONAL INFORMATION FOR 3 CRACKERS: Calories: 110 cal; Protein: 5 g; Carbohydrates: 10 g; Fat: 6 g; Fiber: 5 g; Sodium: 4 mg.

KEY NUTRIENTS: Thiamine: .18 mg; Niacin: 1.01 mg; Pantothenic Acid: .6 mg; Vitamin B6: .12 mg; Folate: 54.68 mcg; Vitamin E: 2.77 mg; Iron: 1.56 mg; Magnesium: 63.97 mg; Zinc: 1.16 mg.

Brown Rice Crackers

These flaky, delicious crackers are vegan and gluten-free.

1 1/2 cups brown rice flour
2/3 cup cooked brown rice
1 tablespoon flaxseeds (optional)
1/4 teaspoon sea salt
1/4 cup oil
1/3 to 1/2 cup water

Preheat oven to 375°F. Lightly oil a large baking sheet. In bowl or food processor, mix flour, rice, flaxseeds, salt, and oil until combined. Add water a little at a time until dough holds together. Turn out onto floured surface and knead a few times to form a ball. Press or roll dough onto prepared baking sheet to 1/8-inch thickness. With a sharp knife, score dough into 1 1/2-inch squares. Bake 20 to 25 minutes, or until bottoms are golden brown. Cool before removing from pan.

Makes about 3 dozen

APPROXIMATE NUTRITIONAL INFORMATION FOR 3 CRACKERS: Calories: 112 cal; Protein: 2 g; Carbohydrates: 14 g; Fat: 5 g; Fiber: 1 g; Sodium: 47 mg.

Rye-Corn Crackers

These zingy wheat-free crackers are great with soup or salads.

1/2 cup rye flour
1/2 cup corn flour
1/4 teaspoon sea salt
1/3 teaspoon chili powder
1/3 teaspoon ground cumin
1/2 teaspoon baking soda
3 tablespoons cold unsalted butter or coconut oil
4 to 5 tablespoons cold water

Preheat oven to 350°F. Lightly oil a large baking sheet. In bowl or food processor, mix flours, sea salt, chili powder, cumin, and baking soda. Cut in butter or coconut oil until mixture resembles coarse meal. Add water a little at a time until dough holds together. Turn out onto floured surface and knead a few times to form a ball. Press or roll dough onto prepared baking sheet to about 1/8-inch thickness. With a sharp knife, score dough into 1 1/2 x 2-inch rectangles. Bake 10 to 15 minutes, or until edges are golden brown. Cool before removing from pan. They will get crisper as they cool.

Makes about 2 dozen

APPROXIMATE NUTRITIONAL INFORMATION FOR 3 CRACKERS: Calories: 87 cal; Protein: 1 g; Carbohydrates: 11 g; Fat: 5 g; Fiber: 2 g; Sodium: 149 mg.

Cinnamon Graham Crackers

1/4 cup softened unsalted butter or coconut oil
1/4 cup maple syrup, brown rice syrup, agave nectar, or honey
1 egg or egg replacer
2 cups whole wheat pastry flour
1/2 teaspoon baking soda
1 teaspoon ground cinnamon
1/4 teaspoon sea salt

Preheat oven to 350°F. Lightly oil a 9 x 13-inch baking sheet. Beat butter or oil and sweetener together until light and fluffy. Add egg and beat until smooth. In separate bowl, whisk flour, baking soda, cinnamon, and sea salt together. Use low speed on mixer to beat flour mixture into liquid mixture. The dough will be crumbly but should hold together when pressed in your hand. If it's too dry, add a little water.

Press dough into prepared baking sheet. Score into squares a little over 2 inches. Prick each square several times with a fork. Bake for 15 minutes, or until edges are golden. Cool and break into squares.

Makes 2 dozen

APPROXIMATE NUTRITIONAL INFORMATION FOR 2 CRACKERS: Calories: 108 cal; Protein: 3 g; Carbohydrates: 15 g; Fat: 7 g; Fiber: 2 g; Sodium: 105 mg.

Gingerbread Bars

These moist, delicious treats can be made gluten-free.

1 cup pitted prunes, packed
Boiling water
2 tablespoons oil
1/2 cup blackstrap molasses
1 egg or egg replacer
3/4 cup plain yogurt (dairy or nondairy)
2 cups brown rice, barley, or whole wheat flour
1/2 teaspoon baking soda
1 1/2 teaspoons baking powder
2 teaspoons powdered ginger
1 teaspoon ground cinnamon
1/4 teaspoon ground cloves
1/4 teaspoon ground nutmeg
1/2 teaspoon sea salt
1/4 cup chopped crystallized ginger

Place prunes in heatproof bowl. Pour in just enough boiling water to cover prunes. Let sit 15 to 30 minutes.

Preheat oven to 350°F. Oil a 9 x13-inch baking pan. Grind prunes and water to paste in food processor. Mix prunes, oil, and molasses together. Beat in egg and yogurt. In separate bowl, sift flour, baking soda, baking powder, ginger, cinnamon, cloves, nutmeg, and salt together. Add flour mixture to prune mixture. Fold in crystallized ginger. Pour into prepared pan. Bake 25 minutes, or until knife inserted into center comes out dry. Cool before cutting.

Makes 2 dozen

APPROXIMATE NUTRITIONAL INFORMATION FOR 1 BAR: Calories: 85 cal; Protein: 2 g; Carbohydrates: 15 g; Fat: 2 g; Fiber: 1 g; Sodium: 98 mg.

KEY NUTRIENTS: Vitamin B6: .12 mg.

Cranberry-Date Bars

These scrumptious vegan bars are full of fiber and nutrients.

2 cups pitted dates
1/2 cup dried cranberries
Boiling water
1 cup almonds or walnuts
3 cups rolled oats
1 cup whole wheat, barley, or brown rice flour
1/2 cup flavorless oil (grapeseed, safflower, etc.)
3 tablespoons maple, brown rice syrup, or agave nectar
1/4 cup water

Place dates and cranberries in heatproof bowl. Pour over just enough boiling water to cover. Let sit 30 minutes.

Preheat oven to 350°F. Oil a 9 x 13-inch baking dish. Place nuts and oats in food processor and grind to a coarse meal. Add flour and pulse to mix. Drizzle oil, sweetener, and water over top. Mix until combined. Dough should be slightly crumbly but hold together when pressed in your hand. Add more water if too dry. Add flour if too sticky.

Press 2/3 of dough into bottom of prepared pan to form a crust about 1/4 inch thick. Transfer remaining dough to a bowl and reserve for topping. Place date/cranberry mixture with water into food processor and puree. Spread date filling over bottom crust. Sprinkle remaining dough over top and press into date filling. Bake 30 to 35 minutes until edges are golden. Cool before cutting into squares.

Makes 24 bars

APPROXIMATE NUTRITIONAL INFORMATION FOR 1 BAR: Calories: 185 cal; Protein: 4 g; Carbohydrates: 26 g; Fat: 8 g; Fiber: 4 g; Sodium: 1 mg.

KEY NUTRIENTS: Thiamine: .12 mg; Vitamin E: 1.7 mg; Iron: 1.1 mg; Magnesium: 43.47 mg; Zinc: .7 mg.

Granola Bars

These low-fat, lightly sweetened bars are cooked at a low temperature to preserve the nutrients. They are great for snacks, breakfast on the run, or in a lunch box.

3/4 cup raisins or chopped dried fruit
Boiling water
3 cups rolled oats
1/2 cup sunflower seeds
1/2 cup unsweetened coconut flakes
1 teaspoon ground cinnamon or pumpkin pie spice
1/2 cup honey, maple syrup, brown rice syrup, or agave nectar
1/3 cup peanut butter, almond butter, or tahini
1/4 cup raisin soak water

Place raisins in small heat-proof bowl or measuring cup. Add just enough boiling water to cover fruit. Preheat oven to 250°F. Oil a 9 x 13-inch baking dish. Drain raisins but reserve soak water. In large mixing bowl, combine oats, seeds, coconut, cinnamon, and fruit.

Place sweetener, nut or seed butter, and 1/4 cup raisin soak water in small saucepan. Warm over low heat, stirring until smooth. Pour over oat mixture. Mix thoroughly. Press into prepared baking dish. Bake for one hour. If crispy bars are preferred, bake an extra 15 minutes. Score into squares immediately upon removing from oven. Let cool. Bars will harden as they cool.

Makes 18

APPROXIMATE NUTRITIONAL INFORMATION FOR 1 BAR: Calories: 163 cal; Protein: 5 g; Carbohydrates: 24 g; Fat: 7 g; Fiber: 3 g; Sodium: 4 mg.

KEY NUTRIENTS: Thiamine: .2 mg; Pantothenic Acid: .46 mg; Vitamin E: 2.18 mg; Iron: 1.14 mg; Magnesium: 37.98 mg; Zinc: .67 mg.

Carob Brownies

1/2 cup melted unsalted butter or oil
4 eggs or egg replacer
1/3 cup honey, brown rice syrup, or agave nectar
2 teaspoons vanilla extract
1 cup carob powder
1/4 cup uncooked farina (or Cream of Wheat®)
1/4 cup water
1/2 cup whole wheat flour
3/4 cup ground raw almonds
1/2 cup chopped walnuts

Preheat oven to 325°F. Oil a 9-inch square baking pan. Beat together melted butter or oil, eggs, sweetener, and vanilla until smooth. Sift carob powder into bowl. Add farina and water. Mix well. Stir in flour, almonds, and walnuts until just mixed. Pour into prepared pan and bake for about 30 minutes, or just until the middle is firm to the touch. Do not overbake or they will be dry.

Makes 16

Note: If you don't have farina, you can substitute finely ground bulgar, rice, or millet. Use a coffee grinder or blender to grind the grain to powder.

APPROXIMATE NUTRITIONAL INFORMATION FOR 1 BAR: Calories: 182 cal; Protein: 4 g; Carbohydrates: 18 g; Fat: 12 g; Fiber: 4 g; Sodium: 19 mg.

KEY NUTRIENTS: Vitamin A: 77.63 mcg; Vitamin D: .65 mcg; Vitamin E: 1.77 mg; Magnesium: 30.25 mg; Zinc: .61 mg.

Pumpkin Cheesecake Bars

These are incredibly rich and creamy but not heavy like regular cheese cake.

Crust:
1 1/4 cups pecans
1 tablespoon unsalted butter or coconut oil
1 tablespoon maple syrup

Filling:
8 ounces cream cheese or Neufchâtel cheese
1/3 cup maple syrup
1 1/2 tablespoons flour (any kind)
2/3 cup cooked and mashed pumpkin (canned is fine)
1 /4 teaspoon vanilla extract
1 teaspoon pumpkin pie spice

Preheat oven to 350°F. Lightly oil an 8-inch square baking dish. Grind pecans in food processor to a coarse meal. Add butter or coconut oil and maple syrup. Pulse until dough holds together. Press into bottom and 1/4 inch up side of prepared pan. Bake 20 minutes. Cool on wire rack while you make filling. Leave oven on.

In food processor or with mixer, beat cream cheese until smooth. Add remaining ingredients and beat until smooth. Pour mixture into cooled crust. Bake 30 minutes, or until center is firm to the touch. Cool on wire rack for 30 minutes. Place in refrigerator and cool 1 hour or overnight.

Makes 16 bars

APPROXIMATE NUTRITIONAL INFORMATION FOR 1 BAR: Calories: 140 cal; Protein: 2 g; Carbohydrates: 8 g; Fat: 12 g; Fiber: 1 g; Sodium: 43 mg.

KEY NUTRIENTS: Vitamin A: 72.54 mcg.

Energy Bars

1/4 cup sesame seeds
1/4 cup sunflower seeds
1/2 cup raisins
1/2 cup dried figs
1/2 cup peanut butter, almond butter, or tahini

Place sesame seeds, sunflower seeds, raisins, and figs in food processor with metal blade. Chop until everything is ground together. Add nut or seed butter and mix until combined. Roll mixture into balls or press into 8-inch round cake pan and cut into 1-inch squares. Keep refrigerated.

Makes about 3 dozen

Note: Nuts can be substituted for seeds and other dried fruit can be substituted for raisins and figs.

Variation

Coconut Energy Bars: Add 1/2 cup unsweetened coconut to mixture. Add a little coconut milk if necessary to help balls hold together.

APPROXIMATE NUTRITIONAL INFORMATION FOR 2 BARS: Calories: 93 cal; Protein: 3 g; Carbohydrates: 9 g; Fat: 6 g; Fiber: 2 g; Sodium: 4 mg.

KEY NUTRIENTS: Vitamin E: 1.08 mg.

Carob-Nut Balls

These are great energy boosters. Keep a batch in your refrigerator and take a few along when you go out.

1/4 cup almonds
1/4 cup walnuts
1 cup raisins
4 dried figs or dates, pits removed
1/4 cup carob powder
2 teaspoons blackstrap molasses
1/2 teaspoon vanilla extract
1/8 teaspoon ground cardamom
1 teaspoon minced fresh ginger or 1/8 teaspoon powdered
Pinch sea salt
About 2 tablespoons water
Carob powder or unsweetened shredded coconut for rolling

Place almonds and walnuts in food processor with metal blade and pulse to chop. Add raisins, figs or dates, molasses, vanilla, cardamom, ginger, and sea salt. Process until everything is uniformly chopped. Add water a little at a time until mixture holds together. Roll into 1-inch balls. Roll balls in shredded coconut or carob powder if desired. Keep balls refrigerated if you are plan to keep them around more than a day or two.

Makes about 2 dozen

Note: Other nuts or seeds can be substituted for the almonds and walnuts.

APPROXIMATE NUTRITIONAL INFORMATION FOR 2 BALLS: CALORIES: 187 cal; Protein: 3 g; Carbohydrates: 36 g; Fat: 6 g; Fiber: 6 g; Sodium: 31 mg.

KEY NUTRIENTS: Vitamin E: 1.88 mg; Calcium: 90.45 mg; Iron: 1.74 mg; Magnesium: 46.74 mg.

Coconut-Almond Shortbread

These amazing wheat-free treats are so luscious, you won't believe they are good for you.

1/2 cup softened coconut oil or unsalted butter
2 tablespoons almond butter
1/4 cup honey, brown rice syrup, or agave nectar
1/3 teaspoon almond or vanilla extract
1 cup brown rice flour
1 cup rolled oats
1 cup unsweetened shredded coconut

Preheat oven to 350°F. Beat together coconut oil or butter with almond butter, sweetener, and almond or vanilla extract until smooth. Add remaining ingredients and mix until combined. You may need to use your hands to knead this dough a few times so it will hold together. Place dough on unoiled baking sheet. Press into an 8-inch disk. With sharp knife, cut dough into 12 wedges but don't separate. Prick each wedge several times with a fork. Bake 25 minutes, or until edges are golden brown. Cool before separating wedges.

Makes 1 dozen

Note: If nut allergies are a problem, tahini can be substituted for the almond butter.

APPROXIMATE NUTRITIONAL INFORMATION FOR 1 WEDGE: Calories: 209 cal; Protein: 2 g; Carbohydrates: 18 g; Fat: 15 g; Fiber: 2 g; Sodium: 4 mg.

Flourless Sesame-Almond Cookies

These delicious crispy cookies are gluten- and egg-free.

1/2 cup sesame seeds
1 cup almonds
1/2 cup softened unsalted butter or coconut oil
1/2 teaspoon sea salt
1 cup arrowroot powder
1/4 cup + 2 tablespoons evaporated cane juice
1 teaspoon almond extract
1/2 teaspoon vanilla extract
1 tablespoon grated orange rind (optional)
2 to 3 tablespoons water or orange juice

Preheat oven to 300°F. Oil 1 or 2 large cookie sheets. In food processor or blender, grind sesame seeds and almonds to powder. In mixing bowl or food processor, mix ground seeds and almonds with butter or coconut oil, sea salt, arrowroot powder, evaporated cane juice, almond extract, vanilla, and grated orange rind. Add water or juice, a little at a time, until dough holds together. Place walnut-size balls on prepared baking sheet leaving about 3 inches in between. Press balls with fork twice to form a criss-cross pattern. Bake 20 to 22 minutes, or until bottom and edges are golden.

Makes about 2 1/2 dozen

APPROXIMATE NUTRITIONAL INFORMATION FOR 2 COOKIES: Calories: 374 cal; Protein: 3 g; Carbohydrates: 16 g; Fat: 13 g; Fiber: 2 g; Sodium: 75 mg.

KEY NUTRIENTS: Vitamin E: 2.71 mg; Iron: 3.53 mg; Magnesium: 43.39 mg; Zinc: . 7 mg.

Sunflower-Sesame Molasses Cookies

These are cookies you can feel good about. This makes a big batch so store some in the freezer for later.

1 cup sunflower seeds, toasted
1/2 cup sesame seeds, toasted
1 3/4 cups whole wheat flour
1 1/2 teaspoons pumpkin pie spice
1/2 teaspoon sea salt
1/2 teaspoon baking soda
1/2 cup oil
1/3 cup maple syrup, brown rice syrup, agave nectar, or honey
1/3 cup blackstrap molasses
1 egg or egg replacer
1 teaspoon vanilla extract
2 tablespoons milk or yogurt (dairy or nondairy)

Preheat oven to 350°F. Oil cookie sheet(s). Coarsely chop sunflower and sesame seeds in food processor, blender, or by hand. Place in large mixing bowl with flour, spice, salt, and baking soda and whisk together. In separate bowl, beat together oil, sweetener, molasses, egg, vanilla, and milk or yogurt. Add liquid ingredients to flour mixture. Stir until combined. Scoop by tablespoonfuls onto prepared cookie sheet. Bake 12 minutes, or until bottoms are golden. Cool on wire rack.

Makes 4 1/2 dozen

Note: If you don't have pumpkin pie spice, use 3/4 teaspoon cinnamon, 1/2 teaspoon cardamom, and 1/4 teaspoon ground nutmeg.

APPROXIMATE NUTRITIONAL INFORMATION FOR 2 COOKIES: Calories: 137 cal; Protein: 3 g; Carbohydrates: 13 g; Fat: 9 g; Fiber: 2 g; Sodium: 73 mg.

KEY NUTRIENTS: Iron: 1.91 mg; Magnesium: 36.9 mg; Zinc: .79 mg.

Cranberry-Pumpkin Cookies

These wheat-free cookies are a good source of vitamin A.

1/3 cup maple syrup, brown rice syrup, agave nectar, or honey
1/2 cup softened unsalted butter or coconut oil
1 teaspoon vanilla extract
1 egg or egg replacer
1 cup mashed cooked pumpkin (canned is fine)
1 3/4 cups barley or brown rice flour
2 teaspoons baking powder
1/2 teaspoon baking soda
1 1/2 teaspoons pumpkin pie spice
3/4 cup dried cranberries
1/2 cup chopped walnuts or pecans

Preheat oven to 375°F. Beat together sweetener and butter or coconut oil until smooth. Add vanilla, egg, and pumpkin and beat well. In separate bowl, sift together flour, baking powder, baking soda, and pumpkin pie spice. Stir flour mixture into liquid ingredients. Fold in dried cranberries and nuts. Drop by tablespoonfuls onto unoiled cookie sheets. Bake about 10 minutes, or until bottoms are golden. Cool on wire rack.

Makes about 3 dozen

Note: If you don't have pumpkin pie spice, use 3/4 teaspoon cinnamon, 1/2 teaspoon cardamom, and 1/4 teaspoon ground nutmeg.

APPROXIMATE NUTRITIONAL INFORMATION FOR 2 COOKIES: Calories: 156 cal; Protein: 3 g; Carbohydrates: 20 g; Fat: 8 g; Fiber: 2 g; Sodium: 73 mg.

KEY NUTRIENTS: Vitamin A: 67.68 mcg.

Everything Cookies

These easy cookies are bursting with different tastes, textures, and flavors.

1/2 cup softened unsalted butter or coconut oil
1/2 cup evaporated cane juice
1 egg or egg replacer
1 1/2 teaspoons vanilla extract
1 cup brown rice flour, barley flour, or whole wheat pastry flour
1 cup rolled oats (or other rolled grain)
1/2 teaspoon sea salt
3/4 teaspoon baking powder
1/3 cup raisins
1/3 cup chocolate chips or unsweetened carob chips
1/3 cup sunflower seeds or chopped walnuts

Preheat oven to 375°F. Oil cookie sheet. Beat together butter and evaporated cane juice until creamy. Beat in egg and vanilla. In separate bowl, whisk together flour, oats, sea salt, and baking powder. Mix flour mixture into liquid ingredients until combined. Stir in remaining ingredients. Drop by tablespoonfuls on prepared baking sheet leaving space between cookies for slight spreading. Bake 6 to 8 minutes, or until bottoms are golden. Let sit one minute before removing to wire rack to cool.

Makes about 2 1/2 dozen

APPROXIMATE NUTRITIONAL INFORMATION FOR 2 COOKIES: Calories: 438 cal; Protein: 3 g; Carbohydrates: 24 g; Fat: 10 g; Fiber: 2 g; Sodium: 99 mg.

KEY NUTRIENTS: Vitamin A: 64.15 mcg; Thiamine: .17 mg; Pantothenic Acid: .5 mg; Vitamin B6: .12 mg; Vitamin E: 1.9 mg; Iron: 4.04 mg; Magnesium: 32.67 mg.

DESSERTS

Here are some easy treats for those occasions when you want a nice dessert. This chapter contains scrumptious cakes, comforting crisps and pies, creamy puddings, and quick fruit desserts. There are even recipes to make your own sorbets and ice creams in a food processor. Every dish is made with healthful ingredients and no refined sugar so you really can have your cake and eat it too!

Cake, Crisps, and Pies

Applesauce Cake
Gluten-Free Bundt Cake with
  Apricot-Orange Glaze
Lemon-Lime Tofu "Cheesecake"
Strawberry-Almond Shortcake
Apricot Buckle
Apple Crisp
Basic Pie Crust
Coconut Sweet Potato Pie
Pecan Pie

Fruit, Puddings, and Frozen Treats

Ambrosia
Fresh Fig Dessert
Millet-Coconut Pudding
Squash Stewed in Coconut Milk
Tapioca Pudding
Strawberry Mousse
Mango Sorbet
Piña Colada Sorbet
Better Than Ice Cream
Better Than Frozen Yogurt

Dessert Toppings

Whipped Cream
Whipped Tofu Topping
Vanilla Yogurt Dessert Topping

Cakes, Crisps, and Pies

Applesauce Cake

This moist, spiced cake is easy to make and vegan too.

1/4 cup oil
1/2 cup maple syrup, brown rice syrup, or agave nectar
1 teaspoon vanilla extract
1 cup unsweetened applesauce
3/4 cup raisins
3/4 cup chopped walnuts
2 cups whole wheat or whole wheat pastry flour
1 teaspoon baking powder
1/2 teaspoon baking soda
1/2 teaspoon sea salt
3/4 teaspoon ground cinnamon
1/4 teaspoon ground nutmeg
1/4 teaspoon ground cloves
1/4 teaspoon powdered ginger

Preheat oven to 350°F. Oil a 10-inch round cake pan or 8- or 9-inch square baking pan. Beat oil, maple syrup, and vanilla together until smooth. Stir in applesauce, raisins, and walnuts. In separate bowl, sift remaining ingredients together. Dough will be stiff. Spread into prepared pan. Bake 30 minutes, or until cake pulls away from edges of pan and knife inserted in center comes out dry. Cool on rack. Serve cake plain or with whipped tofu topping. It's also delicious frosted.

Makes 12 servings

APPROXIMATE NUTRITIONAL INFORMATION FOR 1 SERVING: Calories: 229 cal; Protein: 4 g; Carbohydrates: 34 g; Fat: 10 g; Fiber: 4 g; Sodium: 172 mg.

KEY NUTRIENTS: Thiamine: .13 mg; Niacin: 1.53 mg; Vitamin B6: .14 mg; Iron: 1.45 mg; Magnesium: 43.05 mg; Zinc: .85 mg.

Gluten-Free Bundt Cake with Apricot-Orange Glaze

This cake is so moist and delicious, no one will guess it has no wheat or eggs in it. It is good on its own or with the glaze.

1/2 cup very soft unsalted butter or coconut oil
3/4 cup maple syrup, brown rice syrup, agave nectar, or honey
2 tablespoons flaxseeds, ground
1/4 cup water
1/4 cup orange juice
Grated peel of 1 orange
1 cup plain yogurt (dairy or nondairy)
2 teaspoons vanilla extract
2 1/2 cups brown rice flour
1 teaspoon baking powder
1/2 teaspoon baking soda
1/4 teaspoon sea salt
1 teaspoon ground cinnamon
1 teaspoon ground cardamom
1/4 teaspoon ground nutmeg

Apricot-Orange Glaze:
1/2 cup 20-Minute Apricot Jam (page 268) or prepared apricot jam or preserves
3 to 4 tablespoons orange juice

Preheat oven to 350°F. Oil a bundt pan. Beat butter or oil and sweetener together until smooth. In small bowl, mix ground flax and water. Add to butter mixture along with orange juice and peel, yogurt, and vanilla. Beat well. In separate bowl, sift remaining ingredients together. Stir liquid ingredients into flour mixture. Pour into prepared pan and bake 45 minutes, or until tester inserted in cake comes out dry. Let cool 10 minutes, then remove cake from pan.

Place glaze ingredients in saucepan. Stir together over low heat until warm and thinned out. Spoon glaze over cake if desired. Serve warm or room temperature.

Makes 12 servings

APPROXIMATE NUTRITIONAL INFORMATION FOR 1 SERVING: Calories: 286 cal; Protein: 4 g; Carbohydrates: 46 g; Fat: 10 g; Fiber: 3 g; Sodium: 142 mg.

KEY NUTRIENTS: Vitamin A: 118.54 mcg; Thiamine: .16 mg; Niacin: 2.33 mg; Pantothenic Acid: .7 mg; Vitamin B6: .28 mg; Iron: 1.44 mg; Magnesium: 50.33 mg; Zinc: 1.06 mg.

Lemon-Lime Tofu "Cheesecake"

You won't miss the cheese in this luscious dessert.

Crust:
3/4 cup rolled oats
1/4 cup almonds
1/4 cup whole wheat flour
4 tablespoons unsalted butter or coconut oil
1 teaspoon honey, brown rice syrup, or agave nectar

Filling:
2 (12-ounce) packages silken tofu
1/4 cup fresh-squeezed lemon juice (1 lemon)
1/3 cup fresh-squeezed lime juice (2 limes)
1/2 cup honey, brown rice syrup, or agave nectar
1 tablespoon arrowroot powder or cornstarch
1 teaspoon powdered ginger
2 teaspoons vanilla extract
1/4 cup oil
Pinch sea salt

Topping:
1/4 cup chopped almonds

Preheat oven to 350°F. Chop oats and almonds in food processor or blender until mixture resembles coarse crumbs. Add flour. Melt together butter or oil and sweetener. Stir into oat mixture. Press into bottom of 9-inch pie plate.

Puree filling ingredients in food processor or blender until smooth. Pour into pie crust and spread evenly. Sprinkle with chopped almonds. Bake for 30 minutes. Cool to set. Chill at least one hour.

Makes 8 servings

APPROXIMATE NUTRITIONAL INFORMATION FOR 1 SERVING: Calories: 331 cal; Protein: 10 g; Carbohydrates: 32 g; Fat: 20 g; Fiber: 3 g; Sodium: 50 mg.

KEY NUTRIENTS: Thiamine: .18 mg; Riboflavin: .13 mg; Vitamin C: 6.75 mg; Vitamin E: 2.71 mg; Iron: 1.74 mg; Magnesium: 65.03 mg; Zinc: 1.17 mg.

Strawberry-Almond Shortcake

This dessert can be made with or without dairy products. Either way, it's delicious and good for you.

4 cups sliced strawberries
1 to 2 tablespoons honey, brown rice syrup, agave nectar, or maple syrup
1/2 cup almonds
3/4 cup rolled oats
1 1/4 cups whole wheat pastry flour
2 teaspoons baking powder
1/8 teaspoon sea salt
5 tablespoons cold unsalted butter or coconut oil, cut into small pieces
1 egg or egg replacer
1/2 cup milk (dairy or nondairy)
2 tablespoons honey, brown rice syrup, agave nectar, or maple syrup
Vanilla Yogurt Dessert Topping (page 347), Whipped Cream (page 346),
   or Whipped Tofu Topping (page 347)

Toss strawberries and 1 to 2 tablespoons sweetener gently until fruit is coated. (Use more sweetener if fruit is tart, less if it is sweet.)

Preheat oven to 375°F. Oil baking sheet. Grind almonds and oats to coarse meal in food processor or blender. Mix in flour, baking powder, and salt. In mixing bowl or food processor, cut in butter until mixture resembles coarse meal.

In separate bowl, beat egg, milk, and 2 tablespoons sweetener together. Add to flour mixture. Stir gently just until mixed. Scoop out 1/4-cup balls of dough (I use an ice cream scoop) and place on prepared baking sheet. Flatten slightly to about 1 inch high. Bake 15 minutes, or until edges and bottoms are golden. Cool slightly.

Split warm biscuits in half horizontally. Place one half on plate. Cover with fruit and then a layer of topping of choice. Place other biscuit half on top. Add a little more topping and fruit.

Makes 8 servings

Variations

Strawberry-Banana-Almond Shortcake: Substitute 2 cups sliced bananas for 2 cups sliced strawberries.

Peach-Almond Shortcake: Substitute 2 cups sliced peaches for strawberries.

Peach-Blackberry-Almond Shortcake: Substitute 2 cups sliced peaches and 2 cups blackberries for strawberries.

Mixed Berry-Almond Shortcake: Substitute 4 cups mixed berries (raspberries, blackberries, blueberries, strawberries, etc.) for strawberries.

APPROXIMATE NUTRITIONAL INFORMATION FOR 1 SERVING: Calories: 304 cal; Protein: 9 g; Carbohydrates: 35 g; Fat: 18 g; Fiber: 5 g; Sodium: 153 mg.

KEY NUTRIENTS: Vitamin A: 105.75 mcg; Thiamine: .12 mg; Riboflavin: .28 mg; Pantothenic Acid: .78 mg; Vitamin B6: .1 mg; Vitamin B12: .36 mcg; Vitamin C: 47.6 mg; Vitamin D: 33 mcg; Vitamin E: 2.77 mg; Calcium: 146.28 mg; Iron: 1.71 mg; Magnesium: 54.08 mg; Zinc: 1.13 mg.

Apricot Buckle

This shortcake-type dessert is made all in one pan. It is best hot, so plan to eat it within 20 minutes of removing from oven (or reheat it before serving).

Cake layer:
1 cup whole wheat flour
1 cup whole wheat pastry flour
2 teaspoons baking powder
1/2 teaspoon baking soda
1/2 teaspoon sea salt
5 tablespoons cold unsalted butter or coconut oil, cut into small pieces
1 egg or equivalent egg replacer
1/2 cup plain yogurt (dairy or nondairy)
1/2 cup milk (dairy or nondairy)
3 tablespoons maple syrup, honey, brown rice syrup, or agave nectar

Fruit layer:
3 cups sliced apricots
1 tablespoon maple syrup, honey, brown rice syrup, or agave nectar
1/2 teaspoon ground cinnamon
2 tablespoons unsalted butter or coconut oil

Preheat oven to 425°F. Place flours, baking powder, baking soda, and salt in mixing bowl or food processor. Whisk or pulse to mix. Cut in butter or oil until mixture resembles coarse meal. In separate bowl, beat egg, yogurt, milk, and sweetener together until smooth. Add egg mixture to flour mixture and mix just until dough holds together.

Toss apricots with sweetener and cinnamon. Melt butter or oil in 9-inch cast iron skillet over medium heat, or in a 9-inch cake pan in the oven. Remove from heat and spread apricots in even layer over bottom. Spread dough over top of apricots to cover completely. Bake 20 minutes, or until cake is golden brown. Serve warm with your choice of topping (pages 346–347).

Makes 8 servings

Note: This is a wonderful dish for company. Make the dough and prepare the fruit ahead of time and keep refrigerated. Then just assemble and cook when you're ready to eat.

Variation

Peach Buckle: Substitute peaches for apricots.

APPROXIMATE NUTRITIONAL INFORMATION FOR 1 SERVING: Calories: 263 cal; Protein: 6 g; Carbohydrates: 34 g; Fat: 14 g; Fiber: 4 g; Sodium: 315 mg.

KEY NUTRIENTS: Vitamin A: 276.89 mcg; Thiamine: .1 mg; Riboflavin: .14 mg; Niacin: 1.36 mg; Pantothenic Acid: .5 mg; Vitamin B6: .1 mg; Vitamin C: 6.49 mg; Vitamin D: .33 mcg; Vitamin E: 1.03 mg; Iron: 1.63 mg; Magnesium: 30.34 mg; Zinc: .82 mg.

Apple Crisp

This quick and easy dessert is very low in sugar and contains lots of fiber.

6 cups peeled, cored, and sliced apples (6 to 8 apples)
2 tablespoons lemon juice
1 tablespoon water or apple juice
1 tablespoon maple syrup, brown rice syrup, agave nectar, or honey
1 teaspoon ground cinnamon

Topping:
1 cup rolled oats
1/2 cup wheat germ
1 cup chopped walnuts
1/2 teaspoon ground nutmeg
1/4 teaspoon ground cloves
1/4 teaspoon sea salt
4 tablespoons unsalted butter or oil
3 tablespoons maple syrup, brown rice syrup, agave nectar, or honey

Preheat oven to 350°F. Lightly oil an 8- or 9-inch square baking dish. Toss apples with lemon juice, apple juice or water, sweetener, and cinnamon. Spread in bottom of pan.

Mix oats, wheat germ, nuts, spices, and salt in food processor with metal blade or by hand. Heat butter or oil and mix with sweetener until smooth. Add to oat mixture and stir until completely combined. Cover apples with topping. Bake for 30 minutes or until golden. Serve with your choice of topping (pages 346–347).

Makes 9 servings

Variation: Use pears, peaches, plums, or a mixture of fruits instead of the apples.

APPROXIMATE NUTRITIONAL INFORMATION FOR 1 SERVING: Calories: 259 cal; Protein: 5 g; Carbohydrates: 28 g; Fat: 15 g; Fiber: 6 g; Sodium: 63 mg.

KEY NUTRIENTS: Thiamine: .26 mg; Vitamin B6: .12 mg; Folate: 36.55 mcg; Vitamin E: 3.46 mg; Iron: 1.51 mg; Magnesium: 56.16 mg; Zinc: .72 mg.

Basic Pie Crust

6 tablespoons cold unsalted butter or coconut oil
1 1/4 cup whole wheat pastry flour
3 to 4 tablespoons ice cold water

Cut butter or coconut oil into flour until mixture resembles coarse meal. Add water a little at a time until dough holds together when pressed in your hand. Keep dough chilled if not using immediately.

Makes 1 (8- or 9-inch) pie crust

Prebaked Pie Crust: Preheat oven to 350°F. Roll out crust and press into pie pan. Flute or pinch edges. With a fork, pierce the bottom of the crust several times. Bake 15 minutes for partially prebaked crust. Bake 30 minutes for completely prebaked crust, or until golden.

Note: You can also place weights in the crust to keep it from puffing. Place a piece of foil over crust and fill it with dried beans or rice. Remove about 5 to 10 minutes before end of baking time.

APPROXIMATE NUTRITIONAL INFORMATION FOR 1/8 CRUST: Calories: 140 cal; Protein: 3 g; Carbohydrates: 14 g; Fat: 9 g; Fiber: 2 g; Sodium: 2 mg.

KEY NUTRIENTS: Vitamin A: 80.3 mcg; Niacin: 1.2 mg.

Working with coconut oil

Store your coconut oil at room temperature, which keeps it fairly soft and easy to handle. Cold coconut oil is very difficult to measure accurately. When a recipe calls for cold coconut oil, measure the oil at room temperature and then place that amount in the refrigerator or freezer to harden.

Coconut Sweet Potato Pie

This simple pie is good warm but my family really loves it chilled. If you don't like coconut, see the note below.

1 (8- or 9-inch) Basic Pie Crust, partially prebaked (page 333)
3 cups mashed, cooked sweet potatoes (about 3 medium)
2 eggs, slightly beaten, or egg replacer
1/3 cup light coconut milk
3 tablespoons maple syrup, brown rice syrup, agave nectar, or honey
1 tablespoon unsweetened shredded coconut

Preheat oven to 350°F. Prepare and partially prebake pie crust. Place sweet potatoes, eggs, coconut milk, and sweetener in food processor or blender. Puree until smooth. Pour filling into prepared crust. Sprinkle with shredded coconut. Bake about 45 minutes, or until edges are golden. Cool at least 15 minutes before cutting. Serve warm or cold.

Makes 8 servings

Note: If you don't like coconut, use milk or cream (dairy or nondairy) instead of coconut milk and omit the shredded coconut.

APPROXIMATE NUTRITIONAL INFORMATION FOR 1 SERVING: Calories: 319 cal; Protein: 6 g; Carbohydrates: 49 g; Fat: 12 g; Fiber: 5 g; Sodium: 35 mg.

KEY NUTRIENTS: Vitamin A: 2201.33 mcg; Thiamine: .16 mg; Riboflavin: .28 mg; Niacin: 2 mg; Pantothenic Acid: 1.02 mg; Vitamin B6: .38 mg; Vitamin C: 21.84 mg; Vitamin D: .65 mcg; Iron: 1.77 mg; Magnesium: 40.29 mg; Zinc: 1.04 mg.

Pecan Pie

Treat yourself to this luscious dessert. It supplies protein, vitamins, minerals, and good fats. Try it with any of the toppings on pages 346–347.

1 (8- or 9-inch) Basic Pie Crust (page 333)
3/4 cup pecan halves
3 eggs
1/4 cup unsalted butter or coconut oil, melted
1/4 cup blackstrap molasses
1/2 cup maple syrup, honey, or brown rice syrup
1 teaspoon vanilla extract
Few drops brown rice vinegar
3/4 cup chopped pecans

Preheat oven to 350°F. Roll out pie crust and place in 8- or 9-inch pie pan. Place pecan halves in pie crust, rounded side up. Beat together eggs, melted butter or oil, molasses, sweetener, vanilla, and vinegar. Stir in chopped pecans. Pour filling into pie crust. Bake 30 to 40 minutes, or until center is set. Cool at least 15 minutes before serving.

Makes 8 servings

APPROXIMATE NUTRITIONAL INFORMATION FOR 1 SERVING: Calories: 444 cal; Protein: 7 g; Carbohydrates: 36 g; Fat: 32 g; Fiber: 4 g; Sodium: 33 mg.

KEY NUTRIENTS: Vitamin A: 171.3 mcg; Thiamine: .24 mg; Riboflavin: .17 mg; Niacin: 1.57 mg; Pantothenic Acid: .72 mg; Vitamin B6: .21 mg; Vitamin B12: .21 mcg; Vitamin D: .98 mcg; Vitamin E: 1.57 mg; Calcium: 137.87 mg; Iron: 3.72 mg; Magnesium: 75.89 mg; Zinc: 1.83 mg.

Fruit, Puddings, and Frozen Treats

Ambrosia

2 cups or 1 (15-ounce) can pineapple chunks
1 cup mandarin orange sections
2 bananas, peeled and sliced
1/2 cup unsweetened coconut flakes
1/2 cup pineapple or orange juice

Toss all ingredients together. Keep chilled until ready to serve. Serve plain or with one of the Dessert Toppings (pages 346–347).

Makes 4 servings

APPROXIMATE NUTRITIONAL INFORMATION FOR 1 SERVING: Calories: 224 cal; Protein: 2 g; Carbohydrates: 39 g; Fat: 8 g; Fiber: 5 g; Sodium: 12 mg.

KEY NUTRIENTS: Vitamin B6: .44 mg; Vitamin C: 35.48 mg; Iron: 1.13 mg; Magnesium: 38.42 mg.

Fresh Fig Dessert

This delicious treat can also be made without yogurt. Just use a little more orange juice.

8 fresh, ripe figs
2 oranges, peeled and sectioned
1/3 cup coarsely chopped walnuts
2 tablespoons orange juice
2 tablespoons yogurt (dairy or nondairy)

Cut figs in half lengthwise and then cut each half in half lengthwise to form wedges. Place in bowl with oranges. Sprinkle walnuts over the top. Whisk orange juice and yogurt together until smooth. Toss fruit gently with dressing until coated.

Makes 4 servings

Note: If figs are not in season, use 2 pears, apples, or bananas instead of figs.

APPROXIMATE NUTRITIONAL INFORMATION FOR 1 SERVING: Calories: 178 cal; Protein: 3 g; Carbohydrates: 29 g; Fat: 7 g; Fiber: 6 g; Sodium: 5 mg.

KEY NUTRIENTS: Thiamine: .16 mg; Riboflavin: .1 mg; Pantothenic Acid: .57 mg; Vitamin B6: .21 mg; Folate: 38.31 mcg; Vitamin C: 40.89 mg; Vitamin E: 1.35 mg; Magnesium: 41.12 mg.

Millet-Coconut Pudding

This light, creamy pudding is delicious for breakfast or a snack as well as dessert.

3/4 cup millet
3 cups water
1 (14-ounce) can light coconut milk
1/4 teaspoon sea salt
1 teaspoon vanilla extract
2 to 3 tablespoons maple syrup, brown rice syrup, agave nectar, or honey
1/4 teaspoon ground nutmeg
1/2 cup unsweetened shredded coconut
2 cups fresh berries or sliced fruit (blackberries, strawberries mangoes, peaches, bananas, etc.)

Optional toppings:
2 to 3 tablespoons shredded coconut or chopped macadamia nuts

Place millet, water, coconut milk, and salt in heavy bottomed pan. Bring to a boil over high heat. Reduce heat to the very lowest setting. Simmer uncovered one hour, or until pudding thickens. Stir occasionally to prevent scorching. Place warm or cold pudding in serving dishes. Spoon fruit on pudding. Sprinkle coconut or chopped macadamia nuts (or both) over fruit.

Makes 6 servings

Note: Other dairy or nondairy milk can be substituted for coconut milk.

APPROXIMATE NUTRITIONAL INFORMATION FOR 1 SERVING: Calories: 234 cal; Protein: 4 g; Carbohydrates: 31 g; Fat: 11 g; Fiber: 6 g; Sodium: 97 mg.

KEY NUTRIENTS: Thiamine: .12 mg; Riboflavin: .1 mg; Niacin: 1.42 mg; Pantothenic Acid: .39 mg; Vitamin B6: .15 mg; Folate: 38.27 mcg; Vitamin C: 15.5 mg; Iron: 1.4 mg; Magnesium: 45.08 mg; Zinc: .71 mg.

Squash Stewed in Coconut Milk

This sweet, warm dessert is perfect in fall or winter. Coconut milk provides calcium, iron, magnesium, and other minerals. Squash is full of beta carotein. Be sure to add the pumpkin seeds for protein.

3 cups light coconut milk
1/2 teaspoon sea salt
1/4 teaspoon ground cinnamon
2 teaspoons maple syrup, brown rice syrup, agave nectar, or honey (optional)
1 medium hubbard, kabucha, or butternut squash, cubed (7 to 8 cups)
1/2 cup toasted pumpkin seeds

Place coconut milk, salt, cinnamon, and sweetener in pan. Bring to a gentle boil over medium heat while you prepare the squash. Peel hubbard or butternut squash if using. Kabucha doesn't need to be peeled – just wash it. Cut off stem ends. Cut open squash and remove pulp and seeds. Cut squash into 1-inch cubes. Add to coconut milk mixture and return to boil. Reduce heat to low and simmer 10 minutes, or until squash is tender. Don't stir the mixture so squash cubes can retain their shape. Ladle squash and liquid into bowls and sprinkle seeds over the top.

Makes 8 servings

Note: Many markets sell fresh or frozen precut squash.

APPROXIMATE NUTRITIONAL INFORMATION FOR 1 SERVING: Calories: 149 cal; Protein: 4 g; Carbohydrates: 11 g; Fat: 10 g; Fiber: 0 g; Sodium: 147 mg.

KEY NUTRIENTS: Vitamin A: 551.38 mcg; Vitamin C: 18.14 mg; Iron: 1.73 mg; Magnesium: 65.43 mg; Zinc: .78 mg.

Tapioca Pudding

I devoured this during both of my pregnancies. It's a great protein- and calcium-rich snack.

3 cups milk (dairy or nondairy)
2/3 cup granulated tapioca
1/4 teaspoon sea salt
2 eggs
1/4 to 1/3 teaspoon liquid stevia extract or to taste
1/2 teaspoon vanilla extract

Place milk, tapioca, and sea salt in medium pan. Bring to boil over medium heat, stirring often. Reduce heat to low and simmer 2 minutes. Beat eggs, stevia, and vanilla together. Beat some tapioca mixture into beaten egg mixture a little at a time to prevent curdling. Stir egg mixture into mixture in pan. Simmer about 5 minutes, or until thickened. Remove from heat and cool 15 minutes. Pour into serving dishes. Serve warm or chilled.

Makes 6 servings

Note: To sweeten tapioca with honey, brown rice syrup, agave nectar, or maple syrup instead of stevia, add 1/4 cup sweetener with egg mixture. Add a little extra granulated tapioca.

Variation

Vegan Tapioca Pudding: Use nondairy milk and omit eggs. Add an additional tablespoon granulated tapioca.

APPROXIMATE NUTRITIONAL INFORMATION FOR 1 SERVING: Calories: 164 cal; Protein: 6 g; Carbohydrates: 21 g; Fat: 6 g; Fiber: 0 g; Sodium: 173 mg.

KEY NUTRIENTS: Vitamin A: 73.31 mcg; Riboflavin: .28 mg; Vitamin B12: .61 mcg; Vitamin D: .87 mcg; Calcium: 156.72 mg; Zinc: .67 mg.

Strawberry Mousse

2 1/4 cups apple juice, divided
1 tablespoon agar agar flakes
1 tablespoon cashew butter or tahini
1 cup sliced strawberries
1/2 cup Whipped Cream (page 346) or Whipped Tofu Cream (page 347) (optional)
4 whole strawberries for garnish

Pour 2 cups apple juice into small pan. Sprinkle agar agar flakes over top. Bring to a boil over medium heat. Cook 5 minutes, stirring occasionally. Remove from heat. Place remaining 1/4 cup apple juice, cashew butter or tahini, and strawberries in blender or food processor. Pulse to puree. Leave it a little chunky if you like. Stir puree into apple juice mixture in pan. Pour the mousse into 4 individual serving dishes. Chill at least one hour, or until firm. Top with a dollop of whipped topping if desired. Garnish with whole strawberries.

Makes 4 servings

APPROXIMATE NUTRITIONAL INFORMATION FOR 1 SERVING: Calories: 153 cal; Protein: 1 g; Carbohydrates: 21 g; Fat: 8 g; Fiber: 1 g; Sodium: 21 mg.

KEY NUTRIENTS: Vitamin A: 64.23 mcg; Vitamin C: 30.42 mg; Vitamin D: .77 mcg.

Freezing Fruit

Frozen fruit is essential for sorbets and Better Than Ice Cream, and makes smoothies cold and thick. Freezing is a great way to use up ripe fruit that might otherwise go bad. Frozen fruit keeps for months, so buy extra fruit in season and freeze it so you'll always be ready to make smoothies or sorbets.

Start the preparation and freezing process at least six hours before you are planning to use the fruit.

Apricot, Nectarine, Peach: Remove pit and slice.
Banana: Peel and slice.
Strawberries: Wash, hull, and leave whole.
Berries: Wash and leave whole.
Mango: Remove peel and pit. Cut into chunks.
Melon, Papaya: Remove peel, seeds, and pulp. Cut into chunks,
Pineapple: Remove peel and core. Cut into chunks. For canned pineapple chunks, drain and freeze.

Prepare fruit as suggested above. Lay fruit on baking sheet and place in freezer until completely frozen (1 to 2 hours). Remove fruit from pan. Store in freezer bags or containers.

Mango Sorbet

2 cups frozen, diced mango
1/4 to 1/2 cup unsweetened pineapple juice

In a food processor, pulse fruit until coarsely chopped. Add juice a little at a time through top of processor, and puree until creamy. Serve immediately, or freeze in individual-size containers for later.

Makes 4 servings

Note: This is best eaten right after it is made. If you want to save it for later, place in individual containers and leave at room temperature about 10 minutes before eating. It can also be poured into popsicle molds.

Variations

Mango Ice Cream: Substitute milk (dairy, rice, soy, almond, or coconut) for pineapple juice.
Mango Frozen Yogurt: Substitute plain or vanilla-flavored yogurt (dairy or nondairy) for pineapple juice.

APPROXIMATE NUTRITIONAL INFORMATION FOR 1 SERVING: Calories: 61 cal; Protein: 0 g; Carbohydrates: 16 g; Fat: 0 g; Fiber: 1 g; Sodium: 2 mg.

KEY NUTRIENTS: Vitamin A: 320.92 mcg; Vitamin C: 26.6 mg.

Piña Colada Sorbet

1 cup pineapple chunks (fresh or canned)
1 1/2 cups frozen diced mango or peaches
1/4 cup unsweetened shredded coconut

Place all ingredients in food processor and puree until smooth.

Makes 4 servings

Note: This is best eaten right after it is made. If you want to save it for later, place in individual containers and leave at room temperature about 10 minutes before eating.

APPROXIMATE NUTRITIONAL INFORMATION FOR 1 SERVING: Calories: 98 cal; Protein: 1 g; Carbohydrates: 17 g; Fat: 4 g; Fiber: 3 g; Sodium: 4 mg.

KEY NUTRIENTS: Vitamin A: 241.47 mcg; Vitamin C: 23.19 mg.

Better Than Ice Cream

1/2 cup nuts (almonds, walnuts, pecans, etc.) (optional)
1 cup frozen sliced bananas
1 cup diced peaches or frozen berries
1/2 teaspoon vanilla extract
1/4 to 1/2 cup milk (dairy or nondairy)

Place nuts in food processor and pulse until coarsely chopped. Add bananas and berries or peaches. Pulse until fruit is coarsely chopped. Add milk a little at a time through top of processor, and puree until creamy.

Makes 4 servings

Note: This is best eaten right after it is made. If you want to save it for later, place in individual containers and leave at room temperature about 10 minutes before eating.

Variation

Better Than Frozen Yogurt: Substitute plain or flavored yogurt (dairy or nondairy) for milk.

APPROXIMATE NUTRITIONAL INFORMATION FOR 1 SERVING: Calories: 166 cal; Protein: 5 g; Carbohydrates: 18 g; Fat: 10 g; Fiber: 4 g; Sodium: 8 mg.

KEY NUTRIENTS: Riboflavin: .22 mg; Niacin: 1.33 mg; Vitamin B6: .25 mg; Vitamin C: 6.45 mg; Vitamin E: 5.06 mg; Magnesium: 64.65 mg; Zinc: .77 mg.

Dessert Toppings

Whipped Cream

The secret to making whipped cream is to make sure all ingredients and equipment are cold. I usually put the bowl and the beaters or whisk in the freezer until I'm ready to start. It's best to make whipped cream right before you want to use it. If you must prepare it in advance, keep it refrigerated.

1 cup heavy cream
1/2 teaspoon vanilla or almond extract (optional)
2 drops liquid stevia extract (or to taste)

Pour all ingredients into a cold nonplastic bowl. Using wire whisk or beaters, whip until mixture forms soft peaks.

Makes about 2 cups

Note: If you don't have stevia, use a teaspoon or two of honey, maple syrup, brown rice syrup, agave nectar, or evaporated cane juice.

APPROXIMATE NUTRITIONAL INFORMATION FOR 2 TABLESPOONS: Calories: 52 cal; Protein: 0 g; Carbohydrates: 0 g; Fat: 6 g; Fiber: 0 g; Sodium: 6 mg.

KEY NUTRIENTS: Vitamin A: 62.62 mcg; Vitamin D: .77 mcg.

Whipped Tofu Topping

This is a delicious nondairy alternative to whipped cream. Keep blending until it is really creamy.

8 ounces silken tofu
2 tablespoons maple syrup, brown rice syrup, agave nectar, or honey
2 tablespoons oil
1 teaspoon vanilla or almond extract
1 tablespoon soy or other nondairy milk, if needed

Puree tofu, sweetener, oil, and vanilla or almond extract in blender or food processor until very smooth and creamy. Add milk if necessary for creamy texture. Chill for at least one hour before using. Mixture will firm slightly as it chills.

Makes about 1 cup

Note: A few drops of liquid stevia extract can be substituted for other sweeteners.

APPROXIMATE NUTRITIONAL INFORMATION FOR 2 TABLESPOONS: Calories: 60 cal; Protein: 1 g; Carbohydrates: 4 g; Fat: 4 g; Fiber: 0 g; Sodium: 2 mg.

Vanilla Yogurt Dessert Topping

This is a delicious, healthy alternative to whipped cream or ice cream with pies or desserts. The tanginess is a good contrast to the sweetness of the dessert and the beneficial enzymes help digestion.

2 cups plain yogurt (dairy, soy, or cashew)
1 teaspoon vanilla
1 tablespoon maple syrup, brown rice syrup, agave nectar, or honey

Place all ingredients in small bowl and mix well. Keep refrigerated until ready to serve.

Makes 2 cups.

BEVERAGES

 This section contains instructions to make basics like rice, almond, and soy milk which can be used in place of dairy milk for drinking, on cereal, or in recipes. There are suggestions for warm milk drinks to help you to relax and refreshing cold beverages to quench your thirst. Nutrient-rich smoothies make excellent snacks and can be prepared quickly. They are handy to take in the car or to drink while breastfeeding. There is also a selection of teas and tonics that can be taken to promote healthy pregnancy and lactation, and to relieve some common discomforts. Remember to drink plenty of water while pregnant and especially while lactating.

Dairy and Nondairy Milks

Brown Rice Milk
Almond Milk
Instant Soy Milk
Carob Cocoa
Spiced Warm Milk

Thirst Quenchers

Iced Herbal Tea
Lemonade
Mint Lemonade
Mixed Fruit Ade
Watermelon Blast-Off
Better Than Ginger Ale
Better Than Lemon-Lime Soda
Better Than Orange Soda

Smoothies and Shakes

Watermelon-Strawberry Cooler
Super C Smoothie
Creamsicle Smoothie
Melon Mint Cooler
Fruity Yogurt Smoothie
Meal Shake
Ginger-Peach Smoothie
Everything Smoothie
Peanut Butter-Banana Shake
Fresh Fig and Orange Smoothie
Creamy Greens Smoothie
Tomato-Watercress Blend

Teas and Tonics

Every Day Pregnancy Tea
Last Trimester Pregnancy Tea
Nursing Tea
Iron Booster Tonic
Rose Hip Tea
Morning Sickness Tea
Anti-Nausea Tea
Ginger Root Tea
Unblocker Tea
Fennel Tea
Tummy Tea
Insomnia Tea
Afterpain Tea
Apple Cider Vinegar Tonic
Chia Energy Drink
Rejuvelac

Dairy and Nondairy Milks

Brown Rice Milk

You won't believe how easy it is to make your own rice milk. It is delicious warm as well as cold.

1/2 cup brown rice
8 cups water
1/2 teaspoon sea salt
1 cup or more cold water
3 tablespoons brown rice syrup, maple syrup, agave nectar, or honey
1/2 teaspoon ground cinnamon (optional)

Place rice, 8 cups water, and salt in pan. Cover and bring to a boil over high heat. Reduce heat to low and simmer 3 hours, or until rice is very soft. (You can also do this in a slow cooker overnight.)

In a blender, puree rice mixture with remaining ingredients. (You will have to do it in two batches.) Puree each batch 2 to 3 minutes, or until rice is completely liquefied. Add more water if a thinner consistency is desired. Keep refrigerated.

Makes about 6 cups

Note: A few drops of liquid stevia can be used to sweeten the milk instead of syrup or honey.

APPROXIMATE NUTRITIONAL INFORMATION FOR 1 CUP: Calories: 78 cal; Protein: 1 g; Carbohydrates: 17 g; Fat: 0 g; Fiber: 1 g; Sodium: 191 mg.

Almond Milk

You can substitute almond milk for dairy or soy milk in most recipes. Soaking the almonds makes them more digestible.

1/2 cup raw almonds
2 cups water
Liquid stevia extract, maple syrup, brown rice syrup, agave nectar, or honey to taste
(optional)

Soak almonds in water 8 to 24 hours. Drain. Place almonds in blender and grind as finely as possible. (Wet nuts don't grind as well as dry ones but that's okay.) Add water and blend until smooth. Add sweetener if desired and blend to combine. Use as is in smoothies, cereals, or cooking. For a smooth drinking texture, pour milk through a fine strainer. Nut pulp can be added to hot or cold cereal, breads or muffins. (It also makes a great facial scrub.) Keep milk refrigerated. It will keep for about 5 days.

Makes 2 cups

Variation

Sunflower Milk: Substitute raw sunflower seeds for almonds.

APPROXIMATE NUTRITIONAL INFORMATION FOR 1 CUP: Calories: 205 cal; Protein: 8 g; Carbohydrates: 7 g; Fat: 18 g; Fiber: 4 g; Sodium: 0 mg.

KEY NUTRIENTS: Riboflavin: .29 mg; Niacin: 1.39 mg; Vitamin E: 9.29 mg; Iron: 1.53 mg; Magnesium: 97.63 mg; Zinc: 1.19 mg.

Instant Soy Milk

This has a strong taste so I prefer to use it for baking or to make creamy soups and sauces.

4 ounces tofu
3/4 cup water
Liquid stevia extract, honey, maple syrup, brown rice syrup, or agave nectar to taste
   (optional)

Place all ingredients in blender. Puree until smooth.

Makes about 1 cup

APPROXIMATE NUTRITIONAL INFORMATION FOR 1 CUP: Calories: 264 cal; Protein: 18 g; Carbohydrates: 5 g; Fat: 10 g; Fiber: 3 g; Sodium: 16 mg.

KEY NUTRIENTS: Thiamine: .18 mg; Riboflavin: .12 mg; Vitamin B6: .1 mg; Folate: 32.89 mcg; Calcium: 774.52 mg; Iron: 11.87 mg; Magnesium: 65.77 mg; Zinc: 1.78 mg.

Carob Cocoa

Carob and molasses are good sources of calcium and iron. This is an excellent drink before bed or any time you need a soothing treat. It's good cold, too.

2 cups milk (dairy or nondairy)
1/4 cup carob powder
1 teaspoon blackstrap molasses
1/8 teaspoon ground nutmeg
1 teaspoon vanilla extract

Place all ingredients in blender and puree until smooth. Pour into pan and heat to desired temperature.

Makes 2 servings

APPROXIMATE NUTRITIONAL INFORMATION FOR 1 SERVING: Calories: 198 cal; Protein: 9 g; Carbohydrates: 25 g; Fat: 9 g; Fiber: 5 g; Sodium: 126 mg.

KEY NUTRIENTS: Vitamin A: 83.09 mcg; Thiamine: .1 mg; Riboflavin: .45 mg; Pantothenic Acid: .8 mg; Vitamin B6: .17 mg; Vitamin B12: .88 mcg; Calcium: 363.83 mg; Iron: 1.08 mg; Magnesium: 45.84 mg; Zinc: 1.08 mg.

Spiced Warm Milk

Warm milk helps to induce sleep and provides calcium.

1 cup milk (dairy or nondairy)
Pinch ground cardamom, nutmeg, and/or cinnamon
Liquid stevia extract, honey, blackstrap molasses, maple syrup, brown rice syrup, or
  agave nectar to taste (optional)

Heat milk in small pan over low heat. Pour into cup and stir in spices and sweetener.

Makes 1 serving

APPROXIMATE NUTRITIONAL INFORMATION FOR 1 SERVING: Calories: 156 cal; Protein: 8 g; Carbohydrates: 11 g; Fat: 9 g; Fiber: 0 g; Sodium: 120 mg.

KEY NUTRIENTS: Vitamin A: 82.96 mcg; Riboflavin: .39 mg; Pantothenic Acid: .76 mg; Vitamin B6: .1 mg; Vitamin B12: .88 mcg; Calcium: 290.36 mg; Magnesium: 31.72 mg; Zinc: .93 mg.

Thirst Quenchers

Iced Herbal Tea

Most herbal teas (like peppermint, rose hips, or hibiscus, for example) are just as delicious cold as warm. We particularly like fruit blends such as Celestial Seasons" Berry Zinger teas.

1 to 2 herbal tea bags or 2 tablespoons loose herbal tea
1 quart boiling water

Place tea in 1-quart heatproof container. (Use a tea ball to hold loose herbal tea.) Pour boiling water over tea. Place a cover or plate on top of container and steep 15 minutes or until desired strength. Remove tea bags or ball. Cool tea until you can comfortably immerse your finger in it. Refrigerate tea until cold or serve immediately over lots of ice. Sweeten with a drop or two of liquid stevia if desired.

Makes 1 quart

APPROXIMATE NUTRITIONAL INFORMATION FOR 1 CUP: Calories: 0 cal; Protein: 0 g; Carbohydrates: 0 g; Fat: 0 g; Fiber: 0 g; Sodium: 0 mg.

Lemonade

I love lemonade but hate all that sugar. Thanks to stevia, there is a healthy way to make this delicious treat. This goes great with Sabzi (page 290).

1/2 cup fresh-squeezed lemon juice (about 4 lemons)
3 1/2 cups cold water
1/4 to 1/3 teaspoon liquid stevia

Mix all ingredients together in a large jar or pitcher. Chill. Serve over ice. Add mint leaves or orange slices for garnish if desired.

Makes 1 quart

APPROXIMATE NUTRITIONAL INFORMATION FOR 1 CUP: Calories: 8 cal; Protein: 0 g; Carbohydrates: 3 g; Fat: 0 g; Fiber: 0 g; Sodium: 0 mg.

KEY NUTRIENTS: Vitamin C: 14.03 mg.

Mint Lemonade

This drink can help relieve nausea during the first trimester.

1/4 cup fresh peppermint leaves or 1 heaping tablespoon dried
3 1/2 cups boiling water
1/2 cup fresh-squeezed lemon juice (about 4 lemons)
1/4 to 1/3 teaspoon liquid stevia

Place peppermint leaves in heatproof jar or pitcher. Pour boiling water over peppermint. Cover and steep 30 minutes. Strain out leaves. Cool tea until you can comfortably immerse your finger in it. Add remaining ingredients. Refrigerate until cold or serve immediately over lots of ice. Serve with fresh peppermint leaves or lemon slices for garnish if desired.

Makes 1 quart

APPROXIMATE NUTRITIONAL INFORMATION FOR 1 CUP: Calories: 8 cal; Protein: 0 g; Carbohydrates: 3 g; Fat: 0 g; Fiber: 0 g; Sodium: 0 mg.

KEY NUTRIENTS: Vitamin C: 14.03 mg.

Mixed Fruit Ade

1/2 cup fresh-squeezed lemon juice (about 4 lemons)
1/4 cup fresh-squeezed orange juice (about 1 orange)
1/4 cup fresh-squeezed lime juice (about 2 limes)
7 1/2 cups cold water
1/2 to 2/3 teaspoon liquid stevia

Mix all ingredients together in a large jar or pitcher. Refrigerate until cold. Serve over ice with fresh mint leaves or orange slices for garnish if desired.

Makes 2 quarts

APPROXIMATE NUTRITIONAL INFORMATION FOR 1 CUP: Calories: 9 cal; Protein: 0 g; Carbohydrates: 3 g; Fat: 0 g; Fiber: 0 g; Sodium: 0 mg.

KEY NUTRIENTS: Vitamin C: 13.14 mg.

Watermelon Blast-Off

This refreshing drink is full of enzymes and beneficial bacteria to promote a healthy digestive system. This is a great choice for those who find Rejuvelac too strong on its own.

2 cups cubed watermelon (seeds removed)
1/2 cup Rejuvelac (page 383)

Place ingredients in blender and puree until smooth.

Makes 1 serving

APPROXIMATE NUTRITIONAL INFORMATION FOR 1 SERVING: Calories: 97 cal; Protein: 2 g; Carbohydrates: 22 g; Fat: 1 g; Fiber: 2 g; Sodium: 6 mg..

KEY NUTRIENTS: Vitamin A: 112.48 mcg; Thiamine: .24 mg; Pantothenic Acid: .64 mg; Vitamin B6: .44 mg; Vitamin C: 29.18 mg; Magnesium: 33.44 mg.

Better Than Ginger Ale

This will help settle a nauseated or upset stomach. Vary the amount of ginger to suit your taste.

1 cup sparkling mineral water
1 to 3 teaspoons ginger juice (see below)
Liquid stevia to taste (optional)

Pour all ingredients in glass and stir to mix. Add ice if desired.

Makes about 1 cup

Variation: Replace 1/4 to 1/2 of the mineral water with apple juice and omit the stevia.

APPROXIMATE NUTRITIONAL INFORMATION FOR 1 CUP: Calories: 0 cal; Protein: 0 g; Carbohydrates: 0 g; Fat: 0 g; Fiber: 0 g; Sodium: 4 mg.

Ginger Juice

Shred unpeeled ginger root with a coarse grater. Gather the shredded ginger in one hand and squeeze tightly to extract liquid. Discard pulp. The fresher the ginger, the more juice it will yield but a 3-inch piece of ginger root yields about 1 tablespoon of juice.

Better Than Lemon-Lime Soda

1 cup sparkling mineral water
1 tablespoon lemon juice
1 tablespoon lime juice
Liquid stevia to taste (optional)

Pour all ingredients in glass and stir to mix. Add ice if desired.

Makes about 1 cup

APPROXIMATE NUTRITIONAL INFORMATION FOR 1 CUP: Calories: 8 cal; Protein: 0 g; Carbohydrates: 3 g; Fat: 0 g; Fiber: 0 g; Sodium: 5 mg.

KEY NUTRIENTS: Vitamin C: 11.52 mg.

Better Than Orange Soda

3/4 cup sparkling mineral water
1/4 cup orange juice
Liquid stevia to taste (optional)

Pour all ingredients in glass and stir to mix. Add ice if desired.

Makes 1 cup

Variation: Try other juices instead of orange, like grape, pineapple, apple, peach, mango, pear, etc.

APPROXIMATE NUTRITIONAL INFORMATION FOR 1 CUP: Calories: 28 cal; Protein: 0 g; Carbohydrates: 6 g; Fat: 0 g; Fiber: 0 g; Sodium: 4 mg.

KEY NUTRIENTS: Vitamin C: 31 mg.

Smoothies and Shakes

Smoothies are a delicious way to get extra servings of protein and nutrients into your diet. They are easy to make and you can drink them while you are doing other things, like folding laundry or breastfeeding. Smoothies are versatile. Use your imagination to come up with new combinations that use your favorite fruits. Frozen fruit makes cold, thick smoothies. See page 342 for instructions on freezing your own fruit.

Watermelon-Strawberry Cooler

This vivid pink smoothie makes a light and refreshing snack and provides calcium and vitamin C.

3 cups diced watermelon, seeds removed
1/2 cup plain yogurt (dairy or nondairy)
8 to 10 frozen strawberries

Place all ingredients in blender and puree until smooth.

Makes 2 servings

Note: This makes great popsicles.

APPROXIMATE NUTRITIONAL INFORMATION FOR 1 SERVING: Calories: 125 cal; Protein: 4 g; Carbohydrates: 23 g; Fat: 3 g; Fiber: 2 g; Sodium: 33 mg.

KEY NUTRIENTS: Vitamin A: 104.17 mcg; Thiamine: .21 mg; Riboflavin: .16 mg; Pantothenic Acid: .89 mg; Vitamin B6: .38 mg; Vitamin B12: .23 mcg; Vitamin C: 49.41 mg; Calcium: 99.07 mg; Magnesium: 37.23 mg.

Super C Smoothie

This smoothie contains the daily recommended dietary intake of vitamin C for nonpregnant women.

1 cup cold orange or pineapple juice
6 to 8 strawberries, fresh or frozen
1 banana, frozen
1/2 cup chopped kale, green cabbage, or watercress

Place all ingredients in blender and puree until smooth.

Makes 2 servings

Variation: Add 1/2 cup plain yogurt or 1/4 cup chopped cashews if desired for protein.

APPROXIMATE NUTRITIONAL INFORMATION FOR 1 SERVING: Calories: 133 cal; Protein: 2 g; Carbohydrates: 33 g; Fat: 1 g; Fiber: 3 g; Sodium: 13 mg.

KEY NUTRIENTS: Vitamin A: 154.88 mcg; Riboflavin: .1 mg; Vitamin B6: .41 mg; Folate: 52.55 mg; Vitamin C: 81.88 mg.

Add any of the following to your smoothie or shake for added nutrients.

- **Yogurt (dairy or nondairy):** for protein, calcium, digestive enzymes
- **Kefir:** for protein, calcium, digestive enzymes
- **Tofu:** for protein, calcium
- **Nuts/seeds:** for protein, vitamins, minerals, essential fatty acids
- **Nut/seed butters:** for protein, vitamins, minerals, essential fatty acids
- **Nutritional yeast flakes:** for protein, B vitamins
- **Spirulina, chlorella, or blue-green algae:** for protein, vitamins, minerals, chlorophyll
- **Barley or wheat grass powder:** for vitamins, minerals, chlorophyll
- **Chopped kale, cabbage, or watercress:** for vitamins A and C, calcium, iron
- **Carrots or sweet potatoes:** for vitamin A
- **Wheat germ:** for vitamin E and fiber
- **Granulated kelp:** for minerals
- **Rejuvelac (page 383):** for digestive enzymes
- **Flaxseed oil:** for omega-3 fatty acids
- **Chia Gel:** for vitamins, minerals, and essential fatty acids

Creamsicle Smoothie

This tangy, creamy drink is really refreshing.

2 oranges, peeled and cut into pieces
1/2 cup yogurt (dairy or nondairy)
1/2 cup ice cubes

Place all ingredients in blender and puree until smooth.

Makes 1 to 2 servings

Note: Silken tofu can be substituted for yogurt if desired.

APPROXIMATE NUTRITIONAL INFORMATION FOR 1 SERVING: Calories: 198 cal; Protein: 7 g; Carbohydrates: 36 g; Fat: 4 g; Fiber: 6 g; Sodium: 56 mg.

KEY NUTRIENTS: Vitamin A: 91.77 mcg; Thiamine: .26 mg; Riboflavin: .28 mg; Pantothenic Acid: 1.13 mg; Vitamin B6: .2 mg; Folate: 87.17 mcg; Vitamin B12: .45 mcg; Vitamin C: 140 mg; Calcium: 253.03 mg; Magnesium: 40.9 mg; Zinc: .91 mg.

Melon Mint Cooler

This light, refreshing smoothie can help soothe an upset or nauseated stomach.

2 cups cold, diced cantaloupe melon
2 cups cold, diced honeydew melon
1 tablespoon chopped fresh peppermint

Place all ingredients in blender and puree until smooth.

Makes 2 servings

Variation: Add 1/2 cup plain yogurt (dairy or nondairy) or silken tofu if desired.

APPROXIMATE NUTRITIONAL INFORMATION FOR 1 SERVING: Calories: 115 cal; Protein: 2 g; Carbohydrates: 29 g; Fat: 1 g; Fiber: 2 g; Sodium: 31 mg.

KEY NUTRIENTS: Vitamin A: 512.52 mcg; Thiamine: .19 mg; Niacin: 1.93 mg; Pantothenic Acid: .55 mg; Vitamin B6: .28 mg; Folate: 37.63 mcg; Vitamin C: 108.25 mg; Magnesium: 29.7 mg.

Fruity Yogurt Smoothie

This creamy, delicious shake supplies protein, calcium, fiber, and folate. I especially like it with Cashew Yogurt (page 272) and a mixture of fruits. Use frozen fruit if you want a thicker smoothie.

3/4 cup plain yogurt (dairy or nondairy)
1/2 cup apple or pineapple juice
2 cups diced fresh or frozen fruit (apricots, berries, peaches, etc.)

Place all ingredients in blender and puree until smooth.

Makes 2 servings

APPROXIMATE NUTRITIONAL INFORMATION FOR 1 SERVING: Calories: 163 cal; Protein: 5 g; Carbohydrates: 29 g; Fat: 4 g; Fiber: 4 g; Sodium: 50 mg.

KEY NUTRIENTS: Vitamin A: 458.21 mcg; Riboflavin: .2 mg; Niacin: 1.06 mg; Pantothenic Acid: .75 mg; Vitamin B6: .12 mg; Vitamin B12: .34 mcg; Vitamin C: 16.96 mg; Vitamin E: 1.55 mg; Calcium: 134.27 mg; Zinc: .97 mg.

Meal Shake

This smoothie is a powerhouse of protein, vitamins, and minerals.

2 tablespoons raw almonds or cashews
1 tablespoon raw sunflower or pumpkin seeds
1 cup milk (dairy or nondairy) or kefir
1/4 cup juice (apple, pineapple, etc.)
1 banana, fresh or frozen
1 cup fresh or frozen berries (strawberries, blueberries, etc.)
1 tablespoon wheat germ
2 teaspoons nutritional yeast flakes
1 teaspoon flaxseed oil or 1 tablespoon chia gel (page 394)
1/4 teaspoon spirulina powder (optional)

Place nuts and seeds in blender and grind to powder. Add remaining ingredients and puree until smooth.

Makes 2 servings

APPROXIMATE NUTRITIONAL INFORMATION FOR 1 SERVING: Calories: 293 cal; Protein: 11 g; Carbohydrates: 34 g; Fat: 15 g; Fiber: 7 g; Sodium: 66 mg.

KEY NUTRIENTS: Thiamine: 2.4 mg; Riboflavin: 2.53 mg; Niacin: 13.72 mg; Pantothenic Acid: 1.13 mg; Vitamin B6: 2.6 mg; Folate: 106.62 mcg; Vitamin B12: 2.19 mcg; Vitamin C: 50.36 mg; Vitamin E: 6.48 mg; Calcium: 186.64 mg; Iron: 1.64 mg; Magnesium: 90.98 mg; Zinc: 1.88 mg.

Ginger-Peach Smoothie

This nutritious smoothie makes an excellent meal or snack. I especially appreciated it my first trimester because the ginger helped with the nausea.

1/4 cup almonds or 2 tablespoons almond butter
1/2 cup water
1/2 cup yogurt (dairy or nondairy)
1 cup frozen diced peaches
1/4 teaspoon powdered ginger
Liquid stevia extract, maple syrup, brown rice syrup, agave nectar, or honey to taste (optional)

Place almonds in blender and grind to powder. Add remaining ingredients and puree until smooth.

Makes 1 serving

APPROXIMATE NUTRITIONAL INFORMATION FOR 1 SERVING: Calories: 353 cal; Protein: 13 g; Carbohydrates: 32 g; Fat: 22 g; Fiber: 8 g; Sodium: 57 mg.

KEY NUTRIENTS: Vitamin A: 128.91 mcg; Thiamine: .15 mg; Riboflavin: .53 mg; Niacin: 3.17 mg; Pantothenic Acid: .89 mg; Vitamin B6: .12 mg; Vitamin B12: .45 mcg; Vitamin C: 11.83 mg; Vitamin E: 10.59 mg; Calcium: 244.77 mg; Iron: 1.77 mg; Magnesium: 124.22 mg; Zinc: 2.15 mg.

Everything Smoothie

This smoothie is a great way to get a couple extra servings of vegetables.

1 cup cold apple juice
1/2 sweet potato (peeled) or 1 carrot, cut into chunks
1 banana (fresh or frozen)
1 orange, peeled and broken into sections
1/4 cup chopped cabbage
2 tablespoons tahini or cashew butter

Place all ingredients in blender and puree until smooth.

Makes 2 servings

APPROXIMATE NUTRITIONAL INFORMATION FOR 1 SERVING: Calories: 266 cal; Protein: 5 g; Carbohydrates: 49 g; Fat: 8 g; Fiber: 6 g; Sodium: 27 mg.

KEY NUTRIENTS: Vitamin A: 672.92 mcg; Thiamine: .3 mg; Riboflavin: .21 mg; Niacin: 1.64 mg; Pantothenic Acid: .63 mg; Vitamin B6: .5 mg; Folate: 54.89 mcg; Vitamin C: 51.17 mg; Calcium: 105.12 mg; Magnesium: 42.98 mg; Zinc: .95 mg.

Peanut Butter-Banana Shake

Both kids and adults like this creamy, delicious shake. It's hard to believe there's no ice cream in it. You can also make it with almond butter, cashew butter, or tahini.

1 cup milk (dairy or nondairy)
1 heaping tablespoon peanut butter
1 to 2 bananas, sliced and frozen

Place all ingredients in blender and puree until smooth.

Makes 1 serving

Variation

Carob Peanut Butter-Banana Shake: Add 2 to 3 teaspoons carob powder.

APPROXIMATE NUTRITIONAL INFORMATION FOR 1 SERVING: Calories: 390 cal; Protein: 15 g; Carbohydrates: 43 g; Fat: 19 g; Fiber: 4 g; Sodium: 127 mg.

KEY NUTRIENTS: Vitamin A: 92.4 mcg; Thiamine: .15 mg; Riboflavin: .51 mg; Pantothenic Acid: 1.07 mg; Vitamin B6: .78 mg; Folate: 34.62 mcg; Vitamin B12: .88 mcg; Vitamin C: 14.4 mg; Calcium: 297.44 mg; Iron: 94 mg; Magnesium: 65.94 mg; Zinc: 1.12 mg.

Fresh Fig and Orange Smoothie

1/2 cup orange juice
1/2 cup plain yogurt (dairy or nondairy)
1 orange, peeled and broken into pieces
5 fresh figs, halved
1/2 cup ice cubes

Place ingredients in the blender in the order listed. Blend until smooth.

Makes 2 servings

Variation: Try one frozen banana instead of the ice cubes. Also, try vanilla yogurt instead of plain.

APPROXIMATE NUTRITIONAL INFORMATION FOR 1 SERVING: Calories: 189 cal; Protein: 4 g; Carbohydrates: 41 g; Fat: 3 g; Fiber: 6 g; Sodium: 30 mg.

KEY NUTRIENTS: Vitamin A: 62.03 mcg; Thiamine: .21 mg; Riboflavin: .19 mg; Pantothenic Acid: .9 mg; Vitamin B6: .23 mg; Folate: 50.04 mcg; Vitamin B12: .23 mcg; Vitamin C: 68.65 mg; Vitamin E: 1.38 mg; Calcium: 150.88 mg; Magnesium: 41.97 mg.

Creamy Greens Smoothie

This smoothie surprises everyone because it tastes so good. You really don't taste the kale at all. This is an excellent snack while breastfeeding because the greens help to increase milk production. Use nutritional yeast flakes fortified with vitamin B12.

1/2 cup pineapple juice
1/2 cup light coconut milk
1 banana, sliced and frozen
2 to 3 kale leaves
2 teaspoons nutritional yeast flakes

Place ingredients in blender and puree until smooth.

Makes 1 to 2 servings

Note: 1 cup pineapple-coconut juice can be substituted for pineapple juice and coconut milk.

APPROXIMATE NUTRITIONAL INFORMATION FOR 1 SERVING: Calories: 292 cal; Protein: 6 g; Carbohydrates: 51 g; Fat: 9 g; Fiber: 5 g; Sodium: 23 mg.

KEY NUTRIENTS: Vitamin A: 307.59 mcg; Thiamine: 4.31 mg; Riboflavin: 4.39 mg; Niacin: 25.61 mg; Vitamin B6: 5 mg; Folate: 137.74 mcg; Vitamin B12: 3.71 mcg; Vitamin C: 90.74 mg; Iron: 1.61 mg; Magnesium: 45.61 mg; Zinc: 1.72 mg.

Tomato-Watercress Blend

This savory blend supplies vitamin C and iron.

1 cup tomato juice
1/2 cup watercress leaves
1 tablespoon lemon or lime juice
Dash Tabasco sauce (optional)

Place ingredients in blender and puree until smooth.

Makes 1 serving

APPROXIMATE NUTRITIONAL INFORMATION FOR 1 SERVING: Calories: 64 cal; Protein: 2 g; Carbohydrates: 13 g; Fat: 0 g; Fiber: 6 g; Sodium: 620 mg.

KEY NUTRIENTS: Vitamin A: 80.21 mcg; Vitamin C: 35.27 mg; Iron: 1.09 mg.

Teas and Tonics

Teas and tonics can help promote healthy pregnancy and lactation and relieve some of the discomforts caused by physical and hormonal changes. The herbs mentioned are available both in bulk and in tea bags at natural foods stores and some supermarkets. They are considered safe during pregnancy and lactation, however, this section is not intended as medical advice. Consult your midwife or physician for medical problems.

Accurate nutrient information was unavailable for the herbs used in the following teas and tonics so no KEY NUTRIENTS are listed.

Note: Traditional Medicinals® makes excellent tea blends specifically for pregnant and lactating women.

Every Day Pregnancy Tea

Drink at least one cup each day before and during pregnancy. Red raspberry leaves provide calcium and iron, help to prevent miscarriage and hemorrhage, ease morning sickness, relax the muscle of the uterus making delivery easier and speedier, and assist in production of breast milk.[11] I like red raspberry leaves on their own, but if you prefer a stronger flavor, try it with the mint. This tea is good hot or cold.

2 to 3 teaspoons dried red raspberry leaves
1 teaspoon dried peppermint leaves or other tea for flavor (optional)

Pour one cup boiling water over tea leaves. Cover and steep 5 minutes.

Makes 1 cup

Note: If you are taking homeopathic remedies, omit the mint because it will counteract the effects.

APPROXIMATE NUTRITIONAL INFORMATION FOR 1 CUP: Calories: 0 cal; Protein: 0 g; Carbohydrates: 0 g; Fat: 0 g; Fiber: 0 g; Sodium: 0 mg.

Last Trimester Pregnancy Tea

Nettle is extremely nutrient-rich and may help to ease leg cramps. Red raspberry tones the uterus. Peppermint boosts your energy.

1 teaspoon dried nettle leaves
1 teaspoon dried red raspberry leaves
1 teaspoon dried peppermint leaves

Pour 2 cups boiling water over leaves. Steep 5 minutes.

Makes 2 cups

Note: If you are taking homeopathic remedies, omit the mint because it will counteract the effects.

APPROXIMATE NUTRITIONAL INFORMATION FOR 1 CUP: Calories: 0 cal; Protein: 0 g; Carbohydrates: 0 g; Fat: 0 g; Fiber: 0 g; Sodium: 0 mg.

Nursing Tea

Fenugreek stimulates milk flow. Red raspberry and nettle supply calcium and other minerals and vitamins. Fennel increases milk production and helps to prevent colic or indigestion in baby.

1 teaspoon fenugreek seeds (optional)
1 teaspoon dried red raspberry leaves
1 teaspoon dried nettle leaves
1 teaspoon fennel seeds

Place herbs in heatproof jar. Pour 2 cups boiling water over herbs. Cover and steep 15 minutes.

Makes 2 cups

APPROXIMATE NUTRITIONAL INFORMATION FOR 1 CUP: Calories: 0 cal; Protein: 0 g; Carbohydrates: 0 g; Fat: 0 g; Fiber: 0 g; Sodium: 0 mg.

Iron Booster Tonic

This iron-rich tea helps to prevent anemia. The recipe makes enough for several days. Keep leftovers refrigerated and reheat as needed.

3 tablespoons dried nettle leaves
1/4 cup dried parsley
2 tablespoons dried red raspberry leaves
2 tablespoons dried peppermint leaves

Place herbs in 1-quart heatproof jar. Fill with boiling water. Cover and infuse at least 8 hours.

Makes 1 quart

APPROXIMATE NUTRITIONAL INFORMATION FOR 1 CUP: Calories: 0 cal; Protein: 0 g; Carbohydrates: 0 g; Fat: 0 g; Fiber: 0 g; Sodium: 0 mg.

Rose Hip Tea

Rose hips are a good source of vitamin C. Drink this along with an iron-rich snack like Sunflower-Sesame Molasses Cookies (page 318) to increase absorption of the iron.

1 tablespoon dried rose hips
1 cinnamon stick
1 cup boiling water

Place rose hips and cinnamon stick in cup. Add boiling water. Cover and steep 5 minutes.

Makes 1 cup

APPROXIMATE NUTRITIONAL INFORMATION FOR 1 CUP: Calories: 0 cal; Protein: 0 g; Carbohydrates: 0 g; Fat: 0 g; Fiber: 0 g; Sodium: 0 mg.

Morning Sickness Tea

1 tablespoon minced fresh ginger
1 teaspoon coriander seeds
1 cup boiling water

Place ginger and coriander in cup. Add boiling water. Cover and steep 10 minutes.

Makes 1 cup

APPROXIMATE NUTRITIONAL INFORMATION FOR 1 CUP: Calories: 0 cal; Protein: 0 g; Carbohydrates: 0 g; Fat: 0 g; Fiber: 0 g; Sodium: 0 mg.

Anti-Nausea Tea

This traditional macrobiotic remedy works amazingly well for morning sickness.

1 cup cold water
1 teaspoon kudzu
1 teaspoon freshly grated ginger
1 teaspoon soy sauce

Place water and kudzu in saucepan over low heat. Stir until kudzu is dissolved. Add remaining ingredients.

Makes 1 cup

APPROXIMATE NUTRITIONAL INFORMATION FOR 1 CUP: Calories: 0 cal; Protein: 0 g; Carbohydrates: 0 g; Fat: 0 g; Fiber: 0 g; Sodium: 0 mg.

Ginger Root Tea

This tea helps to relieve nausea, upset stomach, gas, and heartburn. It aids circulation and is warming.

2 tablespoons minced fresh ginger root
4 cups water

Simmer ginger and water in covered pan for about 15 minutes. Remove from heat. Keep covered and steep one hour. Sweeten with stevia or honey if desired.

Makes 4 cups

APPROXIMATE NUTRITIONAL INFORMATION FOR 1 CUP: Calories: 0 cal; Protein: 0 g; Carbohydrates: 0 g; Fat: 0 g; Fiber: 0 g; Sodium: 0 mg.

Unblocker Tea

Pears are mildly laxative. The fennel and peppermint help reduce gas and aid digestion.

1 tablespoon fennel seeds
2 tablespoons chopped fresh peppermint leaves or 2 teaspoons dried
1 1/2 cups boiling water
1 pear, cored and diced

Place fennel seeds and peppermint in a heatproof jar. Pour boiling water over herbs. Cover and steep 15 minutes. Strain tea and pour in blender with pear. Blend until smooth. Drink warm or add ice cubes to drink cold.

Makes about 2 cups

APPROXIMATE NUTRITIONAL INFORMATION FOR 1 CUP: Calories: 49 cal; Protein: 0 g; Carbohydrates: 13 g; Fat: 0 g; Fiber: 2 g; Sodium: 0 mg.

Fennel Tea

Fennel aids digestion. It relieves heartburn, indigestion, and morning sickness. During lactation, fennel increases milk production and helps to prevent and relieve gas or colic in baby.

1 teaspoon fennel seeds
1 cup boiling water

Place fennel seeds in cup. Pour boiling water over seeds. Cover and steep 15 minutes. Drink warm.

Makes 1 cup

APPROXIMATE NUTRITIONAL INFORMATION FOR 1 CUP: Calories: 0 cal; Protein: 0 g; Carbohydrates: 0 g; Fat: 0 g; Fiber: 0 g; Sodium: 0 mg.

Tummy Tea

These herbs soothe an upset or gassy stomach. This is also a good tea to drink while breastfeeding.

1 teaspoon dried chamomile flowers
1 teaspoon fennel seeds
1 teaspoon dried peppermint leaves
1 cup boiling water

Place herbs in cup. Cover with boiling water. Cover and steep 10 minutes.

Makes 1 cup

APPROXIMATE NUTRITIONAL INFORMATION FOR 1 CUP: Calories: 0 cal; Protein: 0 g; Carbohydrates: 0 g; Fat: 0 g; Fiber: 0 g; Sodium: 0 mg.

Insomnia Tea

I drank this tea while breastfeeding so I would be able to nap when my baby napped. The hops boost your milk supply but they have an extremely bitter taste. Omit them if you can't stand the taste.

1 teaspoon dried hops
1 teaspoon dried skullcap
1 teaspoon dried catnip
2 cups boiling water

Place herbs in heatproof jar. Pour boiling water over herbs. Steep 20 minutes. This can be reheated but do not boil.

Makes 2 cups

APPROXIMATE NUTRITIONAL INFORMATION FOR 1 CUP: Calories: 0 cal; Protein: 0 g; Carbohydrates: 0 g; Fat: 0 g; Fiber: 0 g; Sodium: 0 mg.

Afterpain Tea

If this is not your first child, afterpain cramps can be quite painful. Sip this tea throughout the day and night, especially while breastfeeding which seems to stimulate the cramps. The hops give this a bitter taste so omit them if you want. Sea salt or honey can be added to make it taste better.

1 ounce dried cramp bark
1/4 ounce dried hops flowers
Sea salt or honey to taste (optional)
4 cups boiling water

Place herbs in heatproof quart-size jar. Fill with boiling water. Cover and infuse 8 hours. Strain and refrigerate. Reheat and sip brew as needed to ease pain and encourage rest.

Makes 1 quart

APPROXIMATE NUTRITIONAL INFORMATION FOR 1 CUP: Calories: 0 cal; Protein: 0 g; Carbohydrates: 0 g; Fat: 0 g; Fiber: 0 g; Sodium: 0 mg.

Apple Cider Vinegar Tonic

This is helpful with indigestion, constipation, gas, heartburn, and colds. It is cleansing and energizing. This tonic is most effective when taken on an empty stomach (e.g. first thing in the morning).

1 teaspoon raw, organic apple cider vinegar
1 teaspoon raw honey, brown rice syrup, or agave nectar
1 cup boiling water

Place vinegar and sweetener in a cup. Pour boiling water over and stir until sweetener is dissolved.

Makes 1 cup

APPROXIMATE NUTRITIONAL INFORMATION FOR 1 CUP: Calories: 21 cal; Protein: 0 g; Carbohydrates: 6 g; Fat: 0 g; Fiber: 0 g; Sodium: 0 mg.

Chia Energy Drink

This drink is an excellent way to get energy, fiber, vitamins, minerals, and essential fatty acids. Chia seeds absorb more than nine times their volume in liquid, which helps to prolong hydration and retain electrolytes in body fluids.

Pour 1 tablespoon chia seeds and 1 cup of water or juice in a jar or a glass. Cover and shake well or stir to mix. Let sit about five minutes. Shake or stir again and drink.

Serves 1

APPROXIMATE NUTRITIONAL INFORMATION FOR 1 SERVING: Calories: 57 cal; Protein: 2 g; Carbohydrates: 6 g; Fat: 3 g; Fiber: 0 g; Sodium: 5 mg.

KEY NUTRIENTS: Thiamine: .1 mg; Iron: 1.2 mg; Zinc: .64 mg.

Rejuvelac

This is one of the most active and easy to digest of the fermented foods because it is mostly water. It has a strong, lemony taste that is similar to lemonade. The ginger is good for digestion and gives it a little extra zing. If the taste is too strong, use rejuvelac to replace part of the liquid in a smoothie or try Watermelon Blast-Off (page 359).

1/2 cup soft wheat berries
1 (2-inch) piece fresh ginger root, sliced (optional)
7 cups water

Sprout wheat for 3 days as follows: Soak berries in 2 cups water for 12 hours. Drain. Place berries in quart-size jar. Cover jar with cheesecloth and secure with rubber band. Rinse soaked seeds by filling the jar with water and inverting it to drain through cheesecloth. Position the jar at approximately a 45-degree angle, mouth side down, to allow excess moisture to drain. Place jar out of direct sunlight. Rinse sprouts at least twice daily to provide them with water and wash away by-products of growth.

After 3 days, or when sprouts are about as long as the seeds, remove sprouts and place them in a blender along with the ginger and 3 cups of water. Blend for about 10 seconds, just enough to open the sprouts up a bit. Pour the mixture into a half-gallon jar. Fill the jar with the remaining water. Cover the jar with cheesecloth or a dish towel and let it sit for 3 days in a shady spot. Stir the mixture twice daily to keep the enzymes and live organisms mixed. Smell the rejuvelac each day to monitor its progress. It should have a fresh smell like lemons or sauerkraut. If it smells bad, discard it and start again.

After 3 days, or when it tastes and smells strongly like lemons or sauerkraut, stir the mixture one final time and pour through a strainer. Keep rejuvelac refrigerated in a covered jar but be sure to open the jar every few days to release gasses that will build up. It will last for at least one month.

Sip rejuvelac slowly. If you are not used to eating fermented foods, start with 1/4 to 1/2 cup per day. After a couple of weeks, gradually increase to one cup a day.

Makes 2 quarts

Note: The strained pulp can be used to start another batch. Place pulp in clean half-gallon jar and fill with water. Stir and cover with cheesecloth and ferment as previous batch. It will mature faster – probably in two days. Discard pulp after second batch.

APPROXIMATE NUTRITIONAL INFORMATION FOR 1 CUP: Nutritional information unavailable.

Appendix

Appendix A:
Grain Cooking Chart

Grain (1 cup dry)	Water (cups)	Cooking Time	Cooked Volume (cups)
Barley, hulled	3	$1\frac{3}{4}$ – 2 hours	$3\frac{1}{2}$
Barley, pearled	3	40 mins.	3
Buckwheat groats	2	15 – 20 mins.	$2\frac{1}{2}$
Millet	3	25 – 30 mins.	$3\frac{1}{2}$
Oats, rolled	3	15 mins.	2
Oats, steel cut	3	30 mins.	3
Oats, whole groats	3	$1\frac{3}{4}$ – 2 hours	$3\frac{1}{2}$
Polenta (coarse cornmeal)	4	25 – 30 mins.	3
Quinoa	2	15 – 20 mins.	$2\frac{1}{2}$
Rice, brown	$2\frac{1}{4}$	35 – 45 mins.	3
Wheat, berries	3	2 hours	$2\frac{1}{2}$
Wheat, bulgur	2	15 – 20 mins.	$2\frac{1}{2}$

Preparation Instructions:

1) Optionally, wash grain as follows: Measure grain and pour it into the pot or a large bowl. Add about 3 times as much water as grain and swish it around with your hands to remove dust and debris. Pour off some of the water to get rid of floating debris. Pour the grain into a fine strainer to drain. Repeat if needed. Rinse out the pot before putting drained grain back in.

Note: Although washing is optional, quinoa should be rinsed to remove the bitter coating (saponin). Never wash buckwheat because it becomes gooey.

2) Add water (or other liquid, like stock) to grain. Cover pot and bring to a boil over high heat.

3) Reduce heat to lowest setting and simmer until liquid is absorbed.

4) Test grain. It should be chewy but tender. If tough or hard, add some boiling liquid, cover and continue cooking until tender.

Tips:

- Cook grain in pot with a heavy bottom to prevent scorching.
- Stir little, if at all, to prevent grain from becoming gummy.
- Keep cooked grain covered in pot until ready to use. Grain will retain heat for at least 1 hour.
- Bring out the flavor of the grain by dry roasting. This also helps grains to remain separate when cooked. Place dry or washed grain in pot over medium heat. Use a wooden spoon to stir the grain. As moisture evaporates, move grains more quickly. Toast until grains begin to pop and give off a nutty aroma.
- Presoak long-cooking grains like wheat berries, hulled barley, and oat groats to reduce cooking time and improve digestibility. Soaking also helps to neutralize phytates. Add the correct amount of liquid to the pot along with the grain. Soak 2 to 24 hours. You can also add 2 tablespoons whey, yogurt, or lemon juice when soaking.
- Grains can be cooked in a slow cooker. Large, firm grains (barley, wheat berries, etc.) work best. Small grains (millet, quinoa, etc.) tend to become mushy (good if you want porridge). Cook grains 3 to 5 hours on high setting, or 8 to 10 hours on low setting.
- Cooked grains freeze well. Make extra and freeze in amounts needed for a meal. Frozen grains can be added to soups, stews, casseroles, salads, or burritos.
- Use leftover grain to make Cranberry-Pear Crunch Cereal (page 51) or Cold Grain Cereal (page 60).
- To deter insects from infesting your grain, keep them refrigerated or place a bay leaf in jar or bag.

Appendix B:
Bean and Legume Cooking Chart

Bean	Water	Cooking Time	Cooked Volume	Soaking Required
(1 cup dry)	(cups)		(cups)	
Adzuki	$3\frac{1}{2}$	45 – 60 mins.	3	no
Anasazi	3	$2\frac{1}{2}$ hours	2	yes
Black-eyed Pea	$3\frac{1}{2}$	1 hour	$2\frac{1}{4}$	no
Black Turtle	$3\frac{1}{2}$	$1\frac{1}{2}$ hours	$2\frac{1}{2}$	yes
Chickpeas (or Garbanzo)	4	2 – 3 hours	3	yes
Kidney	3	$1\frac{1}{2}$ – 2 hours	2	yes
Lentil	3	45 mins.	2	no
Lima	3	$1 - 1\frac{1}{2}$ hours	$2\frac{1}{2}$	no
Pea, split	4	1 hour	$2\frac{1}{4}$	no
Pinto	3	$1\frac{1}{2}$ hours	2	yes
Soybean	4	2 – 3 hours	$2\frac{1}{2}$	yes
White (Great Northern, Navy)	3	1 hour	$2 - 2\frac{1}{2}$	yes

Preparation Instructions:

1) Sift through beans. Pick out damaged beans, pebbles, and other debris. Rinse beans.
2) If soaking is required, place beans in large bowl or pot with at least three times their volume of water.
3) When ready to cook, pick out any floating beans and drain soak water. Place beans in pan with recommended amount of cooking water.
4) Bring uncovered beans to boil over high heat. Turn heat to lowest setting. Cover pot and simmer beans for recommended cooking time, or until beans are tender. Stir as little as possible so beans do not become mushy.
5) Do not add salt or seasonings until beans are tender. Salt, sugar, fat, and acidic foods prevent beans from softening.

Tips:

- Soak beans to neutralize phytates so minerals are better absorbed.
- Change soak water once or twice to help reduce the oligosacharides which can cause gas.
- Cook beans in cast iron or other heavy-bottomed pot to avoid scorching.
- A strip of kombu sea vegetable cooked with beans helps to tenderize beans and improve digestibility.
- Beans can be cooked in a slow cooker. Use 1 part beans to 4 parts water (measure before beans are soaked). For unsoaked beans, cook 4 to 6 hours on high setting, or 12 to 14 hours on low setting. For presoaked beans, cook 3 to 5 hours on high setting, or 8 to 12 hours on low setting.
- Cooked beans can be frozen. Make extra and place meal-size amounts in freezer containers. Frozen beans can be added to soups, stews, casseroles, salads, or used in burritos.
- To deter insects from infesting your beans, place a bay leaf in the jar with the beans or store beans in the refrigerator.

Appendix C:
Vegetarian Substitution Guide

Instead of:	Try:
Butter	On toast, grains, vegetables, etc.: tahini, olive oil, flaxseed oil, non-hydrogenated soy or rice margarines
	For baking: coconut oil, nonhydrogenated soy or rice margarines, cold-pressed vegetable oils
Eggs	Instead of scrambled or fried eggs: tofu For baking: Ener-G® egg replacer, 1 tablespoon ground flaxseed mixed with 3 tablespoons water for each egg, mashed tofu, mashed banana
Dairy milk	Soy, rice, oat, almond, or coconut milk
Buttermilk	Put 1 tablespoon vinegar or lemon juice in measuring cup and fill rest of measure with dairy or nondairy milk
Dairy yogurt	Soy or cashew yogurt*
Sour cream	Plain dairy* or nondairy yogurt*
Ricotta cheese	Pureed tofu and olive oil
Cottage cheese	Tofu cottage cheese*
Cream cheese	On bagels, muffins, etc.: nut or seed butter, soy or rice cream cheese substitutes, yogurt cheese*
	For baking: soy or rice cream cheese substitutes, yogurt cheese, tofu
Hard cheese	Soy, rice or almond cheese
Meat, poultry, or fish	Tempeh, tofu, seitan, beans
Beef or chicken stock	Vegetable stock*, vegetable bouillon, water
Gelatin	Agar agar flakes
Honey	Brown rice syrup, maple syrup, agave nectar
Ice cream	Sorbet*, Better Than Ice Cream*, soy or rice ice cream substitutes

= Items can also be made from recipes in this book

Appendix D:
High Protein Recipes

The following recipes contain at least 20 percent (14 grams) per serving of the RDI for protein for pregnant or lactating women.

Cantaloupe Surprise
Cottage Cheese Sundae
Sesame French Toast
French Toast Sandwich
Scrambled Eggs Plus
Broccoli-Mushroom Scramble
Curried Spinach Scramble
Basic Omelet
Tomato-Herb Omelet
Veggie Breakfast Burrito
Scrambled Tofu
Golden Tofu on Toast
Herbed Cottage Cheese and Avocado
    Sandwich
Egg or Tofu Salad Sandwich
Quick Tofu Sandwich
Garbanzo Bean Salad Pocket
Beanball Submarine Sandwich
Open-Face Bagel Melt
Veggie-Apple Melt
Tempeh Rueben
Veggie Dog and Sauerkraut
Stuffed Bell Peppers
Baked Potato Lunch
Quick Asian Noodles
Tofu and Udon Noodles with Sesame-
    Peanut Dressing
Herbed Split Pea Soup

Tortilla Soup
Seitan "Chicken" and Barley Stew
Coconut-Tempeh Stew
Mild Yellow Curry Stew
Better Than "Beef" Stew
Tofu-Vegetable Pot Pie
Sesame-Tofu Quiche with Broccoli and
    Mushrooms
Tempeh, Apple, Potato, and Kraut
    Casserole
Broccoli-Noodle Casserole
Roasted Eggplant and Zucchini Parmesan
Tofu Enchiladas
Fajitas
High-Protein Pasta
Garbanzos and Pasta in Tomato-Basil
    Sauce
Mushroom Stroganoff
Saucy Noodles and Vegetables
Pumpkin Seed Pesto Ravioli
Lima-Vegetable Lasagna
Butternut Lasagna
Seitan "Chicken" and Cashews
Kung Pao Tofu
Tofu Cottage Cheese
Instant Soy Milk
Peanut Butter-Banana Shake

Appendix E:
High Calcium Recipes

The following recipes contain at least 10 percent (120 mg) per serving of the RDI for calcium for pregnant or lactating women.

Papaya Delight
Cottage Cheese Sundae
Sesame French Toast
Vegan French Toast
French Toast Sandwich
Tomato-Herb Omelet
Scrambled Tofu
Golden Tofu on Toast
Molasses Toast
Savory Bagel Sandwich
English Muffin Cheesecake
English Muffin Melt
Egg or Tofu Salad Sandwich
Tahini-Vegetable Sandwich
Avocado-Cheese Sandwich
Quick Tofu Sandwich
Beanball Submarine Sandwich
Bean Quesadilla
Open-Face Bagel Melt
Creamy Watercress and Tomato Toast
Tempeh Rueben
Quick Asian Noodles
Tofu and Udon Noodles with Sesame-Peanut
    Dressing
Miso-Noodle Soup
"Cream" of Spinach and Millet Soup
Squash and White Bean Soup
Sea Vegetable Soup
Mild Yellow Curry Stew
Braised Greens with Sesame
Tofu-Vegetable Pot Pie
Asparagus Quiche with Brown Rice Crust
Potato-Kale Quiche
Yogurt-Spinach Quiche

Sesame-Tofu Quiche with Broccoli and
    Mushrooms
Spanakopitta
Kale and Rice Casserole
Tempeh, Apple, Potato, and Kraut Casserole
Broccoli-Noodle Casserole
Roasted Eggplant and Zucchini Parmesan
Tofu Enchiladas
Fajitas
High-Protein Pasta
Vegan Paht Si-Yu
Saucy Noodles and Vegetables
Pumpkin Seed Pesto Ravioli
Butternut Lasagna
Kung Pao Tofu
Tofu Vegetable Stir-Fry
Baked Ginger-Orange Tofu
Creamy Watercress Dip or Spread
Yogurt
Tofu Cottage Cheese
Light Cheese Sauce
Strawberry-Almond Shortcake
Pecan Pie
Tapioca Pudding
Instant Soy Milk
Carob Cocoa
Spiced Warm Milk
Creamsicle Smoothie
Fruity Yogurt Smoothie
Meal Shake
Ginger-Peach Smoothie
Peanut Butter-Banana Shake
Fresh Fig and Orange Smoothie

Appendix F:
High Iron Recipes

The following recipes contain at least 10 percent (2.7 mg) per serving of the RDI for iron for pregnant women.

High-Protein Porridge
Winter Müesli
Millet Crunch Granola
Cottage Cheese Sundae
Whole Grain Pancakes
Sesame French Toast
Vegan French Toast
French Toast Sandwich
Veggie Breakfast Burrito
Scrambled Tofu
Golden Tofu on Toast
Molasses Toast
Bean Salad Sandwich
Egg or Tofu Salad Sandwich
Quick Tofu Sandwich
Spinach-Hummus Wrap
Garbanzo Bean Salad Pocket
Egg and Avocado Sandwich
Bean and Avocado Tortilla
Creamy Watercress and Tomato Toast
Tempeh Rueben
Quick Asian Noodles
Tofu and Udon Noodles with Sesame-Peanut
  Dressing
Miso-Noodle Soup
Squash and White Bean Soup
Ginger-Lentil Soup
Black Bean and Corn Soup
Tortilla Soup
Garbanzo Stew
Seitan "Chicken" and Barley Stew
Ratatouille
Adzuki-Squash Stew
Coconut-Tempeh Stew

Mild Yellow Curry Stew
Better Than "Beef" Stew
Basic Quinoa
Sesame-Carrot Quinoa Pilaf
Oven Fries
Tamale Pie
Shepherd's Pie
Tofu-Vegetable Pot Pie
Sesame-Tofu Quiche with Broccoli and
  Mushrooms
Spanakopitta
Tempeh, Apple, Potato, and Kraut Casserole
Broccoli-Noodle Casserole
Roasted Eggplant and Zucchini Parmesan
Tofu Enchiladas
Fajitas
High-Protein Pasta
Vegan Paht Si-Yu
Saucy Noodles and Vegetables
Pumpkin Seed Pesto Ravioli
Butternut Lasagna
Kung Pao Tofu
Tofu Vegetable Stir-Fry
Baked Ginger-Orange Tofu
Creamy Watercress Dip or Spread
Yogurt
Tofu Cottage Cheese
Instant Soy Milk
Carob Cocoa
Spiced Warm Milk
Creamsicle Smoothie
Ginger-Peach Smoothie
Peanut Butter-Banana Shake

Ingredient Guide

This section contains most of the ingredients used in this book. You will find nutritional highlights, purchasing information, storage instructions, and tips for use. Buy whole foods in bulk whenever possible. Not only will it save you money, but by minimizing the amount of packaging, you will help preserve the environment for our children.

Agar Agar: Agar agar (or kanten) is a marine algae that can be used as a gelling agent. It is rich in calcium, iodine, iron, phosphorus, and vitamins A, B complex, C, D and K. Agar agar soothes the digestive tract and helps expel toxic and radioactive pollutants from the body. It has no taste or aroma and contains no calories.

Agave Nectar: Agave nectar is a syrup extracted from agave cactus plants. It is metabolized more slowly than sugar so it is less likely to cause blood sugar fluctuations. Agave nectar can replace **honey, maple syrup,** or brown **rice syrup** in any recipe. When replacing sugar, use 3/4 cups agave nectar for 1 cup of sugar in a recipe. Be sure to reduce recipe liquids by about 1/3 as well. Agave nectar is available at natural foods markets. Agave nectar should be kept refrigerated once opened.

Adzuki Bean: Adzuki (or aduki) beans are one of the easier beans to digest. They don't need to be soaked before cooking. Adzuki beans contain protein, iron, calcium, and other minerals and vitamins. Adzuki beans are available at natural foods stores. See the Bean and Legume Cooking Chart in the Appendix for information on preparation and storage.

Almonds and Almond Butter: Almonds contain protein, calcium, iron, potassium, phosphorus, and some B vitamins. Almond butter is a good choice for those with peanut allergies. Many people find it more digestible than peanut butter as well. Look for almond butter with no added sugar or hydrogenated oils. Many natural foods stores have machines that grind fresh nut butter. For information on toasting, grinding, or storage of almonds, see **Nuts**.

Amaranth: Amaranth is a high-protein, energizing grain that is excellent as a breakfast food. It is also a good source of calcium and fiber. Amaranth is available at natural foods stores.

Amasake: Amasake is a fermented rice drink that is naturally sweet. It is available plain or flavored. You can drink it as is, or use it in smoothies, puddings, and nondairy ice creams. It is found in the refrigerator or freezer section of natural foods stores.

Arame: The sea vegetable arame is an excellent source of protein and contains vitamin A, B complex, and all the minerals. It has a mild, sweet taste and is delicious alone or combined with vegetables. Arame comes dehydrated and keeps well for at least one year. It is available at natural foods stores or Asian food markets.

Arrowroot Powder: Arrowroot powder (or arrowroot flour) is dried and powdered root from the arrowroot plant. It is easy to digest and contains calcium and trace minerals. It thickens liquids when heated and can be used instead of cornstarch (which is highly refined). Arrowroot powder is available at natural foods stores. Cornstarch can be substituted for arrowroot in any recipe if desired.

Avocado: Avocados are a good source of protein, monosaturated fat, and vitamin E. They are excellent in salads, sandwiches, or mashed into guacamole. Avocados are ripe when a slight dent remains after pressing the rind with your finger. To ripen avocados, place in paper bag. Refrigerate only when ripe. After cutting avocado, place in a tightly covered container with pit in and store in refrigerator. The exposed edges may turn dark from oxidation but are safe to eat.

Barley: *Hulled barley* is more nutritious than *pearled barley* although it takes longer to cook. Hulled barley is a good source of fiber, B vitamins, minerals, and protein. Hulled barley is available at natural foods stores. See the Grain Cooking Chart in the Appendix for information on preparation and storage.

Beans and Legumes: Beans and legumes are a good source of protein, B vitamins, and minerals such as calcium and iron. Beans are inexpensive, keep well, and are very filling. Buy organic, unprocessed beans (lentils, split peas, black beans, etc.). Store uncooked beans in cool dry place or in the refrigerator. Soaked and cooked beans are preferable to canned versions, which are processed using high temperature and pressures. If you use canned beans for convenience, be sure to drain and rinse them. As an alternative to canned beans, cook up batches of beans from scratch and freeze them in two-cup-size containers (about the same amount as a can). Then you'll have the convenience and a better product. See the Bean and Legume Cooking Chart in the Appendix for information on preparation and storage.

Bread: Whole grain bread contains B vitamins, protein, iron, and fiber. Read bread labels carefully. Even whole grain breads may contain artificial colors, additives, and preservatives. Sprouted breads (like Ezekiel 4:9® bread) or natural sourdough breads are the best choices because the phytic acid from the grain has been neutralized. If you are allergic to wheat, try spelt, barley, or other whole grain varieties.

Brown Rice Syrup: See **Rice Syrup, Brown**.

Buckwheat: Buckwheat is a good source of protein, B vitamins, and vitamin E. It is a very hardy and warming grain. Whole buckwheat groats are the hulled grain. Roasted buckwheat groats are called kasha. Buckwheat groats are available at natural foods stores. See the Grain Cooking Chart in the Appendix for information on preparation and storage.

Bulgur: Bulgur is wheat that has been soaked, cooked, dried, and cracked so it cooks quickly. It is good source of B vitamins. Bulgur is available at natural foods stores. See the Grain Cooking Chart in the Appendix for information on preparation and storage.

Butter: Butter is a good source of the fat-soluble vitamins A and D. For baking, use unsalted butter. As with all dairy products, buy organic.

Chamomile Flowers: Chamomile tea can help promote sleep and ease an upset stomach. Dried chamomile flowers are available in bulk and in tea bags at natural foods stores and most supermarkets.

Carob: Carob is an excellent source of calcium and supplies protein, vitamins A and B, and other minerals. Carob is a good substitute for chocolate in recipes because it does not contain caffeine. Since carob is naturally sweet, less sugar is needed. Use ground nutmeg to enhance the flavor of carob. Carob powder and unsweetened carob chips can be found at natural foods stores.

Cashews and Cashew Butter: Cashews supply protein, magnesium, phosphorus, and potassium. Cashew butter is a delicious alternative to peanut butter as a spread or in baking. For information on toasting, grinding, or storage of cashews, see **Nuts**.

Cheese: Cheese supplies protein and calcium. Choose organic cheese that comes from cows not given growth hormones or antibiotics. Cheeses with active cultures (yogurt cheese, cottage cheese, etc.) are the most digestible and beneficial. Avoid processed cheeses because they contain chemicals, artificial flavors, and artificial colors. Soy, rice, and almond cheese substitutes are available for those avoiding dairy.

Chia Seeds: The tiny black chia seeds supply protein, carbohydrates, fiber, vitamins (especially B vitamins), minerals (especially calcium and boron), essential fatty acids, and phytochemicals. To make *Chia Gel*: Whisk 1 part chia seeds with 9 parts water. Let mixture sit 10 minutes, or until it gels. The gel can be kept tightly covered in the refrigerator and added to cereals, soups, baked goods, and beverages to boost your energy.

Coconut: Dried and shredded coconut provides fiber, protein, minerals, and folate. It is a delicious addition to baked goods and adds a natural sweetness. Unsweetened coconut is available at natural foods stores and some supermarkets.

Coconut Milk: Coconut milk contains protein, minerals, and folate. It is a delicious substitute for dairy milk in smoothies, puddings, and baking. It is the base for many Thai-style soups and curries. Canned coconut milk (regular or light) is available at most markets and natural foods stores.

Coconut Oil: Coconut oil is very high in lauric acid which has antimicrobial, antibacterial, and antifungal properties. It remains solid at room temperature and is an excellent substitute for butter in baking. Coconut oil is also good for high-temperature cooking. Coconut oil can be kept at room temperature for months without becoming rancid. Refrigerated coconut oil becomes very hard and can be difficult to measure. When a recipe calls for cold coconut oil (such as for pie crust), measure the oil first and then refrigerate or freeze it. Look for unrefined, cold-pressed coconut oil at natural foods stores.

Dark Green Leafy Vegetables: See **Vegetables, Dark Green Leafy**

Dulse: Of all the sea vegetables, dulse is the best source of iron. It is also rich in phosphorus, potassium, magnesium, protein, and vitamin A. It contains B vitamins, vitamin C, vitamin E, and trace elements. Dulse may be eaten as is, hydrated, or cooked. It comes dehydrated and keeps well for at least one year. Dulse is available at natural foods stores or Asian food markets.

Eggs: Eggs contain extremely useable protein, iron, and most vitamins and minerals. Buy free-range, organic eggs that are free of chemical residue and supply more nutrients than commercial eggs. *Omega-3 enriched eggs* are from chickens fed a special diet to increase the omega-3 fatty acid content of the eggs. Large eggs were used in all recipes in this book.

Egg Replacer: *Ener-G® Egg Replacer* (available at natural food stores) is an excellent vegan substitute for eggs in baking and was used for testing the recipes in this book. **Flaxseeds** also make an excellent replacement for eggs. 1 tablespoon ground flaxseeds mixed with 3 tablespoons water = 1 egg.

Evaporated Cane Juice (unrefined): Unrefined evaporated cane juice (or rapadura) is similar to sugar but contains vitamins, minerals, and other nutrients. It can replace refined, raw, or brown sugar in any recipe. Unrefined evaporated cane juice can be found at natural foods stores.

Fennel Seeds: Fennel seeds aid digestion and can help relieve gas. They can be found in bulk or in tea bags at most markets and natural foods stores.

Flaxseed Oil: Flaxseed oil contains omega-3 essential fatty acids, which are important for your health as well as your baby's brain development. Flaxseed oil should never be heated. It can be used instead of butter on cooked grains, toast, vegetables, etc., to add flavor and nutrition. It can also be used in salad dressings. Flaxseed oil is prone to rancidity and should always be kept refrigerated. Flaxseed oil should be used in moderation during pregnancy as it is a uterine stimulant.

Flaxseeds: Flaxseeds are one of the best plant sources of omega-3 fatty acids. Flaxseeds have laxative properties and are a uterine stimulant so it is important not to eat too much during pregnancy. Limit flaxseed consumption to about 1 tablespoon a day while pregnant. Since flaxseeds are so small, they must be ground for the nutrients to be absorbed. For instructions on grinding or toasting seeds, see **Seeds**.

Flour: Flour can be made from just about any grain or bean, and even from nuts and seeds. *Whole wheat flour* is most commonly used because of its performance in baked goods but *spelt* or *rye* flours work just about as well in any recipe calling for wheat, and those with wheat allergies may be able to tolerate them. *Whole wheat pastry flour* contains less gluten than regular whole wheat flour and will yield a lighter product. It is not suitable for yeast-risen recipes. *Unbleached flour* is wheat flour with the germ and bran (and most of the nutrition) removed. Never use *bleached flour* which is whitened with chemicals. *Barley flour* and *oat flour* contain some gluten and work adequately as wheat substitutes in most baked goods. For yeast-risen products, however, at least half wheat or spelt is needed for a proper rise. For those who must avoid gluten, *brown rice flour, quinoa flour,* and *millet flour* are good choices; however they will not work in yeast-risen breads. Whole grain flour can become rancid so store flour in a cool place, or in the refrigerator or freezer. Whole wheat flour is available at most supermarkets. All whole grain flours are available at natural foods stores.

Fruit: Most fruits are good sources of fiber, vitamin A, and vitamin C, as well as other vitamins and minerals. Fresh fruit is the most nutritious; frozen is the next best. Canned fruit should be the last choice because the high temperatures used in processing destroy most of the nutrients. *Buy organic*. Most fruits are heavily sprayed and washing doesn't remove all the residue. Strawberries, grapes, and apples are more chemically treated than other fruits. Peel nonorganic fruit before eating, especially those with a waxy finish. Generally, domestic produce contains fewer chemicals than imported. If you can't get organic, buy local.

Garbanzo Beans: Garbanzo beans (or chickpeas) are extremely high in vitamin C and iron. They are also excellent sources of calcium, potassium, and vitamin A. Garbanzo beans are available dried or canned at supermarkets and natural foods stores. See the Bean and Legume Cooking Chart in the Appendix for information on preparation and storage.

Ghee: Ghee is clarified butter which contains butterfat but none of the milk solids. It can usually be tolerated by those who are lactose intolerant. Ghee is excellent for high-temperature cooking and can be used like butter for sautéing, on toast, and over grains or vegetables. It is very stable and keeps well at room temperature.

Ginger: Ginger root boosts circulation, aids digestion, and helps alleviate nausea. Fresh ginger comes in tubers or roots. The fresher the root, the juicier it will be. Ginger root does not need to be refrigerated. Powdered ginger is available also. 1 tablespoon of minced, fresh ginger = 1/8 teaspoon powdered ginger. Both fresh and powdered ginger are available at most supermarkets and natural foods stores.

Grains: (See also specific types.) Unrefined grains are an excellent source of complex carbohydrates, fiber, B vitamins, and minerals. Many grains are also good sources of protein. Avoid refined grains, which have little nutrient value. Whole grains can become rancid so store in a cool place or in the refrigerator. See the Grain Cooking Chart in the Appendix for information on preparation and storage. Whole grains can be found at natural foods stores and some supermarkets.

Grapeseed Oil: Grapeseed oil is a stable oil with a high smoke point. It is excellent for high-temperature cooking such as stir-fries or in baking. Purchase cold- or expeller-pressed oil. Whole grains can be found at natural foods stores and some supermarkets.

Herbs: Herbs (especially fresh) add delicious flavor to meals. Herbs are easy to grow in containers or in the ground. The herbs used most in this book are **parsley**, cilantro, thyme, rosemary, dill, oregano, and basil. Avoid *sage* during lactation as it can reduce milk supply. Herbs can also be used for tea. Many have medicinal purposes. Herbs beneficial for pregnancy and lactation are **red raspberry leaf, nettle, chamomile flowers, fennel, peppermint,** and **ginger.**

Hiziki: Hiziki (or hijiki) is the most mineral-rich of all sea vegetables. You don't need to use a lot because hijiki expands up to four times when soaked in water. It can be cooked alone in water or with vegetables or grains. Because of its high calcium and iron content, it is very beneficial during pregnancy. It comes dehydrated and keeps well for at least one year. Hiziki is available at natural foods stores or Asian food markets.

Honey: Honey is a natural sweetener produced by bees. It is sweeter than sugar so use

1/4 to 1/2 less than you would sugar. If honey hardens or crystallizes, place jar in hot water over low heat to soften. Raw honey contains the most nutrients; however, never give raw honey to an infant. Brown **Rice Syrup** and **Agave Nectar** can be substituted for honey in any recipe.

Juice: Juice is not a whole food as the fiber of the fruit or vegetable has been removed. In most cases, it is preferable to eat the whole fruit because the fiber helps slow the sugar absorption in your body. Use fruit juice to sweeten foods instead of sugar or in smoothies (be sure to add fiber and fat to slow the sugar absorption). Vegetable juices contain less sugar and can provide a vitamin and energy boost. Freshly squeezed juice from organic produce is best. Next best is organic juice with no added sweeteners.

Kale: Kale is an excellent source of calcium, iron, magnesium, vitamin A, vitamin C, folate, and fiber. Of all the leafy green vegetables, kale is the richest in the phytochemical lutein. Known mostly for its prevention of eye disease, lutein is now thought to be more protective against cancer than beta-carotein. Kale is also one of the highest sources of antioxidant flavonoids which help ward off heart disease and regulate blood pressure. Kale is available year round but is especially good in the winter because the cold makes it sweeter. Kale comes in bunches of long, dark green leaves. The most common variety is curly around the edges. I prefer the smoother varieties like *Dinosaur* or *Red Russian* because they are tender and milder when lightly steamed or added to a stir-fry. Choose bunches of fresh, green leaves, favoring the smaller, more tender leaves over the large, coarser ones. Keep refrigerated and use within a few days. For longer storage, mince washed and dried kale in food processor to texture of parsley and freeze.

Kefir: Kefir is cultured milk similar to yogurt but of a thin enough consistency to drink. Because of the enzymes and bacteria, kefir is much easier to digest than milk. Kefir is available plain or flavored at most natural foods stores. You can also make it yourself. Kefir and kefir starter is available at natural foods stores.

Kelp: Kelp is an excellent source of calcium and iodine. It is available in a granulated form which makes it easy to use. Because of its high sodium content, it can be used to replace some or all of the salt in any dish. Use 1/4 to 1/2 as much granulated kelp as you would salt. Don't use too much or your dish will get a fishy taste. Kelp is available at natural foods markets and Asian food markets.

Kombu: The sea vegetable kombu is high in potassium, iodine, calcium, vitamin A and vitamin C. Kombu tenderizes food and enhances flavors. Add a strip when cooking beans to soften them and make them more easily digestible. Add to a stew or soup to sweeten root vegetables. It comes in dehydrated strips and keeps well for at least one year. Kombu is available at natural foods stores or Asian food markets.

Kuzu: Kuzu (or kudzu) is a powdered root used to thicken foods, similar to cornstarch or arrowroot. It must be dissolved in cold water. Kuzo is available at natural foods stores, usually in the Asian or macrobiotic foods section.

Legumes: (See **Beans and Legumes**.)

Lentils: Lentils are excellent sources of protein, calcium, iron, as well as other vitamins and minerals. They do not need to be soaked before cooking. See the Bean and Legume Cooking Chart in the Appendix for information on preparation and storage.

Lettuce: Iceberg lettuce contains virtually no nutrition so choose *romaine, green leaf, red leaf,* and *butterhead* varieties instead. These supply vitamin A and other nutrients. Wash lettuce well to remove dirt and grit. Dry in salad spinner so dressing will adhere better.

Maple Syrup: Maple syrup is rich in trace minerals and imparts a delicious flavor to baked goods and sweets. It is sweeter than sugar so you don't need to use as much. Look for maple syrup that has been processed without formaldehyde. Brown **rice syrup, agave nectar,** and **honey** can be used instead of maple syrup in any recipe.

Milk: Milk supplies protein and calcium. Some people find milk difficult to digest or are allergic to it. Cultured milk products like **kefir** and **yogurt** are easier to digest and contain beneficial enzymes and bacteria. Buy organic dairy products because commercial cows are treated with growth hormones and antibiotics that may end up in your milk. Nondairy milk substitutes made from soy, rice, nuts or seeds can be made or purchased.

Millet: Millet is a good source of protein and iron. Its high alkaline content makes it easy to digest. Millet is also said to be effective for easing morning sickness. Millet is available at natural foods stores. See the Grain Cooking Chart in the Appendix for information on preparation and storage.

Miso: Miso is a good source of vegetable protein because it contains eight amino acids. It has a salty, sweet taste that adds flavor to soups, sauces, and salad dressings. Buy only unpasteurized and naturally fermented miso which contains live enzymes to aid digestion. Miso is made from a variety of grains or beans and ranges from white to deep brown. Basically, the lighter the color, the sweeter and lighter the taste. Never boil miso. When using in soup or sauce, add it after soup or sauce is cooked. Remove the dish from heat. Mix desired amount of miso with a small amount of water or soup broth until it forms a smooth paste. Stir paste into the soup or sauce. When reheating, do not boil. Miso is available in the refrigerated and macrobiotic foods sections of natural foods stores and some supermarkets.

Molasses: Blackstrap molasses is the byproduct of sugarcane processing. It is an excellent source of calcium and iron, as well as other minerals. Be sure to use organic molasses as commercial sugar is heavily pesticized.

Nettle: Nettle leaves provide just about every vitamin and mineral necessary for health, including calcium, iron, and vitamin K. It also has an exceptional chlorophyll content. Nettle tea is beneficial before, during, and after pregnancy because it can increase fertility, nourish mother and fetus, ease leg cramps and muscle spasms, help with pain during labor, prevent and reduce hemorrhoids, and increase breastmilk production. Nettle is available in bulk and in tea bags at natural foods stores.

Nori: The sea vegetable nori is most commonly used to wrap sushi. It comes in sheets that can be used as is or toasted slightly over a flame. Nori contains more vitamin A than carrots and is higher in protein than soybeans. It is also high in vitamins C and D, as well as many minerals and trace elements. If that isn't enough, it emulsifies fat, aids digestion, and contains the enzyme cholesterase which breaks down cholesterol. Nori is available at most markets in the Asian foods section.

Nutritional Yeast: Nutritional yeast is a complete protein and an excellent source of B vitamins. If you are vegan, be sure to use a brand fortified with vitamin B12 (like Red Star® Vegetarian Support Formula). Nutritional yeast comes in flakes and can be added to grains, soups, sauces, smoothies, salads, cereals, or sprinkled on popcorn. Nutritional yeast flakes are available at natural foods stores.

Nuts and Nut Butters: (See also individual types.) Nuts are excellent sources of protein, vitamins, minerals, and essential fatty acids. Nuts are a great addition to baked goods, cereals, grain dishes, and salads. To improve digestibility, nuts can be soaked in water overnight. To *chop* nuts, use a knife or food processor. To *grind* nuts, use a blender, seed grinder, or coffee grinder. To *toast* nuts, chop them first if desired. Place in dry skillet over medium heat. Cook, stirring occasionally, for 5 to 10 minutes, or until they are golden and give off a nutty aroma. Hulled nuts should be stored in refrigerator or freezer to prevent rancidity. Unhulled nuts can be stored up to a year in a cool, dry place.

Nut butters are wonderful on toast, crackers, or as a dip for raw fruit or vegetables. Avoid nut butters with additives like hydrogenated oils or sugar. Many natural foods stores offer machines that grind whole nuts to butter while you wait, guaranteeing you a fresh product with no additives. It is also easy to make your own nut butter (recipe on page 267). Nut butters should be kept refrigerated to prevent them from becoming rancid.

Oats: Oats are a good source of protein, B vitamins, calcium, iron, and magnesium. Oats are soothing to the mucus membranes and digestive system. They are also a mild laxative. Oats contain more phytic acid than most other grains. Soaking oats before cooking helps to neutralize the phytates. Rolled oats are commonly used to make oatmeal and in baked goods. Whole oat groats are also available and can be used like barley. Oat flour can be made by grinding rolled oats in a blender or food processor. Oats have an antioxidant that delays rancidity so they have a longer shelf life than other grains. See the Grain Cooking Chart in the Appendix for information on preparation and storage.

Oils: (See also individual types.) Oils supply fatty acids and the fat soluble vitamins A, D, E, and K. In general, monosaturated (e.g., olive) and saturated (e.g., coconut, ghee) fats are more stable and less prone to rancidity than polyunsaturated oils (e.g., corn, flax). **Olive oil** is best used uncooked in salad dressings or at moderate heat as for sautéing. For high heat cooking, use **ghee**, unrefined **coconut oil**, high-oleic **safflower oil**, high-oleic **sunflower oil**, or grapeseed oil. Toasted sesame oil gives a delicious flavor to stir-fries and salad dressings. **Flaxseed oil** contains omega-3 essential fatty acids which are important for your health as well as your baby's brain development. Coconut oil, grapeseed, high-oleic safflower, or high-oleic sunflower oils are good choices for baking. Always purchase cold- or expeller-pressed oils and avoid hydrogenated oils. Buy oil (especially polyunsaturated oils) in smaller bottles and use quickly. Oils can be kept refrigerated. If they harden (as olive oil will), leave at room temperature for an hour or so before using.

Olive Oil: Olive oil contains oleic acid which is good for the heart. It is rich in antioxidants. Choose extra virgin olive oil, preferably organic. Use olive oil in salad dressings or for sautéing. Olive oil is not suitable for high-heat cooking.

Papaya: Papayas are an excellent source of vitamins A and C, as well as potassium. Papaya contains the papain enzyme which aids digestion. Ripen papaya at room temperature until soft to the touch. Keep ripe papayas refrigerated.

Parsley: Parsley is a good source of vitamin A, vitamin C, and iron. It also aids digestion. Keep fresh parsley refrigerated and wash before using. Washed and well-dried parsley can be minced and kept in the freezer for longer storage.

Parsnips: Parsnips look like large, yellow carrots. They provide fiber, vitamin A, vitamin C, calcium, and potassium. They have a strong, sweet flavor and can be substituted for some or all of the carrots or potatoes in a recipe.

Pasta: Pasta is easy to prepare and is liked by most children and adults. Look for pasta made from whole wheat, brown rice, quinoa and other whole grains. Experiment with different brands as quality and texture varies. Whole grain pastas are available at natural foods stores and some supermarkets.

Peanuts and Peanut Butter: Peanuts are a good source of protein, pantothenic acid, B vitamins, vitamin E, and iron. Commercial peanuts are heavily sprayed, so always buy organic. Look for peanuts from dry areas as they are less likely to have mold. When you buy peanut butter, make sure it has no added sugar or hydrogenated oils. Many natural foods stores have machines that grind fresh nut butter for you, or you can make your own (recipe page 267). If food allergies are common in your family, you may want to avoid peanuts while pregnant as there are theories that pregnant women who consume peanut products may expose the fetus to peanut allergens. If there is a predisposition to allergies, the infant could develop a peanut allergy. **Almond butter, cashew butter, pumpkin seed butter**, or **tahini** (sesame butter) can replace peanut butter in any of the recipes in this book.

Peppermint: Peppermint leaves aid digestion and can help relieve nausea. Fresh or dried leaves can be used for tea. Fresh leaves are delicious in salads like tabouli. Dried peppermint leaves are available in bulk at natural foods stores and in tea bags at most supermarkets. Fresh leaves are available in the produce department of many markets. Peppermint is easy to grow in a container or garden.

Pickles: Naturally fermented pickles aid digestion and promote production of beneficial bacteria in the intestine. They can be purchased at natural foods stores; however, if they are pasteurized, the beneficial enzymes are destroyed. Many natural foods markets now carry unpasteurized cultured vegetables and pickles in the refrigerated or frozen foods sections.

Pine Nuts: Pine nuts (also piñon or pignoli) are good sources of protein, vitamin A, B vitamins, as well as minerals. Toasted pine nuts are delicious on salads, and in grain and pasta dishes. See **Nuts** for more information on toasting and storage.

Pineapples: Pineapples supply vitamins A, B complex, and C, as well as fiber. They also contain an enzyme that aids digestion. Pineapples are not usually sprayed so this is one of the few fruits that are okay if not organic.

Pumpkin Seeds and Pumpkin Seed Butter: Pumpkin seeds (also pepitos) are an excellent source of protein, iron, zinc, and vitamin A. They also contain omega-3 fatty acids. They are especially good toasted and sprinkled over salads, grains, or vegetables. Pumpkin Seed Butter is a delicious alternative to peanut butter and is available at many natural foods and specialty stores. For information on toasting, grinding, or storage, see **Seeds**.

Quinoa: Quinoa is a high-protein grain. It is also a good source of B complex vitamins, vitamin E, calcium, and other minerals. Quinoa is available at natural foods stores. See the Grain Cooking Chart in the Appendix for information on preparation and storage.

Red Raspberry Leaves: Red raspberry leaves supply vitamin C, calcium, and iron, as well as other vitamins and minerals. Red raspberry leaves are a uterine tonic that can help increase fertility, prevent miscarriage and hemorrhage, ease morning sickness, and tone uterine muscles for an easier labor. For breastfeeding mothers, the high mineral content can aid milk production. Fresh or dried leaves can be used to make tea. Buy leaves in bulk or in tea bags at natural foods stores.

Rice, Brown: Brown rice is the whole rice kernel with only the hull removed. It is an excellent source of B vitamins and contains iron, vitamin E, and some protein. Brown rice is available in short-grain, medium-grain, long-grain, basmati, and sweet varieties. Brown rice is available at supermarkets and natural foods stores. See the Grain Cooking Chart in the Appendix for information on preparation and storage.

Rice Syrup, Brown: Brown rice syrup contains B vitamins and minerals. It is similar in texture to honey and can be used to replace honey, agave nectar, or maple syrup in any recipe. It is absorbed more slowly into your system than sugar, honey, and maple syrup and has a mild taste that won't overpower other flavors. Brown rice syrup can be found at natural foods stores. It does not need to be refrigerated.

Safflower Oil: Safflower oil is a good all-purpose oil, fine for stir-frying or baking. It is high in vitamin E and linoleic acid. Use *cold-pressed* oils and look for *high-oleic* safflower oil which is the most stable.

Sea Salt: Unrefined Celtic sea salt contains essential minerals and trace elements. Avoid commercial table salt which has been chemically stripped of nutrients and has more chemicals added for cosmetic reasons. Most of the sea salt sold in natural foods and specialty stores is refined so be sure to look for *unrefined Celtic* sea salt.

Sea Vegetables: (See also individual types.) Sea vegetables are exceptional sources of minerals, vitamins, and protein. They help strengthen bones and teeth, and improve nerve transmission and digestion. Sea Veg Mix (page 282) makes it easy to incorporate sea vegetables into your meals. Dehydrated sea vegetables are available at natural foods stores.

Seeds and Seed Butters: (See also individual types.) Seeds are excellent sources of protein, vitamins, minerals, and essential fatty acids. To improve digestibility, seeds can be soaked in water overnight. To *toast* seeds, place them in a dry skillet over medium heat. Cook and stir occasionally for 5 to 10 minutes, until they are golden and give off a nutty aroma. To *grind* seeds, use a blender, seed grinder, or coffee grinder. Hulled seeds should be stored in refrigerator or freezer to prevent rancidity.

Seed butters are wonderful on toast, crackers, or as a dip for raw fruit or vegetables. Avoid seed butters with additives like hydrogenated oils or sugar. Seed butters are available at natural foods stores and some supermarkets. It is also easy to make your own seed butter (see recipe on page 267).

Seitan: Seitan is a concentrated protein made from wheat gluten. The texture is similar to chicken or turkey. Seitan is usually stocked near the tofu in the refrigerated section of natural foods stores.

Sesame Oil: Toasted sesame oil gives a delicious flavor to stir-fries and salad dressings. It is relatively stable but should be purchased in small, dark-colored bottles. Because of its strong flavor, only a little of this oil is normally used and it is often mixed with other milder flavored oils.

Sesame Seeds: Sesame seeds are extremely high in protein, iron, vitamin E. Unhulled seeds are very high in calcium but also contain oxalic acid so not all of the calcium is absorbed. Since the seeds are so small, they must be ground for the nutrients to be absorbed. For instructions on toasting or grinding seeds, see **Seeds**. Sesame seeds can also be ground into a butter called **Tahini**.

Soy milk: Soy milk provides protein and is usually enriched with calcium, vitamin B12, vitamin D, and other nutrients. Soy milk can replace dairy milk in most recipes. Look for milk made from organic soybeans to ensure they have not been genetically engineered. Do not buy soy milk made from soy protein isolates, which are created using a highly chemical process. Soy milk is available at most supermarkets and natural foods stores.

Soy Sauce: Choose *tamari* or *Shoyu* soy sauces. Both are naturally fermented but tamari is typically wheat-free while Shoyu usually contains wheat. Avoid common soy sauce. It is chemically fermented, contains additives and coloring, and may even contain additional salt.

Stevia: Stevia is a naturally sweet herb that tastes faintly of licorice. It comes in liquid or powder form. Only tiny amounts are needed to sweeten food. If too much is used, food will have a bitter taste. For the recipes in this book, use liquid stevia extract labeled "no bitter aftertaste." Stevia is available at natural foods stores and some supermarkets.

Sunflower Oil: Sunflower oil is a good all-purpose oil, fine for stir-frying or baking. It is high in vitamin E and linoleic acid. Only use *cold-pressed* oil and look for *high-oleic* sunflower oil, which is the most stable. See **Oils** for information on storage.

Sunflower Seeds: Sunflower seeds are very high in protein. They are good sources of calcium, iron, and vitamins A, D, and E. For information on toasting, grinding, or storage, see **Seeds**.

Sunflower Sprouts: Sunflower sprouts that you buy at natural foods stores or farmers markets are actually very young sunflower plants. They are rich in chlorophyll, minerals, and vitamins A and C. Sunflower sprouts are delicious on sandwiches and salads. They keep for about a week in your refrigerator.

Sweeteners: (See also individual types.) **Fruit, juice,** juice concentrate, brown **rice syrup,** pure **maple syrup, honey, agave nectar,** blackstrap **molasses,** unrefined **evaporated cane juice,** and **stevia** are suggested to sweeten food. Highly refined sweeteners such as *white sugar, raw sugar, turbinado sugar, brown sugar, corn syrup, high fructose corn syrup,* and *fructose* should be used sparingly if at all. Avoid *artificial sweeteners. Saccharin* has been shown to cause cancer in animals and many reports of adverse reactions to *aspartame* have been filed with the FDA.

Tahini: Tahini (or sesame seed butter) is extremely high in protein, iron, and vitamin E. It is an excellent substitute for peanut butter on toast or crackers. It gives a delicious creamy flavor to soups, sauces, and salad dressings. Tahini may be made with either raw or roasted sesame seeds. Unroasted seeds make a sweeter tahini and roasted seeds make a nutty tahini. Tahini is available at natural foods stores and many supermarkets.

Tempeh: Tempeh supplies protein and B vitamins. Tempeh is one of the most beneficial soy products since it is naturally cultured which neutralizes the phytates in the soy. Tempeh has a meaty, chewy texture that makes it a good substitute for meat. Tempeh is available in the refrigerated section of natural foods stores.

Tofu: Tofu is a good source of protein, calcium, and iron, as well as other minerals and vitamins. Many tofus are made using calcium sulfate as a coagulant, which increases the calcium content significantly. Use firm tofu in recipes unless otherwise specified. Soft or silken tofu works well in puddings or purees. Buy tofu made from organic soybeans to ensure they have not been genetically engineered. Tofu is available at supermarkets and natural foods stores.

Vegetables: Vegetables are good sources of vitamins, minerals, antioxidants, and fiber. Fresh vegetables are the most nutritious. Frozen is next best. The only canned vegetables I recommend are tomatoes and pumpkin. Buy organic vegetables whenever possible. Most produce is heavily sprayed and washing doesn't remove all the residue. Peel nonorganic produce before eating, especially those with a waxy finish. Generally, domestic produce contains fewer chemicals than imported. If you can't get organic, buy local.

Vegetables, Dark Green Leafy: Dark green leafy vegetables include **kale**, collard greens, chard, watercress, mustard greens, dandelion greens, spinach, beet greens, etc. They are excellent sources of fiber, vitamins A and C, folate, and most minerals especially calcium and iron. They also contain phytochemicals like lutein and beta-carotein. Eating dark green leafy vegetables increases the quantity and richness of breastmilk. Choose bunches of fresh, green leaves. Choose the smaller, more tender leaves over the large, coarser ones. Keep refrigerated and use within a few days. For longer storage, mince washed and dried greens in food processor to texture of parsley and freeze.

Wakame: The sea vegetable wakame is high in protein, iron, calcium, vitamins, and trace minerals. It comes in dehydrated strips and keeps well for at least one year. Wakame is available at natural foods stores and Asian food markets.

Walnuts: Walnuts are good sources of omega-3 fatty acids. They also contain protein, zinc, calcium, and potassium. For information on toasting, grinding, or storage, see **Nuts**.

Watercress: Watercress is an exceptional source of minerals, including calcium and iron. It is also an excellent source of vitamin A and vitamin C. Watercress can be helpful in the prevention and treatment of edema. Watercress is available at most supermarkets in bunches, similar to parsley. Look for fresh, green leaves. Keep refrigerated and use within a few days. Wash watercress well before using. When raw, it has a spicy taste that becomes mild when cooked.

Wheat: Whole wheat is a good source of B vitamins, vitamin E, trace minerals, and protein. Wheat berries can be soaked and cooked similar to barley. Hard wheat contains more protein than soft wheat because of the higher gluten content. *Spelt* or *rye* berries or flour can be substituted for whole wheat. See the *Grain Cooking Chart* in the Appendix for information on preparation and storage of wheat berries. See **Flour** for more information on whole wheat flour.

Yogurt: Yogurt can be made from cow's milk, goat's milk, soy milk, or even nuts and seeds. When buying yogurt look for organic, nonhomogenized yogurt with live, active cultures. Homemade yogurt (page 270) is easy to make and contains more vigorous cultures than store-bought.

References

1. Phyllis A. Balch, CNC, *Prescription for Dietary Wellness – Second Edition* (New York: Avery, 2003), pp 268-269.

2. Dostalova, L., Vitamin status during puerperium and lactation. *Annals of Nutrition and Metabolism* (Basel, Switzerland) 28: Nov/Dec 1984: pp 385-408.

3. Susan S. Weed, *Wise Woman Herbal for the Childbearing Year* (Woodstock, NY: Ash Tree Publishing, 1986), p 85.

4. Carol Simontacchi, *The Crazy Makers* (New York: Tarcher/Putnam, 2000), p 79.

5. Dean Raffelock, D.C., Dipl.Ac., CN, Robert Rountree, M.D., and Virginia Hopkins with Melissa Block, *A Natural Guide to Pregnancy and Postpartum Health* (New York: Avery, 2002), p 97.

6. Messina, Mark and Virginia, *The Dietitian's Guide to Vegetarian Diets.* (Gaithersburg, Md.: Aspen Publishers, 1996), p 28.

7. Dean Raffelock, D.C., Dipl.Ac., CN, Robert Rountree, M.D., and Virginia Hopkins with Melissa Block, *A Natural Guide to Pregnancy and Postpartum Health* (New York: Avery, 2002), p 99.

8. Jacques de Langre, Ph.D., *Seasalt's Hidden Powers* (Asheville, NC: Happiness Press, 1994), p 12.

9. Sally Fallon, *Nourishing Traditions* (Washington, DC: New Trends Publishing, Inc., 2001), pp 440-441.

10. Rebecca Wood, *The Whole Foods Encyclopedia* (New York: Prentice Hall Press, 1988), p 61.

11. Susan S. Weed, *Wise Woman Herbal for the Childbearing Year* (Woodstock, NY: Ash Tree Publishing, 1986), pp 18-19.

Sources and Resources

Fertility, Pregnancy, and Lactation

The Complete Book of Pregnancy and Childbirth — New Edition, by Sheila Kitzinger. Knopf, 1996.

Gentle Birth Choices: A Guide to Making Informed Decisions About Birthing Centers, Birth Attendants, Water Birth, Home Birth, Hospital Birth, by Barbara Harper, R.N. Healing Art Press, 1994.

Giving Birth: A Journey into the World of Mothers and Midwives, by Catherine Taylor. Perigee, 2002.

Having a Baby Naturally: The Mothering Magazine Guide to Pregnancy and Childbirth, by Peggy O'Mara. Atria Books, 2003.

Natural Family Living: The Mothering Magazine Guide to Parenting, by Peggy O'Mara with Jane McConnell. Pocket Books, 2000.

A Natural Guide to Pregnancy and Postpartum Health, by Dean Raffelock, D.C., Dipl.Ac., CN, Robert Rountree, M.D., and Virginia Hopkins with Melissa Block. New York: Avery, 2002.

The Nursing Mother's Companion, by Kathleen Huggins, R.N., M.S. The Harvard Common Press, 1999.

Spiritual Midwifery — Fourth Edition, by Ina May Gaskin. Book Publishing Company, 2002.

Total Nutrition During Pregnancy, by Betty and Si Kamen. Appleton-Century-Crofts, 1981.

What to Expect When You're Expecting, by Heidi Murkoff, Arlene Eisenberg, and Sandee Hathaway, B.S.N. Workman Publishing Company, Inc., 2002.

Wise Woman Herbal for the Childbearing Year, by Susan S. Weed. Ash Tree Publishing, 1986.

Your Fertility Signals: Using Them to Achieve or Avoid Pregnancy Naturally, by Merryl Winstein. Smooth Stone Press, 1999.

Nutrition and Whole Foods Cooking

A Celebration of Wellness, by James Levin, M.D. and Natalie Cederquist. Avery, 1992.

Cooking the Whole Foods Way, by Christina Pirello. HP Books, 1997.

Eating Expectantly: A Practical and Tasty Guide to Prenatal Nutrition, by Bridget Swinney, MS, RD. Meadowbrook Press, 2000.

Every Woman's Guide to Eating During Pregnancy, by Martha Rose Shulman and Jane L. Davis, M.D. Houghton Mifflin Company, 2002.

Feeding the Healthy Vegetarian Family, by Ken Haedrich. Bantam Books, 1998.

The Food Allergy Survival Guide, by Vesanto Melina, Jo Stepaniak, and Dina Aronson. The Book Publishing Company, 2004.

How It All Vegan: Irresistible Recipes for an Animal-Free Diet, by Sarah Kramer and Tanya Barnard. Arsenal Pulp Press, 1999.

The New Laurel's Kitchen, by Laurel Robertson, Carol Flinders, and Brian Ruppenthal. Ten Speed Press, 1986.

The New Whole Foods Encyclopedia: A Comprehensive Resource for Healthy Eating, by Rebecca Wood. Penguin, 1999.

Nourishing Traditions – Second Edition, by Sally Fallon. New Trends Publishing, Inc., 2001.

Nutrition Almanac - Fifth Edition, by Lavon J. Dunne. McGraw-Hill, 2002.

Prescription for Dietary Wellness – Second Edition, by Phyllis A. Balch, CNC. Avery, 2003.

Rodale's Basic Natural Foods Cookbook, edited by Charles Gerras. Simon & Schuster, 1984.

Simply Natural Baby Food: Easy Recipes for Delicious Meals Your Infant and Toddler Will Love, by Cathe Olson. GOCO Publishing, 2003.

Vegan Handbook, edited by Debra Wasserman and Reed Mangels, Ph.D., R.D. The Vegetarian Resource Group, 2000.

The Whole Grain Cookbook, by A.D. Livingston. The Lyons Press, 2000.

Index

About the Author

Cathe Olson has studied nutrition and cookery both formally and informally for over fifteen years, specializing in vegetarian, macrobiotic, and whole foods diets. Cathe has cooked at natural foods restaurants and delis in both the San Francisco Bay and Central Coast areas of California. She is the author of *Simply Natural Baby Food: Easy Recipes for Delicious Meals Your Infant and Toddler Will Love*, as well as numerous articles on nutrition and healthy eating.

Cathe, her husband, Gary, and daughters Aimie and Emily raise organic vegetables, herbs, fruit, and free-range hens on their farm in Suey Creek, California.

Cathe welcomes your questions and comments. Email her at cathe@simplynaturalbooks.com or contact her through the Web site at www.simplynaturalbooks.com.